SILENCE AND STILLNESS IN EVERY SEASON

Other books by Paul Harris

GENEALOGICAL HISTORY OF THE HARRIS FAMILY OF WORCESTER, ENGLAND

BRIEF TO THE BISHOPS: CANADIAN CATHOLIC LAYMEN SPEAK THEIR MINDS

JOHN MAIN BY THOSE WHO KNEW HIM

CHRISTIAN MEDITATION BY THOSE WHO PRACTICE IT

THE FIRE OF SILENCE AND STILLNESS: AN ANTHOLOGY OF QUOTATIONS FOR THE SPIRITUAL JOURNEY

CHRISTIAN MEDITATION: CONTEMPLATIVE PRAYER FOR A NEW GENERATION

SILENCE AND STILLNESS IN EVERY SEASON

Daily Readings with John Main

Edited by

Paul Harris

DARTON · LONGMAN + TODD

First published in 1997 by
Darton, Longman and Todd Ltd
1 Spencer Court
140–142 Wandsworth High Street
London SW18 4JJ

ISBN 0–232–52255–3

A catalogue record for this book is available
from the British Library

Phototypeset in 10.5 on 13.5 Simoncini Garamond by
Intype London Ltd
Printed and bound in Great Britain by
Page Bros, Norwich

❈ CONTENTS

This collection of daily readings by Benedictine monk Dom John Main (1926–1982) reinforces the great inspiration which his taped talks have given to so many people seeking a contemplative spiritual path at the end of the twentieth century. John Main always pointed to the need for a spiritual guide or teacher and in these daily readings we do indeed find a *personal* relationship with a spiritual guide and teacher who leads us into the daily discipline of silence, stillness and simplicity in prayer.

There is a mystery involved in all personal relationships and between a teacher and a follower. Time and time again those seeking a spiritual path mention the significance of a particular book by John Main or the influence of listening to his voice for the first time. But John Main was always pointing to a teacher beyond himself – Jesus. John Main's firm conviction was that the Spirit was the primary teacher. But in reminding ourselves of the role of the Spirit we must also be aware that God uses the creative talents of human beings to do his work on earth. In each age God raises up *teachers* and in the twentieth century John Main continues to lead men and women around the world to 'a country beyond words and beyond names' – to the age-old path of contemplative prayer.

A number of examples of John Main's spiritual influence come from the book *John Main by Those Who Knew Him*. Layman Tom Abraham, one of the original members of the first meditation group at Ealing Abbey in London, recounts his first meeting with John Main. Says Tom:

> When he began to speak about meditation it was with authority and assurance and no pussyfooting around. His message was clear, simple and straightforward. This was the teacher I had been looking for. All I can say is that the way of the mantra, that great leap of unconditional love, changed my life forever.

Irishman Father Patrick Murray remembers the exact time and date of first hearing John Main on tape for the first time, 3:30 pm, June 25, 1979 in Dar es Salaam, Africa. Says Father Patrick:

As soon as I heard John Main's voice, the very sound, the very tonality of his voice struck something deep within my very being. And as I listened to him as he explained the significance of the mantra (which I did not fully understand at the time) there was something in my inner self that said it all made sense. I sensed deep within that even if I did not understand, he was saying something significant and that I would like to meet this man.

Jill Black, who lives in the Barossa Valley, north of Adelaide, Australia, recounts the following story:

About five years ago a Mercy sister put a copy of John Main's book *Word Into Silence* into my hand and urged me to read it. I took the book home, put it on my bedside table, and then avoided it for many weeks. I was always conscious of the fact that it was there, but physically unable to open it. Looking back, I am certain that I knew intuitively how much it would change my life. When I did begin to read it, I was amazed. There were all the answers to all my questions, the very things I had been asking God about. So many people around the world have felt the same way, that they have been waiting all their lives to hear John Main's teaching. Herein lies his genius. He speaks in an authentic voice, so much so that his listeners are left in no doubt that he speaks from a genuine experience of God.

Perhaps what Tom, Fr Patrick and Jill are saying can be summed up in St Paul's inspiring words in a letter to the Corinthians (1 Cor. 2:4–5).

The word I spoke to you, the gospel I proclaimed did not sway you with subtle arguments; it carried conviction by spiritual power, so that your faith might be built, not upon human wisdom but upon the power of God.

PAUL HARRIS
Ottawa, Canada

✤ FOREWORD

In John Main's vision meditation opens an authentic spirituality for a very wide range of people today. This book of his teaching on the spiritual path will help many meditators to stabilise and deepen their daily practice in the two periods of silence, stillness and simplicity which John Main recommended. Each morning and evening these daily readings offer the gentle encouragement and wise inspiration which everyone who has set out on this pilgrimage needs in order to persevere and to discover the fruits of meditation in ordinary, daily life. Many meditators will be very grateful to Paul Harris for the loving work he has put into selecting these readings.

LAURENCE FREEMAN

❧ ACKNOWLEDGEMENTS AND BIBLIOGRAPHY

The editor acknowledges with gratitude the courtesy of the following publishers and organizations who have given special permission to use extracts from their copyright material.

John Main, *Christian Meditation, The Gethsemani Talks*, World Community for Christian Meditation 1977.

John Main, *Community of Love*, Darton, Longman and Todd 1990.

John Main, *The Heart of Creation*, Darton, Longman and Todd 1988, Crossroad 1988.

John Main, *Letters From the Heart*, Crossroad 1982.

John Main, *Moment of Christ*, Darton, Longman and Todd 1984, Crossroad 1984.

John Main, *The Present Christ*, Darton, Longman and Todd 1985.

John Main, *Word Into Silence*, Darton, Longman and Todd 1980, Paulist Press 1981.

John Main, *The Way of Unknowing*, Darton, Longman and Todd 1989, Crossroad 1989.

Paul Harris, *Christian Meditation By Those Who Practice It*, Dimension Books 1993.

Cassette Tapes

John Main, *Christian Meditation: The Essential Teaching*, World Community for Christian Meditation.

John Main, *In The Beginning*, World Community for Christian Meditation.

John Main, *Being On The Way*, World Community for Christian Meditation.

John Main, *Word Made Flesh*, World Community for Christian Meditation.

John Main, *The Door to Silence*, World Community for Christian Meditation.

John Main, *The Last Conferences*, World Community for Christian Meditation.

John Main, *Communitas Series* (5 sets), World Community for Christian Meditation.

John Main, *Fully Alive*, World Community for Christian Meditation.

✤ THE WORLD COMMUNITY FOR CHRISTIAN MEDITATION

International Centre, 23 Kensington Square, London W8 5RN, United Kingdom. Tel: 0171 937 4679. Fax: 0171 937 6790.

Australia: Christian Meditation Community, The Hermitage, Mt Mee Rd., Ocean View, via Dayboro, Queensland. Tel: 07–425–3186.

Belgium: Christelijk Meditatie Centrum, Beiaardlaan 1, 1850 Grimbergen. Tel: 02 269 5071.

Brazil: Meditacco Christa no Brasil, Nucleo Dom John Main, Caixa Postal 33266, 22442–970 Rio De Janeiro RJ, Brasil. Tel: (21) 274–7104.

Canada: Christian Meditation Community, P.O. Box 552, Station NDG, Montreal, Quebec H4A 3P9. Tel: 514 766 0475. Fax: 514 937 8178.
John Main Centre, PO Box 56131, Ottawa, Ontario K1R 7Z0. Tel: 613 236 9437. Fax: 613–236–2821.

India: Christian Meditation Centre, 1/1429 Bilathikulam Road, Calicut 673006 Kerala. Tel: 495 60395.

Ireland: Christian Meditation Centre, 4 Eblana Ave., Dun Laoghaire, Co. Dublin. Tel: 01 2801505.

New Zealand: Christian Meditation Centre, 4 Argyle Rd., Browns Bay, Auckland 1310. Tel:/Fax: 64 9 478 3438.

Philippines: Christian Meditation Centre, 5/f Chronicle Building, Cor. Tektite Road, Meralco Avenue/Pasig, M. Manila. Tel: 02 633 3364. Fax: 02–632 3104.

Singapore: Christian Meditation Centre, 9 Mayfield St., Singapore 438 023. Tel: 65 348 6790.

Thailand: Christian Meditation Centre, 51/1 Sedsiri Road, Bangkok 10400. Tel: 271 3295.

United Kingdom: Christian Meditation Centre, 29 Campden Hill, London W8 7DX. Tel: 0171 937 0014. Fax: 0171 937 6790.

United States: John Main Institute, 7315 Brookville Road, Chevy Chase, MD 20815. Tel: 301 652 8635.
Christian Meditation Centre, 1080 West Irving Park Rd., Roselle, Illinois. Tel: 708 351 2613.

For a full list of all Christian Meditation Centres and Groups please write to the International Centre.

❀ JANUARY 1

The most important thing to know about meditation is *how* to meditate. It is also important, I suppose, to know *why* you should meditate, but in the first place you must know what to do. Let me remind you of this again so that you are as clear as possible in your minds about it. Choose a place that is as quiet as you can find. As far as posture is concerned, the basic rule is to sit with your spine upright. Sit down, either on the floor or in an upright chair, and keep your spine as erect as possible. Close your eyes gently.

To meditate you need to take a word and the word I suggest to you is *maranatha*. Simply, gently repeat that word in silence in your heart, in the depths of your being, and continue repeating it. Listen to it as a sound. Say it; articulate it in silence, clearly, but listen to it as a sound. If you can, you must meditate every morning and every evening. I think it is true to say that you will never learn to meditate unless you do meditate every morning and every evening of every day. You need simply to put that time-slot aside.

The Way of Unknowing

❀ 1 ❀

Meditation is a way of coming to your own centre, coming to the foundation of your own being, and remaining there – still, silent, attentive. Meditation is in essence a way of learning to become awake, to be fully alive and be still. The way to that wakefulness is silence and stillness. This is quite a challenge for people of our time, because most of us have very little experience of silence, and silence can be terribly threatening to people in the transistorised culture that we live in. You have to get used to that silence. That is why the way of meditation is a way of learning to say a word interiorly in your heart.

I think what all of us have to learn is not so much that we have to create silence. The silence is there within us. What we have to do is to enter into it, to become silent, to become the silence. The purpose of meditation and the challenge of meditation is to allow ourselves to become silent enough to allow this interior silence to emerge. Silence is the language of the spirit.

Learning to say your mantra, learning to say your word, leaving behind all other words, ideas, imagination and fantasies, is learning to enter into the presence of the spirit who dwells in your inner heart, who dwells there in love. The Spirit of God dwells in our hearts in silence. And, in humility and in faith, we must enter into that silent presence.

The all-important aim in Christian meditation is to allow God's mysterious and silent presence within us to become more and more not only a reality, but *the* reality in our lives; to let it become that reality which gives meaning, shape and purpose to everything we do, to everything we are.

Word Into Silence

It is very difficult to try to determine what it is that makes a person want to meditate. It has puzzled me over the years. There seem to be so many reasons why people start to meditate. But I think there is only one reason that keeps people meditating. That I think we could describe as a growing commitment to reality.

The longer you meditate, the longer you persevere through the difficulties and the false starts, then the clearer it becomes to you that you *have* to continue if you are going to lead your life in a meaningful and profound way. You must never forget the way of meditation: to say your mantra from the beginning to the end. This is basic, axiomatic, and let nothing dissuade you from the truth of it. In your reading you may come across all sorts of variants and alternatives. But the discipline, the ascesis of meditation places this one demand on us absolutely: that we must leave self behind so completely, leave our thoughts, analyses and feelings behind so completely, that we can be totally at the disposition of the Other. We must do so in an absolute way and that is the demand that the mantra makes upon us: to say it from beginning to the end, in all simplicity and in absolute fidelity.

The Way of Unknowing

Time and again the practical advice of masters of prayer is summed up in the simple injunction: 'Say your mantra. Use this little word.' *The Cloud of Unknowing* advises, 'and pray not in many words but in a little word of one syllable. Fix this word fast to your heart so that it is always there, come what may. With this word you will suppress all thoughts.'

Abbot Chapman, in his famous letter of Michaelmas 1920 from Downside, describes the simple, faithful use of a mantra which he had discovered more from his own courageous perseverance in prayer than from teachers. He had rediscovered a simple enduring tradition of prayer that entered the West through Monasticism, and first entered Western Monasticism through John Cassian in the late fourth century. Cassian himself received it from the holy men of the desert who placed its origin back beyond living memory to Apostolic times.

The venerable tradition of the mantra in Christian prayer is above all attributable to its utter simplicity. It answers all the requirements of the masters' advice on how to pray because it leads us to a harmonious, attentive stillness of mind, body and spirit. It requires no special talent or gift apart from serious intent and the courage to persevere. 'No one', Cassian said, 'is kept away from purity of heart by not being able to read, nor is rustic simplicity any obstacle to it, for it lies close at hand for all if only they will by constant repetition of this phrase keep the mind and heart attentive to God.'

Our mantra is the ancient Aramaic prayer, *Maranatha, Maranatha.* 'Come Lord. Come Lord Jesus.'

Word Into Silence

❧ JANUARY 5

All growth that endures in nature must be thoroughly rooted, and it is the summons of each one of us to be thoroughly rooted in Christ. I think there is a real sense in which meditation is a return to our original innocence. The Fathers described this way as 'purity of heart'. The call of each one of us from Jesus is to find it unclouded by egoism, unclouded by images, unclouded by desire.

Meditation leads us to the clarity that comes from original and eternal simplicity. So we are content simply to be with him, content simply and in a childlike way to say our word, our one word, from the beginning to the end of our meditation.

To begin to meditate requires nothing more than the determination to begin. To begin to discover our roots, to begin to discover our potential, to begin to return to our source. And God is our source. In the simplicity of meditation beyond all thought and imagination we begin to discover in utter simplicity that we are in God; we begin to understand that we are in God in whom we live and move and have our being. We try to describe this growing awareness that we discover in the silence and daily commitment as 'undivided consciousness'.

Meditation is just this state of simplicity that is the fully mature development of our original innocence ... The wonder of the proclamation of Christianity is that every one of us is invited into this same state of simple, loving union with God. This is what Jesus came both to proclaim and to achieve. This is what each of us is invited to be open to.

Moment of Christ

Meeting and meditating with so many who follow the extraordinary and wonderful pilgrimage in the usual course of their ordinary daily lives makes me see more clearly than ever before the true nature of this journey we are making together. We know it as a journey of faith, of expanding capacity to love and to be loved; and so also as an expanding vision of reality.

And we know it too as a way that demands more and more faith. Mountains get steeper the closer you approach the summit and the path narrows. But so also the view becomes vaster, more inspiring and more humbling, strengthening us for the deeper commitment required of us for the last stage of the climb . . .

Meditation, as the way of a life centred faithfully and with discipline on prayer, is our way into this true experience of spirit, of *the* Spirit. As anyone who follows this way soon comes to know for themselves, its demand upon us increases with each step we take along the pilgrimage. As our capacity to receive the revelation increases so too does the natural impulse we feel to make our response, our openness, more generous, more unpossessive.

The strange and wonderful thing is that this demand is unlike any other demand made upon us. Most demands upon us seem to limit our freedom, but this demand is nothing less than an invitation to enter into full liberty of spirit – the liberty we enjoy when we are turned away from self. What seems the demand for absolute surrender is in fact the opportunity for the infinite realization of our potential. But to understand this we cannot flinch from the fact that the demand is absolute and consequently so must our response be.

The Present Christ

Meditation is not the time for words, however beautifully and sincerely phrased. All our words are wholly ineffective when we come to enter into this deep and mysterious communion with God. In order to come into this holy and mysterious communion with the word of God indwelling within us, we must first have the courage to become more and more silent. In a deep, creative silence, we meet God in a way which transcends all our powers of intellect and language. We have to listen, to concentrate, to attend rather than to think.

Silence is really absolutely necessary for the human spirit if it really is to thrive, and not only just to thrive, but to be creative, to have a creative response to life, to our environment, to friends. Because the silence gives our spirit room to breathe, room to be. In silence, you don't have to be justifying yourself, apologizing for yourself, trying to impress anyone. You just have to be, and it's a most marvellous experience when you come to it. And the wonder of it is that in that experience, you are completely free. You are not trying to play any role, you are not trying to fulfil anyone's expectation.

Word Into Silence

❀ JANUARY 8

Throughout Christian history, men and women of prayer have fulfilled a special mission in bringing their contemporaries, and even succeeding generations, to the same enlightenment, the same rebirth in Spirit that Jesus preached. One of these teachers, John Cassian, of the fourth century, has a claim to be one of the most influential teachers of the spiritual life in the West. His special importance as the teacher and inspirer of St Benedict and so of the whole of Western Monasticism derives from the part he played in bringing the spiritual tradition of the East into the living experience of the West.

It was in listening with total attention to the teaching of the Holy Abbot Isaac that Cassian was first fired with an enthusiasm for prayer and the firm resolve to persevere. Abbot Isaac spoke eloquently and sincerely but, as Cassian concludes in his first *Conference*: 'With these words of the holy Isaac we were dazzled rather than satisfied, since we felt that though the excellence of prayer had been shown to us still we had not yet understood its nature and the power by which continuance in it might be gained and kept.'[1]

Cassian and Germanus humbly returned to Abbot Isaac after a few days with the simple question: 'How do we pray? Teach us, show us.' His answer to their question, which can be found in Cassian's tenth *Conference*, had a decisive influence on the Western understanding of prayer down to our own day.

These related aspects of prayer, poverty and redemption leads Cassian to call the condition we enjoy in prayer a 'grand poverty'. 'The mind should unceasingly cling to the mantra', Cassian writes, 'until strengthened by continual use of it, it casts off and rejects the rich and ample matter of all kinds of thought and restricts itself to the poverty of the single verse ... Those who realize this poverty arrive with ready ease at the first of the beautitudes: "Blessed are they who are poor in spirit for theirs is the Kingdom of Heaven." '[2]

Word Into Silence

[1] *Conference* 9:36   [2] Matt. 5:3

❀ 8 ❀

❧ JANUARY 9

There are no half measures. You can't decide to do a bit of meditation. The option is to meditate and to root your life in reality. As far as I can understand it, that is what the Gospel is about. That is what Christian prayer is about. A commitment to life, a commitment to eternal life. As Jesus himself put it, the Kingdom of Heaven is here and now, what we have to do is to be open to it, which is to be committed to it.

A way of limitless life requires on our part openness, generosity and simplicity. Above all, it requires commitment. Not commitment to a cause or ideology but commitment in our own lives to the simplicity of the daily return to the roots of our own existence, a commitment to respond to life with attention, to create the space in our own lives to live fully. What we learn in meditation, in the silence of it and in the simplicity of it, is that we have nothing to fear from the commitment to creating this space.

I think all of us fear commitment because it seems to be a reducing of our options. We say to ourselves, 'Well, if I commit myself to meditating, then I'll not be able to do other things.' But I think what all of us find is that this fear dissolves in the actual commitment to be serious, to be open, to love not out of the shallows of our being, but out of its depths. What we all find in the experience of meditation is that our horizons are expanding, not contracting, and we find, not constraint, but liberty.

Moment of Christ

I want now to address a particular questions that we all encounter. It is the question of distractions. What should you do when you begin to meditate and distracting thoughts come into your mind? The advice that the tradition has to give us is to ignore the distractions and to say your word and to keep on saying your word. Don't waste any energy in trying to furrow your brow and say, 'I will not think of what I'm going to have for dinner', or 'who I'm going to see today', or 'where am I going tomorrow', or whatever the distraction may be. Don't try to use any energy to dispel the distraction. Simply ignore it and the way to ignore it is to say your word.

Moment of Christ

John Cassian speaks of the purpose of meditation as that of restricting the mind to the poverty of the single verse. A little later, he shows his full meaning in an illuminating phrase. He talks about becoming *grandly poor.*[1] Meditation will certainly give you new insights into poverty. As you persevere with the mantra, you will begin to understand more and more deeply, out of your own experience, what Jesus meant when He said, 'Blessed are the poor in spirit.'[2] You will also learn in a very concrete way the meaning of faithfulness as you persevere in fidelity to the repetition of the mantra.

In meditation, then, we declare our own poverty. We renounce words, thoughts, imaginations, and we do so by restricting the mind to the poverty of one word, and thus the process of meditation is simplicity itself. In order to experience its benefits, it is necessary to meditate twice a day and every day, without fail. Twenty minutes is the minimum time for meditation, twenty-five or thirty minutes is about the average time. It is also helpful to meditate regularly in the same place and also at the same time every day because this helps a creative rhythm in our life to grow, with meditation as a kind of pulse-beat sounding the rhythm.

But when all is said and done, the most important thing to bear in mind about meditation is to remain faithfully repeating the mantra throughout the time put aside for it, throughout the time of what the author of *The Cloud of Unknowing* called 'the time of the work'.[3]

Word Into Silence

[1] *Conference* 10:11   [2] *Matt.* 5:3   [3] *The Cloud of Unknowing*, ch. 4–7, 36–40

Why meditation is so important for us is that it helps us to live our lives as a process of integrated growth. To live meaningfully is to know our lives as a constant, deepening maturity. Nothing I suppose is sadder than a person who lives year to year, but somehow never grows up, never truly integrates his or her experience.

Meditation is important because it leads you to that first step in all growth, which is rootedness. By meditating every morning and every evening you set out daily on the way of rootedness. Growth as a whole person unfolds by our becoming rooted in our own deepest, innermost centre. In our society all sorts of helps are given to us to grow intellectually. Not so many are given to us to grow spiritually. To find and become familiar with our spirit, the centre of our personal identity, is to begin to live from the power of that centre; no longer blown around by every wind that happens to ruffle the surface, we learn to be rooted in ourselves. Growth needs planting and rooting and it also needs cultivation. Meditation, because of its highly practical orientation, leads us day in and day out to cultivate the life of the spirit, to return to that rootedness in our centre.

The Way of Unknowing

But I do believe, and believe it is the belief of the tradition (experience and tradition being one again), that the more we 'think' about God, picture him, or stir up our imagination for autonomous visions of him, the less we can experience him. This is not to denigrate theology, philosophy, or art. But these three fruits of our minds and hearts have value for ultimate meaning only so far as they clarify, encourage, or purify our journey to the frontiers of the limited human consciousness. On this frontier we are met by a guide, who is unlimited consciousness, the Person of Jesus Christ. We reach this frontier only if we travel light, if we have left all behind us and if we embrace the one who meets us with absolute trust. At that moment we know from our own experience that He is the Way, the Truth, and the Life.

Letters From the Heart

Why should you meditate? Why should anyone meditate? The tradition that has brought us all together tells us that what each of us needs if we are to live our life fully, if we are to expand our spirit fully, what each of us needs is purity of heart – that clarity of perception that will enable us to see reality as it is, to see ourselves as we are, to see others as they are: the redeemed and loved of God; and to see God as he is: absolute Love. To see all that we require purity of heart which means to say that we need to be able to see straight ahead of us without refracting our vision through the prism of the ego.

Kierkegaard describes purity of heart as the capacity to will one thing. The one thing you must *will* when you are meditating is to say your mantra, to say your word, to go beyond all the self-reflected complexities, all the complexities of the self-reflective consciousness, to be silent and to be still. That is why the bodily stillness is so important as a sacrament, an outward sign of the inward stillness. Purity of heart is simplicity realised.

We all need that, we all need that purity of heart if we are going to have the humility to see what is before our eyes and to see it with absolute clarity of vision. Let me remind you again: each of us, every time we sit down to meditate, is a beginner. We begin as if for the first time again and we lay aside all our fears, all our anxieties, all our hopes, all our plans. We lay everything aside to be open to the supreme purpose of our creation which is to be one, to be one with ourselves, to be one with God and to be one with all creation. The process of meditation is that process of becoming one and the way is the way of the one word: ma-ra-na-tha. Do not be discouraged if you find it difficult to stay with the word, but stay with it. Do not be discouraged if you find distracting thoughts coming into your minds, stay with the word.

Fully Alive

❧ JANUARY 15

Let me remind you again of the importance of the discipline itself. Sitting still is the first step away from egoism, from concern with ourselves, our own bodies. Sit still. You enter into, descend into, areas of simplicity in yourself you hardly suspected were there, areas of humility in yourself you had forgotten were there – your capacity to be childlike, to be trusting and to leave all demands, all desire behind and continue to say your word for the whole time of the meditation. Return to it if you let it go. Do not bother about distractions. There are no short cuts, there is no instant mysticism, but there is for each one of us the infinite love of God welling up in our own heart and that is more than sufficient. Listen to St Paul again:

> So he came and proclaimed the good news: peace to you who were far off and peace to those who are nearby. For through him we both alike have access to the Father in the one Spirit.[1]

That is why we meditate: because we have access to the Father, to our Father, in the one Spirit.

The Door to Silence

[1] Eph. 2:17–18

❀ JANUARY 16

Never forget the purity of heart involved in saying the mantra. Faithfulness to the mantra from the beginning to the end of every meditation brings us to this simplicity and innocence because it enables us to leave self behind. The confidence to proclaim Christ, the discretion needed to see how we should do this today, and the courage to witness to Christ from our own experience of him, arise from our fidelity to meditation each day and to the mantra.

There is nothing less shining in our hearts than the glory of Christ. That glory is not triumphalist but it does triumph over hearts hardened by the wounds of life. Poverty, purity, simplicity are strange weapons to minds trained on images and values of violence. But our survival, spiritually and even physically, depends upon our recovering an awareness of the redeeming power of these qualities of humanity. This is the way of the mantra.

> It is not ourselves that we proclaim; we proclaim Christ Jesus as Lord, and ourselves as your servants, for Jesus' sake. For the same God who said, 'Out of darkness let light shine,' has caused his light to shine within us, to give the light of revelation – the revelation of the glory of God in the face of Jesus Christ.[1]

Word Made Flesh

[1] 2 Cor. 4:5–6

When I read Cassian, I am immediately reminded of the prayer that Jesus approved of when He tells us of the sinner who stood at the back of the temple and prayed in the single phrase: 'Lord, be merciful to me a sinner, Lord be merciful to me a sinner.' He went home 'justified', Jesus tells us, whereas the Pharisee who stood at the front of the temple in loud eloquent prayer did not.[1] The whole of the teaching of Cassian on prayer is based on the Gospels: 'In your prayers do not go on babbling like the heathen, who imagine that the more they say, the more likely they are to be heard. Do not imitate them. Your Father knows what your needs are before you ask him.'[2]

As I have suggested, prayer is not a matter of talking to God, but of listening to Him, or being with Him. It is this simple understanding of prayer that lies behind John Cassian's advice that if we want to pray, to listen, we must become quiet and still, by reciting a short verse over and over again. Cassian received this method as something which was an old, established tradition in his own day and it is an enduring universal tradition. A thousand years after Cassian, the English author of *The Cloud of Unknowing* recommends the repetition of a little word: 'We must pray in the height, depth, length, and breadth of our spirit, [he says] not in many words but in a little word.'[3]

Word Into Silence

---

[1] Luke 18:9–14   [2] Matt. 6:7–8   [3] *The Cloud of Unknowing*, ch. 39

When you meditate your energy must be channelled in a single course, and the way of that course is your word. You can't fully appreciate this advice outside of the experience of meditation. Meditation is, as I have suggested to you, about stillness. It is like the stillness of a pool of water. The distractions that we have when we begin to meditate are only ripples and currents and eddies that disturb the water. But as you begin to meditate, and stillness comes over you, the depth of the water becomes clearer and clearer in the stillness.

The experience of meditation, the experience to which each of us is summoned and which all of us are capable of, is to discover that depth within us which is like a deep pool of water, water of an infinite depth. The marvellous thing about such a pool of water is that when it is still and the sun strikes it, every drop of the water in its infinite depth is like a drop of crystal alive with the light of the sun. That is exactly what we are called to in meditation – to discover the depth of our own spirit and the capacity of our own spirit to be in complete harmony with the God who tells us that he is light. 'I am the light of the world.'[1]

Moment of Christ

[1] John 8:12

For many people the first glance at meditation makes it seem to them that it, too, will soon become another exercise in dull repetition. This summer I was giving a retreat in a convent in Ireland and one of the nuns there, having heard a talk on meditation and the mantra, came to me and said, 'Oh Father, I could never do that. No, no, I could never do it. It would be awful.' Her understanding of the mantra was that it would be totally trivial for her because of its dull repetitiveness. I hope she did begin to meditate, though, despite her fears, because only a little experience of really *learning* to say the mantra (and this is the art of meditation) would have changed her mind – to understand that the art of meditation is simply *setting the mantra free* within your heart. The difficulty of this for us is that we always want to be in control. It is very difficult for us as Westerners to learn to set the mantra free, to let it sound, to let it sing in our heart in a sort of glorious liberty.

For that half an hour every morning and every evening we are focused beyond ourselves. Through the working of the Holy Spirit our spirit is expanding, our heart is enlarging, we are becoming more generous. The change in us comes about because, in meditation, we encounter and embrace the power that makes this change possible. All of us would presumably like to be more kind, more understanding, more selfless, more sympathetic, more compassionate and so on. But, at the same time, we recognise ourselves as weak, mortal, fallible human beings. This recognition often induces us to protect our vulnerability.

What we discover in meditation is the power–source that enables us to live without the anxiety of having to protect ourselves; it is established right at the centre of our own being, in our own hearts. 'God is the centre of my soul.' Now meditation is eminently practical because it requires each one of us to come to know 'from our own experience' what that statement means: 'God is the centre of my soul.'

The Heart of Creation

The way of the mantra is a way of generosity, of expansion and deepening, not in any sense a way of exclusion or narrowmindedness. It is a mystery of this journey that it makes us grow in our sensitivity to the presence of God and the goodness of his working in many unexpected areas of our lives. It is not always easy to explain how this is so, and indeed it cannot really be known outside of the experience. To turn from our thoughts and imagination at the time of prayer and to be wholly faithful to our simple task of saying the 'one little word' – how can you explain by image or concept that this way is into the silence in which God reveals himself in Jesus as the source and foundation of all creation?

Yet we know, when we have followed this way even for a little while, that the poverty of the mantra enriches us in a movement of love that fills every part of our life and awakens us to the mystery in which we are inserted – the mystery that is closed to us as long as we remain centred in ourselves rather than in him.

Letters From the Heart

You must learn to say your word and you must learn to say it with great patience. Part of the problem for most people in the West is that the process itself is so simple. What is required is that you sit down every morning and every evening and you spend about twenty minutes to begin with, then twenty-five, then the optimum period of about half an hour, every morning and every evening. All that matters is that you are on the way, that you are on the pilgrimage – to utter freedom of spirit, total liberty – that you are on the way to wakefulness, to consciousness, that you are on the way to pierce the veil of self-consciousness. That is the freedom: that you are not trapped within yourself. The way forward, the way ahead for you is oneness, with God, in Jesus, through the Spirit.

As I say, the problem for us is that the way is so simple. 'Unless you become like a little child, you cannot enter into the Kingdom of Heaven',[1] Jesus said. I am speaking to you from a tradition that goes back hundreds – thousands – of years, from a tradition that has been followed in every century, in the last two thousand years, by men and women who, by following it, became holy, which is to say they became fully human: compassionate, gentle, forgiving, understanding and, above all, filled with joy. The joy comes from the holiness: that is, from the fact that we have discovered ourselves, found in ourselves, our own true likeness to God; God who, as St John tells us, is love.

The Door to Silence

[1] Matt. 18:3

In beginning to meditate, as in persevering, the essential understanding we need to have grasped is the simplicity of it. The simplicity is just this: that every morning and every evening you give yourself the opportunity to be. You are simple because you are not asking yourself 'what is happening to me now?' You are not analysing yourself, nor are you evaluating yourself. You are not saying 'am I enjoying this?' or 'am I getting anything out of this?' During this time of being, put the self-reflective ego entirely aside.

You will have to begin in faith. There is no way you can evaluate what is happening when you begin. Later, you will not bother to try to evaluate it. Because meditation is a way of faith you cannot just have a curious stab at it, saying your mantra for three minutes, then stopping to see how you're doing. You learn to say your word from the beginning to the end, every day. This is to be done without the strain of force. The art is setting the word free in your heart, not trying to dominate or control with the word. Only say the word and be.

Where does this connect with Christian faith? In Christian terms, we know that God has sent his Spirit to dwell in us through the human consciousness of Jesus. His being is within us. Meditating is simply being open to his being.

> For the same God who said, 'Out of darkness let light shine,' has caused his light to shine within us, to give us the light of revelation – the revelation of the glory of God in the face of Jesus Christ.[1]

This light and glory are to be found in our hearts if only we will learn to be still, to be silent and to be humble. That is the exact purpose of the mantra.

Word Made Flesh

[1] 2 Cor. 4:6

Set your mind on the kingdom before everything else and all else will be given to you as well, says the Gospel.[1] The fact that we are, in our most real being, rooted in the silence of this centre seems to us the most elusive truth of our life. But the problem is our distractedness, our possessiveness. In fact the Spirit waits patiently for us in its own eternal stillness. Our pilgrimage of meditation teaches us that in spirit and in truth we are there already, with our Father who has called us to be there, who created us to be there and who loves us to be there.

Our awakening to this reality is the expansion of our spirit. With expansion comes liberty, the liberty of spirit that pushes forward the range of our limited consciousness by union with the human consciousness of Jesus dwelling with the infinite space of His love in our human heart. Yet there He dwells with the most perfect respect of our freedom, for the destiny being shaped for us in the bosom of His Father and our Father. The liberty is our capacity to enter with undivided consciousness into this destiny and to know it as the perfection of the mystery of love. This knowledge is not theory or speculation, but contact with the most immediate and personal reality. We are not meditating long before our eyes begin to open upon epiphanies of love in our life that before we were too short-sighted to perceive or not generous enough to receive.

The Present Christ

[1] Matt. 6:33

In starting to meditate, we have three preliminary aims. The first is simply to say the mantra for the full duration of the meditation. It will probably take some time to achieve this first stage and we will have to learn patience in the meantime. Meditating is an entirely natural process for all of us, for just as our physical growth takes place in its own natural rhythm, with variations for each individual, so does our prayer life develop quite naturally. We cannot force anything to happen but must simply say the mantra without haste, or expectation.

The second aim is to say the mantra throughout the meditation without interruption, while remaining quite calm in the face of all distractions. In this phase the mantra resembles a plough that continues resolutely across the rough field of our mind, undeflected by any obstruction or disturbance.

And the third of these preliminary aims is to say the mantra for the entire time of the meditation, quite free of all distractions. The surface areas of the mind are now in tune with the deep peacefulness at the core of our being. The same harmonic sounds throughout our being. In this state we have passed beyond thought, beyond imagination, and beyond all images. We simply rest with the Reality, the realised presence of God Himself dwelling within our hearts.

Word Into Silence

If you want to learn to meditate, you must learn to sit still and to say your word from beginning to end. Now what you will find, if you can persevere, is that after a little while of saying the word you will feel a certain peacefulness and relaxation and you will be tempted to say to yourself, 'This is rather good. I'd like just to experience this now and to know what I am feeling now, I'll give up saying the word. I'll just go with the experience.' That is the high road to disaster. You meditate not to experience the experience. You meditate to enter into the experience.

Meditation is a coming to consciousness and a going beyond self-reflective consciousness. Meditation is learning to look out beyond yourself, breaking out of the closed system of self-consciousness, that prison of the ego, and we do so by that discipline of saying the word. When you are saying the word you are not thinking your own thoughts. You are not analysing what is happening to you. You are letting go. Meditation, in the Christian vision of it, is simply launching out into the infinity of God through the Spirit who dwells in our hearts. It is a letting go, a launching out into the deep. And people, in all ages throughout history, have found that it requires an act of faith to leave yourself behind.

Moment of Christ

❀ JANUARY 26

Meditation is the way *par excellence* to handle distractions because the purpose of the one word is simply to bring your mind to peace, silence and concentration. Not to bring it to rest with holy thoughts alone but to transcend what we know as thought altogether. And the mantra, serving this end, is like a plough that goes through your mind pushing everything else aside – 'making the rough places plain'. You remember what Cassian said of its 'casting off and rejecting the rich and ample matter of all manner of thoughts'. It is because the mind is 'light and wandering', as susceptible to thoughts and images as a feather to the slightest breeze, that Cassian enjoins the mantra as the way to transcend distraction and attain stability.

The essence, the art of saying the mantra is: to say it, to sound it, to listen to it and just to ignore the distractions. Give primacy to the mantra above all else. Gradually, as you persevere in saying the mantra, the distractions do become less and less of a reality. My teacher used to say that the first three aims that you have when you begin to meditate are these: first of all, just to say the mantra for the full period of your meditation. That's your first goal and that might take a year, it might take ten years. The second goal is to say your mantra and be perfectly calm in the face of all distractions that come. And the third preliminary aim is to say the mantra for the full time of your meditation with no distractions.

Christian Meditation: The Gethsemani Talks

When we begin to meditate it is natural to wonder, 'How long will this take?' We need to be told – and our living tradition tells us – that it takes no time at all. This is the same as saying that it takes only as long as it takes us to realise that it takes no time. This is why the real use of time is patience. In the moment of pure patience, simple openness, the little ego that keeps us self-centred fades away in the nothing it came from and our spirit, centered in Christ, flows into the plenitude of God as its beginning and its end, its alpha and omega.

Our faith is our patience, our openness to what already is, because we are not waiting so much for God to arrive as for ourselves to realise He is with us in Christ, Emmanuel, God-with-us. What we have to learn is not to 'make God happen' but to become sufficiently still, sufficiently silent, to allow the consciousness of Jesus, His Spirit within us, to expand and push back the frontiers of our limitations, to reveal to us that we are in God.

Letters From the Heart

The word I recommend you to say, the Aramaic word *maranatha*, should be said without moving your lips, that is, said interiorly in your heart, and you should continue to sound it from the beginning to the end of your time of meditation. Meditation is a process of growing, of growing more spiritually aware, and like all processes of growth, it has its own speed, its own pace. It is an organic process.

You have as it were to root the mantra in your heart. Jesus so often spoke of the Word of the Gospel taking root in the hearts of men and women and He tells us it has to fall into receptive soil. In other words, the whole of your being has to be involved in this process. You sound the mantra and by your fidelity in returning to it day after day, you root it in your heart and once rooted, it flourishes. Indeed it flowers.

And the flower of meditation is peace, a profound peace. It is a peace that arises from harmony, from the dynamic harmony that you encounter when you make contact with the ground of your being, because what you discover is that the mantra is roared in your heart, the centre of your being, and your being is rooted in God, the centre of all being.

Moment of Christ

❧ JANUARY 29

The great fourth-century master of prayer, our master, John Cassian, had already noted this danger in alluding to what he called the *pax perniciosa*, the pernicious peace. His graphic phrase points out something that needs to be remembered if we ever think that we can just say, 'So far and no further, this will do.' *Perniciosa* means what it says, namely, destructive or fatal. I am myself convinced that many people do not make the progress they should in prayer, and do not become as free as they are called to be in prayer, simply because they opt for this destructive lethargy, they give up too soon in their toilsome pilgrimage up the mountain side; they abandon the constant saying of the mantra.

When we begin to meditate we must say the mantra for the whole twenty or thirty minutes of our meditation, regardless of whatever mood we are in or whatever reaction we seem to be having. As we progress in fidelity in saying it, we must then sound it for the whole time of our meditation, whatever the distractions or feelings that may arise. Then, as the mantra becomes rooted in our heart, we must listen to it with our whole attention without ceasing.

Word Into Silence

Make no mistake about the commitment to discipline that it entails, the discipline of putting aside every limitation whether in the form of words, ideas, images, insights or symbols.

Meditation is like the practice sessions of an athlete. The iron discipline leads to utter freedom of movement in the art of the performance when the discipline itself is transcended. The difficulty of not understanding this is that it leads people to say things like 'I meditate a bit. In my own way. I say a word occasionally. When it feels right. What's all this fuss about utter commitment?' To this mentality, indeed, saying the mantra for the full period of the meditation seems like a substantial union with the essence of utter rigidity and self-restriction. It seems, they might say, like putting the Holy Spirit in a strait-jacket. But, as anyone who has practised this discipline knows, you cannot even begin to try to put the Holy Spirit in a strait-jacket.

Although you can begin to say the mantra, from beginning to end, you say it until you can say it no longer and then, if there is a strait-jacket around, it is the Holy Spirit who puts you in it: the strait-jacket of unavoidable liberty. In the utter silence there is only God, there is only oneness and it is the oneness that is 'all in all'.

Word Made Flesh

Now let me just tell you this – for those of you who have been coming for some weeks: when you begin to meditate, you begin to become very deeply relaxed. The early Fathers of the Desert used to call their prayer 'resting in the Lord.' In that deep peacefulness, where there is just Jesus and you, you begin to take off the normal suppressing mechanisms of your psyche. Most of us spend quite a lot of our energy suppressing guilts, fears, whatever it may be. When you begin to meditate, after some time those suppressions are taken off and so the fear that you are turning from, or the guilt that you are trying to bury, gradually bubbles up to the surface and so you might find, after your meditation, that instead of feeling more deeply relaxed, you can feel vaguely anxious, vaguely worried, you are not sure why.

The power of meditation is this: as you persevere on the path, the thing that you are suppressing or the fear that you cannot face or the guilt that you do not want to admit to is, as it were, burned away in the fire of Divine Love. Very often, you will never consciously know what it was, but it is gone and it is gone for ever.

Fully Alive

❧ FEBRUARY 1

At no point in history has it been more important to listen to the tradition that reveals prayer as the progressive penetration of the present moment, as a journey ever deeper into the union of love and the progressive shedding of self that leads to that union. But, such is the risk that makes the human being free, even the tradition can teach us nothing of ultimate importance if we do not have some real light from our own experience to read it by.

It is this experience that saves the tradition from ever becoming a mere memory transmitted in print, and that revitalises it for every generation. In the personal act of faith that opens this experience to us, the tradition is invested with human relevance for all and it is relevant because it restores us to that present moment in which we are propelled into the actuality of God.

Letters From the Heart

To learn to meditate the first thing you have to try to understand – and this is the principal challenge to all of us – the first thing is to understand how simple it is. We live in a society that is highly complex. All of us have to deal with a variety of challenges in our life, all of them quite complex. It is very difficult for us to believe in anything that is very simple, very straightforward, very clear. It is very difficult for us to believe that such a teaching could be important and could be effective.

We speak to you as Benedictine monks and our message to you is that we are the inheritance, you and I, in this time, of a long and rich spiritual tradition and it is a tradition that has been passed on and has survived for hundreds of years, despite many attacks on it, despite many misunderstandings of it and despite simple neglect. Because we have been brought up in our society in a largely intellectual climate and tradition we tend to think that once something has been written down it has power to survive on its own.

But what I think we have to understand is this: a tradition does not and cannot survive either merely by being talked about or by being written down. A tradition survives and grows only because men and women can be found who will enter into the experience of the tradition. In other words, we not only inherit a tradition but we have to re-create the tradition in every generation and we re-create by discovering it from our own experience and at that moment of discovery, the tradition lives. It is a living tradition and living, it possesses power. It becomes a living flame that has the power to enlighten, to guide and to warm.

The Door to Silence

❀ FEBRUARY 3

In meditation our way forward to this growing awareness of the Spirit praying within us lies simply in our deepening fidelity to the saying of the mantra. It is the faithful repetition of our word that integrates our whole being. It does so because it brings us to the silence, the concentration, the necessary level of consciousness that enable us to open our mind and heart to the work of the love of God in the depth of our being.

To understand the process once more, begin by sitting down comfortably and calmly and then start to say your mantra in the silence of your mind: *Maranatha*, Ma-ra-na-tha. Repeat the word calmly, serenely, and above all faithfully for the full time of your meditation, that is for about twenty to thirty minutes. We begin by saying the mantra in the mind. For modern Western man who has so restricted himself to the mental modality, there is no other way to begin. But as we progress with simple fidelity, the mantra begins to sound not so much in our head but rather in our heart. That is, it seems to become rooted in the very depths of our being.

Word Into Silence

We must be always careful that thought of the goal does not deflect us from understanding the means necessary to reach it. The means are as utterly simple as to meditate every morning and evening and during the meditation to say our word from beginning to end. Thus we turn from all day-dreaming, from all holy floating and self-dialogue. Thus we gradually submit ourselves to the yoke of poverty. It is the poverty of the 'one little word' which requires the faith of commitment. There are no half-measures possible. You cannot meditate a bit. You either say your word or you do not.

I suppose it is the completeness of the commitment that frightens us. But commit yourself but once and you will know from your own experience the love that casts out all fear. It takes many people years to come to that moment of commitment. Yet whether it takes years, months, weeks, or days is of no importance. All that is of importance is that each of us, as best we can in these earthen vessels, is as open as we can be to the essential truth of union. We are invited to be in the 'all in all'. As far as we can see with our limited insight, the way to the necessary commitment for this union is the way of poverty, silence and humility – the way of the mantra.

Word Made Flesh

Meditation is the great way of purification. Every time we say our mantra, we purify, we clarify our spirit. The process of meditation over a lifetime is the restoration of our spirit to its natural translucency. So often, when we look into our spirit, we see only ourselves. Our spirit is like a mirror and all we see is our own reflection. But the glass must be cleared and cleansed. It is as though the other side of the glass is covered with the sum total of the dross and trivia of a lifetime, with all the images that we have accumulated.

Meditation is a cleansing of the glass so that when we look *at* it we see right *through* it. We see reality unimpeded by any reflection of ourselves. We have to meditate every day, every morning and evening, because we are always accumulating more limiting dross and images. The wonder of the life of Jesus and His message to us is that our spirit need not be constrained by any limits whatsoever. Each of us is called to unlimited development, to expansion and to utter freedom as we soar to total union with God.

It might seem to you as you read these encouragements to meditate, or as you attend a weekly group, or simply meditate every day, that you know all this and have nothing more to learn. There is a real sense in which you do know it and a real sense in which you have nothing more to learn. If you can fully learn and absorb that truth, you have learnt everything! The dynamic of learning it is that, in saying our mantra, in the daily return to the discipline, we gradually find out how to look beyond ourselves. We learn to see with a vision that focuses ahead of us, in God. In that focusing of everything in God (everything that we are), everything in our life becomes aligned on God and is rightly set into its proper place. Meditating is powerful because it leads us into this right order, into this tranquillity and peace.

The Heart of Creation

✤ FEBRUARY 6

The purpose of meditation for each of us is that we come to our own centre. In many traditions, meditation is spoken of as a pilgrimage – a pilgrimage to your own centre, your own heart, and there you learn to remain awake, alive and still. The word 'religion' means a 're-linking', being 'rebound' to your own centre. The importance of meditation is to discover from your own experience that there is only one centre and that the life task for all of us is to find our source and our meaning by discovering and living out of that one centre.

I think that what we have to understand is that returning to our centre, discovering our own centre, is the first task and the first responsibility of every life that is to become fully human. Again, in meditation, in the discipline of it, you will discover from your own experience that to be at one with our own centre means that we are at one with every centre.

The truly spiritual man or woman is one who is in harmony, one who has discovered that harmony within themselves and *lives* this harmony with creation and with God. What we learn in meditation is that to be in our own centre is to be in God. This is not only the great teaching of all Eastern religions but it is the fundamental insight of Christianity. In the words of Jesus, 'The kingdom of heaven is within you.'[1] And the kingdom, in the teaching of Jesus, is an experience. It is an experience of the power of God. It is an experience of the basic energy of the universe. And, again in the vision of Jesus, we understand that this basic power, out of which we are invited to live our own lives vitally, is love.

Moment of Christ

[1] Luke 17:21

I think one of the concepts that can help us to understand the absoluteness of saying the mantra, the absoluteness of the experience of meditation, is the concept of destiny. Prayer, we could perhaps describe as the state of obediential love. The state wherein we are wholly at God's disposition, not desiring, not planning but simply placing ourselves within the fullness of his gift of life, the fullness of his gift of our own unique creation. And each one of us is created for a unique destiny, a unique fulfilment in God and our only task in life is to be wholly open to that destiny. In other words, our task is to live out of the divine energy, to live within the divine plan and to play our part in it fully and generously. You may have been meditating long enough to know that prayer has very little to do with asking for this or asking for that. Prayer is something much more simple than that. It is being at one with God.

Stillness is the way to rootedness and it focuses the challenge that faces all of us, to be rooted in our true self. To put it another way, it is the challenge to be wholly open to the gift of our own creation. Stillness helps us to be rooted in the gift that God has given us in our own being, which we learn by being still in the one place. Coming in to our own selfhood is coming into God. What you will discover in your meditation is the reciprocal harmony that we have with God. Becoming rooted in ourselves, we become rooted in our own proper place in creation and, as a result, rooted in our Creator. St Paul constantly reminds us that the challenge and the task of life is to become 'rooted in Christ',[1] who dwells in our hearts. This is why we have to become rooted in our own hearts. Outward silence and stillness are an effective sign of the inner stillness and silence of inner rootedness.

The Way of Unknowing

---

[1] Eph. 3:17

One of the things that we must clearly understand is that meditation, this pursuit of wisdom and love, must take place in an entirely ordinary, natural way. Meditation must be built into the ordinary fabric of everyday life. We must learn to see the whole of life shot through with the divine, in harmony with the divine. We must also understand that it is our destiny to enter this divine harmony, to be in harmony with God. It is not a question of trying to fit a bit of spirituality into our lives. The spiritual quest, the permanent spiritual invitation is getting our lives, ourselves, into permanent focus with ultimate truth, ultimate goodness. Not in any self-important or exploitative way but in a very simple, childlike way. It is by being still, by paying attention and by becoming mindful of the one who loves us.

To be fit for the great tasks in life we must learn to be faithful in humble tasks. Meditation is a very simple and very humble pilgrimage that prepares us for this focusing of our lives on the divine centre. Our lives are nourished by the spiritual sap, the energy rising from the root of all being. The invitation that each of us has received is to find out who we are, to discover the destiny that we have, to go beyond the limitations of our separate selves and to be united with the One who is all in all. In that going beyond ourselves, we find ourselves. And we find our unlimited capacity for development, for liberty, for love.

The Heart of Creation

In beginning to meditate we have usually to face the question, 'What should my expectations be?' What should we expect to happen? To approach meditation like this, however, is rather like approaching breathing and asking 'what will happen as the result of my breathing?' What happens when you breathe is that you live. Your vitality is assured with every breath. Meditation is very like that. Nothing dramatic happens except that your spirit breathes. You also come to a vitality of spirit very similar to the vitality that your body enjoys as a result of your breathing.

But it is very difficult for us to approach meditation without expecting some kind of pay-off for what we are putting into it. As Westerners we think in terms of the production line and we judge in terms of profit and loss. When we are told to meditate for half an hour morning and evening it seems like a big investment of time and effort and we want to know what the return is going to be. Meditation cannot be reduced to a commodity like this and the spiritual tradition is not a supermarket to shop in or a stock market to gamble on.

Because we think in these terms, however, there can be a real danger that meditation is presented in terms of return and pay-off. Most of the books on meditation in the bookshops offer a whole list of returns from lowering your blood pressure to better exam results and levitation. But whether any of these results, some reasonable, some false, occur at all is not of the slightest importance. The only important thing is that your spirit lives, that it lives wholly and that it realises its union with God and with all.

Word Made Flesh

FEBRUARY 10

I think it is so difficult for us as men and women of the twentieth century because we live in such a materialistic society. It is a society that sees everything in terms of possession and possessing and, even if we happen to be more spiritual in our outlook, we can easily become spiritual materialists. Instead of accumulating money we try to accumulate grace or merit. But this way of prayer is the way of dispossession and of surrender, and that is hard for us because we have been taught success, we have been taught the importance of winning, not losing. But Jesus tells us that if we would find our life we must lose it. And saying our mantra is exactly our response to that command of Jesus to be wholly at his disposition, to give him our undivided attention, to give him our undivided heart, to be in the state of undivided consciousness, which is another way of saying to be at one with him.

St Paul is one of those wise teachers of the contemplative tradition. In writing to the Galatians his case is that our call as Christians is fully to experience the 'glorious liberty of the children of God'. And he asks how do we achieve that freedom, how do we enter and realise it? He replies, 'The only thing that counts is faith active in love.'[1] And the way to that faith, active in love, is 'union with Christ Jesus'. This is what Christian meditation is about. Jesus dwells in our hearts in perfect simplicity. Christian meditation is simply allowing His presence to become the supreme reality of our consciousness. To do that we must learn to be silent, to be still and to be attentive to this presence in our hearts. And the way to that attentiveness is to recite our mantra. To recite it from the beginning of our meditation until the end, without ceasing.

The Way of Unknowing

[1] Gal. 5:6

Consider all the innumerable things that can go wrong in our lives. Then reflect, what can undo these catastrophes? What can heal the inevitable wounds? In every case the answer is 'the power of love'. Love it is that heals, that makes new, that fills us with hope, that delivers us from the prison of our own egoism. In meditation we learn to be still, to be calm, to be recollected and to become aware of the love of God's presence in our hearts. This awareness arises from his revelation, not our manipulation. What we have to do, though, is to be still. His presence is not just another theory, some speculative theology. It is a dynamic personal presence that is to be found in the heart of each one of us, found if only we will be still. Stillness is the door through which we enter the state of transcendence that leads us into the greater reality.

Forgetting about ourselves and encountering this reality, entering into this presence is, quite simply, *the* most important thing in our lives. It is the supreme priority of each day and of each phase in our life because, once we do set out on this path, every part of our life becomes energised with the divine love and this means that we are constantly healed. We are coming into a state of inherent unity. We are constantly being made whole and as a result we are continually discovering new courage to go on living with hope in the goodness of God, and with supreme confidence in His plan being worked out in our lives.

The Heart of Creation

You cannot learn to meditate unless you build it into your life as a regular pattern, as a regular discipline. It requires considerable sacrifice to find that time every morning and evening, indeed considerable discipline. But it is necessary. It is so necessary because the presence of God, in His universe, in His creation, in your heart and my heart, is of such importance that we ignore it at our peril. If we ignore it, we can never make sense of either ourselves or the universe. Because it leads to such meaning, the journey requires seriousness and discipline, which will lead you to a peace and a joy that no words can possibly describe.

Silence, you will discover, is the medium of unity. You will discover in the silence of meditation that your outer life and your inner life are unified. That is why bodily stillness is so important. In meditation you will discover body and spirit in *unity*, then in *union* with God. Nothing is more important for people of our time, or indeed of any time, than to recover this capacity for silence.

The way remains one of absolute simplicity. There is no advanced technique involved or any complicated books that you need to read. The most simple person can undertake this journey. Indeed, the simpler the better to begin with. All you need for the journey is discipline, commitment to the daily return to it and to making that space in your day and in your heart. And you need faith. The basic faith you need is that you *are*, that you are valuable and that you are valued. This is the faith that you are lovable and that you are loved. You need this faith when you begin and as you continue on the pilgrimage your faith will grow, your fears will fall away. The maturing of faith and the falling away of fear depend on your commitment to the mantra, which is another way of saying your determination to leave self behind and to journey into the mystery.

The Way of Unknowing

This discovery of our own spirit, our real self, is an experience that consists of an indescribable joy, the joy of liberation. But the loss of self which makes it possible, the erosion and the shedding of long familiar illusions require those qualities which have so important a place in St Paul's teaching: boldness, courage, faith, commitment and perseverance. It is these qualities, mundane rather than heroic, which enable us to persevere in the daily commitment to the pilgrimage, the fidelity to the twice-daily meditation and the 'grand poverty' to which the mantra leads us. These are not home-grown qualities; they are given to us by love, gifts from the Spirit to lead us to Himself, to deeper love. There is no way to truth or to the Spirit that is not the way of love. God is love.

As we advance into the silence we begin to experience the true meaning of the words of Jesus: 'The one who would find their life must first lose it.'[1] And again: 'Anyone who wishes to be a follower of mine, must leave self behind.'[2] It requires nerve to become really quiet. To learn just to say the mantra and turn away from all thought requires courage. But as we persevere we discover that the poverty of the mantra leads us to a really radical simplicity that makes this courage possible, for we are capable of greater courage than we usually believe of ourselves. But meditation is the prayer of faith, because we have to leave ourselves behind before the Other appears and with no pre-packaged guarantee that He will appear. The essence of poverty consists in this risk of annihilation. This is the leap of faith from ourselves to the Other. This is the risk involved in all loving.

Word Into Silence

[1] Matt. 10:39   [2] Mark 9:34–6

In the journey of meditation as we say our mantra and let go of our thoughts and plans and ideas and imaginings, we learn the value of renunciation, of non-possessiveness, we let go of our own images of self, we let go of our own desires, we let go of our own fears and of our own self-consciousness. This renunciation enables us to enter into communion with the Other and with others at a deep level of reality. The solitude of our meditation is the foundation stone on which we build all communion, true communion with ourselves, with others and with God. It is in the silence of our own heart that we enter into the deep harmony that reveals to us our oneness with all. Listen to St Paul writing to the Colossians:

> Put on the garments that suit God's chosen people, His own, His beloved and those garments are compassion, kindness, humility, gentleness, patience. Be forbearing with one another and forgiving. Where any of you has cause for complaint you must forgive as the Lord forgave you and to crown all there must be love. To bind all together and to complete the whole, let Christ's peace be arbiter in your hearts. For to this peace you were all called as members of a single body.[1]
>
> *The Door to Silence*

[1] Col. 3:12–15

Meditation does call for generosity because it calls for everything. It calls for that abandonment of desire and desiring and, positively, it calls for generous openness to God's destiny for us, to His plan for us, to His love for us. What you discover in meditation is just that – His love for you. So many people when they hear about meditation for the first time think of it as some extraordinarily dry, intellectual, unemotional, unaffective way. But it is none of those things. It is commitment to and openness to infinite love, and that love is like a mighty fountain bursting through in your heart.

The mantra is like the needle of a compass. It heads you always in the direction of your own destiny. It points always to the true direction you must follow, away from self into God and, whichever way your ego may lead you, the compass is always faithful in the direction it points you. The mantra, if you say it with generosity, with faithfulness and with love will always point you in the direction of God and it is only in God that our true destiny can be revealed.

The Way of Unknowing

People who have been meditating for a short time, three or four years, often think that the time quickly comes when you stop saying your mantra and when you just rest, stay in silence. What you must learn, and it is best to learn it when you are beginning, is the absolute necessity of saying your word from the beginning to the end. There are all sorts of problems that are posed for us. If you are a Christian, your ego poses the problem for you: 'Is this really prayer? Am I really praying to God now?' If you are not a Christian your ego poses the question to you, 'Am I really using this time to the best of my advantage? Shouldn't I be analysing the profound insights that are coming to me?' But what you must learn, whether you are a Christian or whether you are not, is that you must be silent. What you will learn is that you have to learn to be silent.

Fully Alive

The aim has always been to stress and, as far as we are able, to prove by our lives that there are no 'methods of prayer.' There is only prayer. There is only one prayer and this is the prayer of Jesus – not words He addresses to His Father but the overflowing plenitude of His relationship with the Father. To talk then, of methods of prayer or of 'our prayer' at all is to miss the essential Christian dimension of prayer revealed to us – that we ourselves do not know how to pray. We have to learn by following the teaching of our Master and He teaches us by taking us into the creative and liberating mystery of His prayer, the stream of love that flows between Him and His Father that is the Spirit.

'Our prayer' is simply our entering into this stream of divine love because of our realisation of our incorporation with Jesus – not because we read about it and think about it, but because we *realise* it. The freedom of spirit that is the fruit and mark of prayer is due to our discovery that the stream of love we have been plunged into and that sweeps us along is the foundational principle of all reality, is Being itself.

Letters From the Heart

My advice is to see your times of meditation not as times that are at your disposition at all. See your meditation, your prayer, not as your own but as the prayer of Jesus. As long as we are self-importantly thinking of our meditation, or our prayer, we have not fully started this pilgrimage. The time is His, the prayer is His. The miracle is that His prayer is ours, and the miracle is worked by simply bringing us to that total and unshakable confidence in the Father which the Gospel describes as hope. We approach meditation with hope rather than desire: without hesitation and with a childlike sense of being available to God.

We learn therefore to say the mantra with this same simplicity. We are not analysing it, or its effect, in a calculating way. We say it with a wholly sincere, self-emptying love. Yet by virtue of this self-emptying we are filled with the power of God and with the knowledge that we are one with God because we are lovable and loved. The only requirement is total selflessness expressed in the total abandoning of all our own thoughts, imagination, insights and, above all, our own prayers. This is our openness to the prayer of Jesus in our heart.

Word Made Flesh

I first learnt to meditate some thirty years or so ago, and my teacher used to say to me – in answer to whatever the question I put to him about meditation – 'Say your mantra, say your word.' The longer I have meditated over the years, the more I have realized the absolute wisdom of what he taught me. Learn just to say your word and keep saying it, keep repeating it throughout the twenty or twenty-five minutes or half an hour of your meditation, and keep repeating it from the beginning to the end. You will eventually be unhooked from your ideas, your concepts, your words, your thoughts, all that amalgam of distraction that is going on in your mind most of the time, and you will come, with patience and with fidelity, to clarity of consciousness.

Whatever phenomena present themselves to you – whether you see colours or hear sounds or see visions, whatever it is – take it as the general principle that it is all utterly unimportant. It has no real significance of any kind, except perhaps that you may need to be a bit more relaxed before you start. One of the things you have to learn in approaching your meditation is to approach it by not expecting anything. A lot of us in the West, when we begin meditating, hope it will bring us to see visions or to understand life with deeper insight, teach us wisdom or knowledge. But you must come to it absolutely generous and absolutely poor in spirit, that is, without demands or any sort of expectations other than this – a conviction that you will come to in the meditation itself – that this is what we were created for. This is what everyone reading this book was created for – to be, and to be in relationship with our Creator.

Moment of Christ

The important thing about meditation is that it is a learning process. It is a process where we enter ever more deeply, ever more richly into *the* mystery. I think that what we all discover from our own experience is that God is Spirit. God is the breath of life. God is presence and He is present deep within our being, in our hearts. If only we persevere we discover that in the power of His Spirit each one of us is regenerated, renewed, recreated so that we become a new creation in Him. 'I have poured out My Spirit upon this people', said the prophet Ezekiel.[1] And the Spirit is the presence of power, the power of love.

Meditation teaches us that this is the foundational wisdom on which to build life and true religion. What we discover is that we can only live our lives fully if we are *always* open to this mysterious presence of the Spirit, and *always* open to the presence more profoundly. That is the pilgrimage we enter upon every time we sit down to meditate. We open our minds, our hearts, our consciousness more permanently to the ultimate reality that *is*, that is now, that is here.

The Heart of Creation

[1] Ezek. 36:27

🎖 FEBRUARY 21

Just listen to these words of St John of the Cross:

> On a dark secret night, starving for love and deep in flame, O happy,
> lucky flight! Unseen I slipped away, my house at last was calm and
> safe. In darkness, free from light, disguised and down a secret way, O
> happy, lucky flight! In darkness I escaped. My house at last was calm
> and safe.[1]

That is the silence of prayer that John of the Cross describes there so
eloquently, so beautifully, in his poetry. The silence of our prayer is our
opportunity to steal away into the night of darkness, into the night where
we are filled with the light that is love. Again, you have all been meditating
long enough to know that all that is required of us is simple fidelity, to
come to our meditation every day in utter simplicity, not to be bothered
about insight, not to be bothered about knowledge because our insight
and our knowledge is always so limited, but to be open to the love of God.
In His love all knowledge and all insight is given and it is given, not upon
any limited scale, but infinitely and it is ours, now and for all eternity.
Because with our heart open to the infinite love of God, our now is indeed
eternal. Simplicity, fidelity and poverty.

The house that we must leave is our ego with all its possessive values,
the self-important values – we must leave it and we must go out into the
infinite liberty of God. How do we do this? Only by having our priorities
absolutely clear in our minds, within our heart, and our priority is this: the
kingdom of God which we seek, not in third place, or second place, not
in the sixth hour or in the third hour, but in the first place and in every
hour. The times of our meditation are like times of epiphany but God is
with us always and we seek Him always and we love Him always. Our
priority must be very clear: His kingdom first.

Fully Alive

[1] John of the Cross. The Ascent to Mount Carmel, Part I

Our daily fidelity to meditation and our fidelity to the mantra throughout the meditation is the sign that we have heard and attended the gospel's call. Each day that rests on the twin pillars of the morning and evening meditation is a step on the pilgrimage from theory into reality, from idea into experience as we turn aside from all complexity, all trivial concerns, simply to be one in Him, with Him and through Him.

The silence releases the power of the glory of God in our heart. Indeed we find the silence itself as a power within us the power of the Spirit who in silence is loving to all, and the silence we find through the poverty of our mantra. As we approach that profound silence reigning in our heart that is the Spirit, we know that it is itself the light, the glory that beckons us onwards. And as we pass more fully into the transforming aura of this silence the greater becomes our wonder, the deeper our joy that we are on this pilgrimage at all.

The Present Christ

The purpose of meditation is that we can learn to live our lives as fully as possible in the presence of God. Learning to live in His presence means also being energised with His energy and as we know from the Gospel His energy is love. Learning to meditate is learning constantly to be in this presence and constantly to live out of that presence. To learn, to learn anything, you have to learn to listen. We have to learn the humility to listen and then to begin the simple tasks involved in learning. If you want to learn a musical instrument you have to learn to play the scales. If you want to learn a language you have to learn the elementary grammar and you have to be content to learn that because without the foundation of that simple learning no progress is possible.

In learning to meditate, perhaps the first thing you have to learn is to sit well, to sit, that is, with a good posture; and the essential rule of posture is that our spine is upright and the essential rule of our sitting is that we sit still and so one of the first things we must learn is a physical stillness of meditation. We sit still, not just so as to get the body out of the way, but so that body and spirit can both be harmoniously involved, unified in our meditation.

Meditation is a complete unity of body and spirit, still and present to God. Now we have to prepare ourselves to meditate and the first preparation is the goodness each of us must practise in our everyday living and that is of great importance: that we learn to prepare ourselves by simple kindness, forgiveness, simple goodness and then the immediate preparation is the quiet of the place where we choose to meditate and the quietness of our body as we prepare for the inner quietness of the spirit, leading us to that total attentiveness of body and spirit.

The Door to Silence

People often ask me 'what sort of progress can I expect to make in my meditation?' I think it is important for us to understand that our progress is not to be found in anything else but stillness and the fruits of stillness. It is inappropriate to seek for progress in the phenomena of meditation. Don't ask yourself 'am I levitating?' or 'am I seeing visions?' That has nothing to do with it and in fact if you are seeing visions or levitating it is more likely due to drinking too much soda water than to the Spirit!

Fidelity to the path of meditation allows us to move beyond this kind of materialistic spirituality. Instead we are able to see our progress in the light of a deeper understanding of the meaning of Scripture. Take, for example, these words of St Paul to the Ephesians:

> So He came and proclaimed the good news: peace to you who are far off, and peace to those who are near by; for through Him we both alike have access to the Father in the one Spirit.[1]

The message for us here is that Jesus has already achieved all this by opening the highway to the Father for us. We do not have to do anything to bring this about. That is the way it is. We have access to the Father in Him and all we have to do is to realise it. Realisation is what meditation is about. The phenomena of 'progress' are utterly unimportant beside the process of realisation which is the opening of our heart, our consciousness, to the great reality that is taking place in our heart. There in our heart the Spirit of Jesus worships and loves the Father and is continuously returning to Him in love.

Word Made Flesh

[1] Eph. 2:17

This is the purpose of our meditation: to lead us to a full awareness of who we are, where we are, to stop hovering in the realms of eternal postponement. We must touch down in the concrete reality of the present moment where our divine splendour is revealed. We must become still. We have to learn how to pay attention steadily and continuously to the reality of our being in the here and now. Père de Caussade called this 'the sacrament of the present moment', and this is what the mantra leads us into, a full awareness of the divine splendour of the eternal present. The mantra is our sacrament of the present moment.

We must always remember that we cannot attempt to force the pace of meditation in any way or to speed up the natural process in which the mantra roots itself in our consciousness by means of our simple fidelity in saying it. We must not be self-consciously asking ourselves, 'How far have I got? Am I saying the mantra or sounding it or listening to it?' If we try to force the pace or to keep a constant self-conscious eye on our progress we are, if there is such a word, non-meditating because we are concentrating on ourselves, putting ourselves first, thinking about ourselves. Meditation requires complete simplicity. We are led to that complete simplicity, but we begin and continue by saying the mantra.

Word Into Silence

❧ FEBRUARY 26

Religious people have often become very confused by thinking that religion demands that they 'placate' God or keep him happy or distract him from punishing them. So religious people tend to get too busy with their ceremonies and liturgies. But we must also learn to be still and to be rooted in the knowledge that we need neither placate God nor distract him. We need only respond to his infinite love. We respond by total attention, by total stillness, not thinking of his love but by being open to it; not thinking of his mercy, but receiving it. The one thing we must understand is that in the time of meditation we need not think about anything. This is the time of the day for total attention, for total openness, for total love.

The Christian experience is, in essence, a certain knowledge that God is love and that He lives in our hearts. Our call, therefore, is more than to dialogue with Him, it is to be in union with Him. To be one with Him, each of us must come to the fullness of our own created oneness. Each of us must experience our own harmony in order that we may be in total harmony with Him. The Christian way is a way where each of us is made whole by becoming completely stable, completely rooted in truth, in love, in goodness, in justice.

The Heart of Creation

Basically, meditation is a way of coming to your own centre, the foundation of your own being, and remaining there – still, silent, attentive. Meditation is in essence a way of learning to become awake, fully alive and yet still. It is the stillness of meditation that leads you forward to that state of wakefulness and the sense of being completely alive that dawns in you because you are in harmony with yourself and, gradually, in harmony with the whole of creation. The experience of meditation puts you in resonance with all life. But the way to that resonance, the way to that wakefulness is silence and stillness.

This is quite a challenge for people of our time, because most of us have very little experience of silence, and silence can be terribly threatening to people in the transistorised culture that we live in. You have to get used to that silence. That is why the way of meditation is a way of learning to say the word interiorly, in your heart. The purpose of repeating the word is to launch you into the silence. So, lay aside all kinds of materialistic ideas about how long this will take. It might take twenty years. But that doesn't matter at all. It might take twenty minutes. That doesn't matter either. The only important thing if you want to re-establish contact with your centre is to be on the way.

Moment of Christ

For our heart to be purely open to supreme reality we require the simplicity of a child, to sit still in the presence of God and to remain open at the beginning of each day. Even so, our day can often drift into distraction, meaninglessness, anxiety or illusion. Then the evening meditation again gathers the scattered parts and binds them together in the love of Christ. So do not think of your meditation as the icing on the cake of your day. It is not 'putting a bit of spirituality' into your life. See it rather as informing your whole day with reality: the supreme reality that we now have access to God with freedom.

We are living in the age when the possibilities for the development of human consciousness have been radically transformed by the resurrection of Christ. Every human consciousness has undergone this transformation because in His risen and universal consciousness we have access to the Father, the source and goal of human life and indeed all creation. We live in an age of the infinite mystery realized in Christ and in us. Meditation is simply openness to that reality.

When we start to meditate we have to learn to say, to sound the mantra from the beginning to the end of the meditation. Every meditation is a new experience of this. Starting to sound the mantra silently in our hearts, we then learn to say it continually. When we find we are not saying it or have become distracted we simply return to it gently but with utter fidelity. It is always new. It is always the same.

So when you think of progress think only of progress in stillness. This is the stillness of fidelity. In your physical posture be as still as you can. As your heart fills with wonder at the unfathomable mystery that we are part of, be more deeply still. Progress is only progress in fidelity.

Word Made Flesh

❦ FEBRUARY 29

Meditation is above all the prayer of simplicity. We must therefore, each one of us, learn to be natural and to allow natural processes to unfold themselves in their own time. So, we each find our own speed for saying the mantra. Most people say it in rhythm with their breathing. The important thing is to articulate it clearly in the silence of your mind a silence that is itself deepening and spreading all the time, and to concentrate on it to the exclusion of all other thoughts. Remember: you begin saying it, you then sound it in your heart and finally you come to listen to it with total attention.

As to frequency you must say the mantra for the entire time of your meditation to the rhythm you find for yourself. You will be tempted to rest on your oars, to float in some anesthetised netherworld of your own. The way to transcend the temptation is absolute fidelity to the mantra. This is the condition of rooting it in your heart.

Christian Meditation: The Gethsemani Talks

Remember that the journey, the spiritual journey, is a journey into the depths of God, into the depths of the divine mystery itself. It is a journey that requires of us only simple faith – the faith to return day after day with childlike attention to our meditation, not demanding anything, not asking for anything, but simply being in the presence. In those times we seek to be still, to be silent, so that we may leave the periphery and return to the centre.

Let me describe to you now the way of meditation itself. In saying the word you enter a great tradition, a tradition of men and women who have meditated over the centuries and who, in meditating, have sought to transcend their own limitations and to enter into the wonder of God, to enter into the heart of the divine energy and to do so by entering their own heart. When we meditate we are still, body and soul, body and spirit, entirely open to the presence of God, knowing that presence to be pure love, pure gentleness, pure forgiveness. In that presence we become who we are: creatures created by God, creatures redeemed by the love of Jesus, creatures who are temples of the Holy Spirit and in that experience we are made utterly free, free to be ourselves, free to love ourselves, our neighbour and God.

Meditation is a leaving behind of all slavery, of all limitations. It is an entry into the freedom of God, into the freedom of the life of the Trinity. All that we need do is open our hearts to that reality and the way is the way of the mantra.

In The Beginning

There are two particularly important truths to get hold of when you are starting. First, that you must say the word from the beginning to the end – and this is essential to understand. In our tradition there is the basic teaching that you must say the word from the beginning to the end of the meditation period. What often happens is that after saying the word for a bit, you begin to feel very peaceful, perhaps very free. The burden of all your ideas and thoughts has been lifted and then you think, 'This freedom, this peace is rather pleasant, I'll just rest in it. I'll let go of the word, I won't say the word. I'll just enjoy the peace.' That is the high road to disaster. And you will waste a lot of time unnecessarily if you do not learn, at the outset, to say your word from the beginning to the end. Secondly, you must learn to meditate every morning and every evening. Again, make no mistake about that, that is the minimum.

When we look at the New Testament, at least when we look at it with eyes enlightened by the spirit of Christ burning in our hearts, we cannot but become intoxicated, amazed at the sheer wonder of the destiny that is given to each of us. But, we must always remember that the condition of being open to this, and of responding to our destiny, is always simplicity, poverty of spirit. It means we are invited by the same destiny to leave behind all complexity, all desire to possess God or to possess spiritual knowledge and to tread the narrow way of dispossession. We require faithfulness. We learn to be faithful by being simply faithful to the daily times of meditation and, during the meditation, to the saying of the mantra.

The Heart of Creation

MARCH 3

My recommendation for your daily meditation is to start with a minimum time of twenty minutes. Try as soon as you can to put it to twenty-five; the ideal time is about half an hour. And take the same time, whether it is twenty, twenty-five or thirty minutes – the same time-slot – every day. A practical instruction to remember is that the best time to meditate is before a meal. So, if you can, in the early morning before breakfast and, if you can, in the early evening before supper or dinner.

God is with His people. God dwells in our midst. And that is why we meditate. To be open to His presence. The presence is eternal. Our awakening to it is daily. We awaken to the great Revelation that transforms human consciousness and existence:

> I heard a loud voice proclaiming, now at last, God has His dwelling among the human race. He will dwell among them and they shall be His people, and God Himself will be with them.[1]

Repeat the mantra silently in your heart and keep it going. You will soon find a steady rhythm by which to say it, either with your breathing or with your heartbeat. Do not bother too much about the technicalities when you begin. Say it, recite it, sound it in your heart silently and the mantra will lead you to silence, to discipline, to concentration. If you are faithful to it it will lead you eventually to the bedrock of your own being. Beyond all the roles that you play, behind all the masks by which we hide, beyond all the images which we have of ourselves, we will find the person God creates and loves in eternity.

To learn to meditate, you have to understand that it involves a daily commitment. There are no short cuts. There is no instant mysticism. Meditating is like breathing and eating. It is part of the fabric of daily life. And as breathing and eating strengthen the body, so meditating strengthens the spirit, purifies it and makes it strong.

The Way of Unknowing

[1] Rev. 21:3

The most important thing to remember is that there is only the prayer of Jesus. This is *the* prayer. His prayer is the torrent of love and power flowing continuously between Jesus and the Father, and that is the Spirit.

This is the first thing for us to try to understand about Christian prayer and of course we cannot understand it. The extraordinary mystery about Christianity is that although we can never understand it we can experience this river of love that pours itself out in the Spirit, and as the Spirit, between Jesus and the Father. We can experience it through the human consciousness of Jesus. This ability to share His consciousness is the Spirit's great gift to us. Indeed it is the meaning of redemption.

Our salvation is precisely that in His human consciousness we are delivered out of our own egotism and isolation. The crucifying sense of our separateness and alienation is penetrated and dispelled by the rising within us of the knowledge of our oneness: one with ourselves, with others, one with the One who *is*. Delivered from our egotistical sense of separateness we enter the mystery of God as we travel in that stream of love.

Word Made Flesh

There are different levels of distraction. There is the distraction that comes just from the immediacy of our lives: the last TV programme we were watching, advertising, newspapers, the conversation we were just having. We must let all that go as we listen to the mantra. Then there are the personal distractions: the problems of our relationships and our family, our friends, our career, the loneliness we may feel. All those, too, we must let go as we come into the presence, the presence of the One who is, who is love. Then there are the spiritual distractions: wondering about our spiritual progress, comparing our experience over against someone else's, analysing the state we are in or whatever. All those distractions we must let go and we let go of them by being really faithful to our mantra. If you find you are thinking about the TV programme or some problem in your family or about your spiritual progress, drop it immediately and return to the mantra ma-ra-na-tha.

The greatest of all distractions is self-consciousness and this arises because of the tendency we all have to look at ourselves, and in meditation we look beyond ourselves to God. The mantra expands our vision beyond ourselves. All those first types of distraction were external. Self-consciousness is internal. The power of meditation is that it tackles the source of all distraction at the root, and the root is self-consciousness. In meditating we learn to stop thinking about ourselves, to go on a journey, looking ahead and staying on the journey and the guarantee of staying on the journey is that we say our mantra, keep saying our mantra and constantly return to it.

The Door to Silence

✿ MARCH 6

Meditation, as we know from John Cassian, from the whole of the tradition, is the way of poverty. We have to leave our 'prayers' behind and enter into *the* prayer, the prayer of Christ. Our way is the way of the one little word, our mantra. All other words, ideas, thoughts, we surrender, we leave behind. Our whole being must enter into this process of emptying: emptying out all distractions, all desire so that we may live and live fully in the mystery of Christ's redemptive love. When we consider the scheme of our redemption, the plan of our redemption, we can easily be totally intoxicated by the scale on which God has achieved our redemption and our potential for development in the power of Christ.

What each of us must find, from our own experience, is that the full vision can only come when our heart is set on God. The vision – make no mistake about it; every one of us is summoned to it – the vision is the blinding light of God's almighty love. We must learn silence, attention, humility, concentration and the vision is to be found in your heart and in my heart. It is not too hard for us, it is not too difficult for us, if only we can bring to the task our daily fidelity.

This is the problem with us Christians of the latter-day world. It seems so much that we would give a half-hour every morning and every evening. It seems so much. But it is nothing compared to the summons, to the vision, and to the love of the One who calls us. If the world is going to be renewed it must be renewed in sanity. If the Church is going to be renewed it must be renewed in sanctity, based on sanity. Every one of us in this room is summoned to this basic sanity and to the fullness of sanctity. Never let anyone lead you away from that vision of your life. In our prayer we discover again our own infinite value in God.

Fully Alive

❀ MARCH 7

Meditation is a universal means to lead us to reality. The reality that we are, the reality that our neighbour is, the reality that history is and the ultimate reality, the reality that is God. Meditation is the means open to everyone who would encounter the Spirit in their own heart. And so I want to encourage each one of you to persevere in meditation. Courage is what we need, the courage above all to abandon all images, especially the images that we have of ourselves, which are the principal stumbling block. The way to abandon all those images is to say our word with deepening fidelity.

To enter into our own selfhood is to enter into God. This is the call given to each one of us, to know ourselves in God. It is an astonishing destiny and it has been given to us in Jesus to know that destiny. Our life's task is to respond to it, in utter seriousness and with total joy. So listen to the word of the tradition. Hold fast to it and reap the harvest of eternal love. That is the good news of the Gospel. Listen to St Luke again:

> The seed in good soil represents those who bring a good and honest heart to the hearing of the Word, hold it fast, and by their perseverance yield a harvest.[1]

The Way of Unknowing

[1] Luke 8:15

In meditation, by learning to say your mantra, you learn to trust, you learn to be. Indeed the joy of meditation is that it is a celebration of being, a celebration of sheer joy in receiving your life as gift, and doing what Blake called kissing 'the joy as it flies'. Prayer is not possessing, not controlling but sheer celebration of being. We come to this celebration because meditation leads us to centredness, to the still point. In each person there is a still point that is me but is not *exclusively* me. What you will learn from your own experience in meditation is that there is only one centre, which is the centre in all centres. This is the understanding we come to in meditation, again out of our own experience, of the profound unity of being, the unity that is in us and the unity in which we have our being.

The commitment in meditation is to be detached from self-conscious preoccupation, through fidelity to the mantra during the meditation itself, and to the twice-daily practice of this *discipline* of detachment. The times of meditation, then, become progressively more simple, more joyous, more centred. And our lives, which are deeply changed through meditation, reveal from our own experience what it means to say 'God is love'. The centre of all centres is the God who is love.

The Heart of Creation

❀ MARCH 9

Meditation, as the way of a life centred faithfully and with discipline on prayer, is our way into this true experience of spirit, of *the* Spirit. As anyone who follows this way soon comes to know for himself, its demands upon us increases with each step we take along the pilgrimage. As our capacity to receive the revelation increases so too does the natural impulse we feel to make our response, our openness, more generous, more un-possessive. The strange and wonderful thing is that this demand is unlike any other demand made upon us. Most demands upon us seem to limit our freedom, but this demand is nothing less than an invitation to enter into full liberty of spirit – the liberty we enjoy when we are turned away from self. What seems the demand for absolute surrender is in fact the opportunity for the infinite realisation of our potential. But to understand this we cannot flinch from the fact that the demand is absolute and consequently so must be our response.

The Present Christ

We must therefore go beyond all concepts of God. We must transcend the language and the insights of the mind because these limit God in our experience. We are called to know God not with our own totally inadequate knowledge but with God's own self-knowledge: the Spirit we receive from Jesus. However perfect or skilled our human mind may be, it is as nothing compared to the wholly ineffable mystery we can enter only by treading the path of simplicity.

It is the simplicity of God, of the divine oneness, that calls us to meditate. It is also our greatest stumbling-block. For how can we with all our complexities know absolute simplicity? The mantra is the way beyond this stumbling-block. It is a sign or symbol of the unity and simplicity of God. In all the classical literature of prayer, in St Teresa, St John of the Cross, Meister Eckhart, for example, we find the common idea that the way to total union and continuous presence is the way of a simple and selfless discipline.

Selflessness is the way of the mantra. It leads us out of the labyrinth of self-consciousness. By its constant repetition it brings us gradually, and with much patience, to the silence where everything is resolved in the utter simplicity of God. In the divine oneness we become one with Him.

Word Made Flesh

For those of us committed to the pilgrimage of meditation we must remember the utter ordinariness of meditation. It is the ordinariness of it, in the daily return to it every morning and every evening, in simplicity of spirit, sitting down to meditate not with demands, not with expectations not for extraordinary phenomena. We sit down to meditate because we know that that is what our spirit requires. It is this ordinariness that gives our meditation its potential for that radical expansion of spirit beyond ourselves into God. That is why the commitment to the simplicity of the practice is of such supreme importance and when we sit down to meditate we leave behind all our analysis, and we are content to *be*, in the presence. If we want to live our lives to the full, then each of us must find our way into this perfect equilibrium of the human and the divine.

Our own humanity must be brought into this harmonious oneness with God, and the inspiring thing about the Christian vision is that this perfect coherence is to be found in the person of Jesus. The mystery of the vision is that this experience of oneness, of wholeness, of harmony is to be found deep within each one of us, to be found within us in the Spirit of God who dwells in our hearts, Our meditation is the outward expression of our inward commitment to the presence of that Spirit of God, dwelling in our hearts.

The Door to Silence

Saying the mantra is learning to die and learning to accept the eternal gift of our being – both in the one act. It is learning that all death is a death to limitation and that if we can die to self we rise to an infinite liberty of love: because love is the creative energy of the universe and also the creative centre of our own being. To find that centre we must go beyond our own self-centredness, we must die to everything that is passing away. As we make this journey and share it with others we enter into the truth that reality is not a final achievement but is a dynamic experience of the passing from self to the other. Only when we have lost our life can we find it.

The wonderful beauty of prayer is that the opening of our heart is as natural as the opening of a flower. Just as to let a flower open and bloom it is only necessary to let it be, so if we simply *are*, if we become and remain still and silent, our heart cannot but be open: the Spirit cannot but pour through into our whole being. It is this we have been created for.

Community of Love

Let me stress for you again the importance of the daily fidelity to meditation, every morning and every evening, and of the fidelity to your word. A priest who was beginning meditation made this point: he said surely if you have a holy thought, a religious thought while you are meditating, surely you should follow it? I think the thing to understand is this, that in saying the mantra with growing and, indeed, perfect fidelity, we are not attending to any thought about God. We are attending to His real presence in our own hearts and in all creation and in attending to that presence any thought is a distraction. Our invitation is to become wholly absorbed in Him, to be one with Him. Listen again to the words of Jesus:

> Set your mind on God's kingdom and His justice before everything else and all the rest will come to you as well. Do not be anxious about tomorrow. Tomorrow will look after itself.[1]

Being On The Way

[1] Matt. 6:33–34

❦ MARCH 14

Our Christian tradition proclaims that the faith each of us has received is that God is not absent but present to us fully in the Jesus whose life lives in our heart. Our prayer, as I have said, is best understood as our awareness of God in Jesus. And so our time of prayer must be a time committed to the fullest openness we are capable of – openness to this real presence and not to the dissipation of 'vain imaginings.'

All our images, and the phantasmagoria where thought and image are combined, derive from our own limited consciousness. All such images link us back to the central image of self, the great illusion we call the ego whose primary force is fear, the inversion of love, and which is the father of lies. It is an illusion because the true self has no image but is complete and undifferentiated consciousness. Our consciousness is limited, fractured, by the false image, the shadow of the ego, and it is set free and made whole by the light of Christ in whom there is no darkness, no separateness of being that can cast a shadow. Of Christ alone can we say that He is the image of God, the supreme Self, because of Him alone can we say that He is one with the Father.

Letters From the Heart

We learn from the faithfulness of our daily meditation how to wait on God and to attend to God in the deepening patience of true presence and mindfulness. In a growing fidelity and clarity of consciousness I urge you to put aside all the irrelevant kinds of speculation: am I enjoying this, am I getting anything out of this, am I becoming wiser or holier?

We know that there is a pilgrimage to make. It is the journey away from self and into the mystery of God. It is an amazing grace that each of us can and does know this, or at least suspect it. To know it is really to know everything because then we have only to begin and to continue. To be on the pilgrimage is everything.

We must learn to become simple, one, whole. We must learn to become peace, so that we become ourselves. In meditation we learn to be and in learning this we learn with unshakable certainty that God is. When you meditate, sit upright, close your eyes and say your word, without speculation, without self-consciousness, without haste, simply like a child, until the end of the meditation.

Word Made Flesh

✿ MARCH 16

This command comes to us from Christ Himself: that he who loves God must also love his neighbour.[1] Let us be quite clear what St John is saying, namely that we cannot love God *or* our neighbour. We love both or neither. And what love means is rejoicing in the otherness of the other because the depth of this awareness is the depth of our communion with the other. In this communion the discovery of our own true self and that of the other is the same discovery. So, in the people we live with we find not objects to be cast in our own superficial likeness but, much more, we find in them our true selves, for our true selves only appear, only become realised when we are wholly turned towards another.

In meditation we develop our capacity to turn our whole being towards the Other. We learn to let our neighbour be just as we learn to let God be. We learn not to manipulate our neighbour but rather to reverence him, to reverence his importance, the wonder of his being; in other words, we learn to love him. Because of this, prayer is the great school of community. In and through a common seriousness and perseverance in prayer we realize the true glory of Christian community.

Word Into Silence

[1] John 13:34–35

Sit down and, in saying your mantra, loosen the chains, the bonds that bind you to unreality, to illusion and to fear. Understand that those bonds have no power over you, if only you are open to the experience of Jesus. His experience is that He is the beloved Son of God. What He has achieved for us is that we can be open to the self-same experience of knowing that we are sons and daughters of a loving, compassionate and understanding Father. In that experience we discover that our meaning is to be fully open to His love, wholly open to the nearness of His mysterious being which is wholly open to our own hearts, to our own centre. For in our centre He is to be found. Meditation, saying the mantra from beginning to end, saying the mantra every morning and every evening, is simply our pilgrimage to that centre where He is and where we are in Him.

Don't worry about how the time is passing. Do not be disappointed if you find that you follow your thoughts instead of saying your mantra. Return to it, return to it gently, return to it constantly. If you want to learn to meditate, if you want to set out on this road of transcendence and one-pointedness, it is essential that you learn the practice of meditating every day of your life, every morning and every evening. The optimum time is half an hour, the minimum time is about twenty minutes.

You will find that in the time of your meditation nothing happens. Say your word and be content to say your word. But in the perseverance along the way of meditation you will begin to understand the truth about one-pointedness, about centredness and from your own experience you will begin to understand what St Paul meant when he said, 'Remember that it is not you who sustain the root: the root sustains you.'[1]

Moment of Christ

[1] Rom. 11:18

Now think for a moment of your own experience of meditation. You know that you begin, you seem to make progress and then you fail. For most of us, all our experience of meditation is contained in starting and stopping, in getting somewhere and finding that we are nowhere, in elation and discouragement. What you have to learn from this experience is that you must simply say your mantra. It is perfectly natural for you to pose the question, 'What good is this doing for me? What progress am I making?', but it is also perfectly useless. Indeed, it is worse than perfectly useless, it is positively counterproductive.

I think that all of us have tried, all of us have wanted to pray and all of us have failed. But at some time we come to the conclusion that the wisdom we receive from the contemplative tradition of prayer is *the* wisdom that turns the failure into triumph. The silence and poverty we experience in our meditation become self-authenticating. We know that we cannot analyse God. We know that we cannot, with finite minds, understand the infinitude of God. But we also know, or at least we soon begin dimly to suspect that we can experience God's love for us. Knowing that sets us on a road that somehow strikes us as authentic and it is this knowledge that keeps us going. It is this experiential knowledge that teaches us, too, that the images manufactured by the ego must all give way. None of them can be taken seriously. Every new strategy of the ego has to be laughed at and dismissed.

The Way of Unknowing

✿ MARCH 19

The practicality of the message of Christian meditation is that by our fidelity to the pilgrimage and by our openness to the indwelling love we come to understand that the great work in life is to communicate this love, to help others to see by its light. If we ourselves understand this and see and judge everything by the light of this love, then we have learned to live our lives with supreme compassion. The way of meditation is at the same time the way of compassion, of simplicity and of joy.

Only one thing is necessary for us to follow this way and that is to tread the pilgrimage with utter seriousness, not half-heartedly but wholeheartedly and single-mindedly. The Christian mystery has always called us to this wholeness and perfect sincerity, where our poverty leads to the riches of the Kingdom and a life lived in active goodness of every kind. St Paul says:

> We ask God that you may receive from Him all wisdom and spiritual understanding for full insight into His will, so that your manner of life may be worthy of the Lord and entirely pleasing to Him. We pray that you may bear fruit in active goodness of every kind, and grow in the knowledge of God. May He strengthen you, in His glorious might, with ample power to meet whatever comes with fortitude, patience and joy; and to give thanks to the Father who has made you fit to share the heritage of God's people in the realm of light.[1]

To enter the realm of the enlightened is our call and we respond to it by entering into our own heart. By entering our own poverty we learn to live our entire lives out of the infinite riches of God.

The Heart of Creation

[1] Col. 1:9–12

There is another important preliminary lesson in learning to meditate: the necessity for stillness. You must learn to be completely still during the meditation. That means, when you sit down choose a really alert posture, with your spine upright; place your arms and hands in a comfortable position, palms upright or facing down with thumb and forefinger joined. Then stay absolutely still. The temptation will come to scratch your nose or straighten your collar or tie or glasses. You will have all sorts of longings to stroke your beard, if you have one, or to rearrange your hair, if you have any.

If you are young enough and your bones are supple enough, you might try some kind of cross-legged position with the spine upright and the whole body peacefully together in a traditional posture, the perfect or lotus posture, for example. When you are beginning this, you may encounter a certain amount of physical discomfort, as well as the urge to scratch your nose. But you have to try to go through that as well as you can. If you are learning to sit in the lotus position, it would be wise to practise outside of meditation and then to sit in an ordinary alert cross-legged position to begin with and not undertake the lotus position during meditation until you have some proficiency in it. Alternatively, choose a chair with a straight back and a comfortable angle for arms and legs. Chair or floor is not of the greatest importance but the posture and stillness is of supreme importance. Posture is an outward sign of your inner commitment to the discipline of meditation.

The Way of Unknowing

The saying of the mantra is an act of pure selflessness. Every time we say the mantra we renounce, we leave behind, our own thoughts, our own concerns, our own hopes, our own fears. In losing these properties or possessions of the self we lose the self. In saying the mantra we become, as the Zen phrase puts it, 'the eye that sees but that cannot see itself'. A person meditating is a person looking straight ahead. One's vision becomes clarified because none of the distorting images of egoism can in any way refract the pure light of God which both enters and emerges from the eye of the heart.

Meditation is the way of love because its meaning and purpose is communion. But we simply cannot find adequate language to talk about meditation and that is why the Buddhist vocabulary, for example, or the sayings of Jesus, are so paradoxical to minds used to the half-truths of mundane experience. Nevertheless it is a true and necessary paradox that we must lose ourselves, we must leave our self absolutely behind in order to find our self.

The word *communion* expresses as perfectly as any the experience of meditation: that we are in a common union. Jesus and ourselves united with the Father. The way of meditation is a way of knowing reality simply because it is only by this most complete and undifferentiated union with the Creator that we can live fully out of our own roots. To live fully is to be conscious of our origin and so live fully out of the power of God. For this awareness we need to be steadfast. We need that steel in the spine that will enable us to return day after day to meditation; not concerned so much with progress or enlightenment or success but with the faithful, humble return to our task.

In meditation as Christians our hearts are directed towards God's love. Each of us has to discover and then to remember, knowing it with absolute clarity and certainty, that we are infinitely lovable and infinitely loved. We must know it, not just as an intellectual proposition but with experiential knowledge, in our own hearts. It is the most important knowledge there is for any of us and that is why meditation is so important.

The Heart of Creation

Through the experience of meditation we come to understand that each of us, meaning every living human being, is in a creative relationship with God through Christ. Meditation has such great importance because as each of us comes closer to Christ the whole fabric of human consciousness is knit more closely together. When we come to see this as individuals we also come to realise that the development of our own personal consciousness and the deepening of our own spiritual journey is not just a personal matter. It partakes of a responsibility for the whole human race.

Meditation teaches us something more: that the more deeply we enter into this mystery of unity the more truly human and humane we become. By deepening our commitment to our own human journey each of us is also deepening our commitment to the whole of humanity, in particular of course to that part of humanity that we encounter in our daily round.

This is to say our commitment is to the universal Christ. Even more, if that is possible, it is a commitment to the whole creation. This means a committed concern and compassion for the beauty of nature, and of the human spirit expressed in art, a respect for the environment and all it encapsulates in terms of value and beauty. Every part of life is deepened as we enter the mystery of the universal Christ.

Word Made Flesh

🎕 MARCH 23

There is the generosity needed to put our whole life into harmony with the spirit in our heart – to see to it that we don't add to the distractions. All of us have distractions arising from our very life. We all have things we are concerned about, things we are worried about, things we are responsible for. So what we must do is put our whole life into harmony with this search, this pilgrimage, which is a pilgrimage to our own heart. It is a pilgrimage that leads us to a freshness of spirit, a clarity of heart and a vitality of spirit.

Meditation is not turning our back on our life or on our responsibilities. Quite the contrary, in meditation we seek to be open fully to the gift of the life that is given us. This is nothing less than the gift of eternal life, eternal life that we are invited to be open to *now*. We need to be responsible people, to be *responsive* people, responsive to the gift of eternal life. As Jesus tells us, eternal life is to know our heavenly Father. In meditation we turn aside from everything that is passing away in order to know what is eternal.

Moment of Christ

What is meditation? In essence it is simply learning to say our word, our mantra, and the problem that most of us have to face is that the way is so simple that we cannot believe it, we cannot trust it. And so we are constantly running to books, to commentaries on books. We are constantly trying to learn about other people's experiences whereas the essence is the practice, the daily practice of learning to say our word, our mantra. Each morning and each evening . . . the art of meditation is learning to say your mantra from the beginning to the end without interruption. You have to learn, and it takes time and patience; you have to learn to let go of your ideas, to let go of the insights you have about yourself, or about God or about meditation. You have to learn what the ancient monastic fathers called 'the art of resting in the Lord'.

The mantra is simply our way to that simple, trust-filled silence, and as I say, we have to learn to say the mantra from the beginning to the end. When you begin you are bound to have questions, you are bound to ask yourself, 'Is this a complete waste of time? Are these monks talking complete nonsense, talking through their hoods?' All you can do is to continue to meditate and ultimately it is the practice itself that is authenticated. It is not what I say or what anyone says. The contact with your own spirit is what authenticates your meditation.

The Door to Silence

We must set our minds on God's kingdom. There have been, in recent times two thinkers who have had a very important influence on our society. One of them is Simone Weil and the other Fritz Schumacker. Simone Weil thought that the most important quality we could acquire in our lifetime was what she described as selfless attention. Fritz Schumacker came to the same conclusion and he described the selfless attention that Simone Weil speaks of simply as 'attention', learning to attend. Both of them were influenced by the tradition from which we speak: the tradition of contemplative prayer, the tradition of meditation coming from the early monastic fathers.

This is the crucial lesson that we have to learn from meditation: to attend wholly and totally, to pay attention. We all know from reading the Sermon on the Mount that each of us must not only change but we must be transformed. We also know from reading St Paul that we can only be transformed in Christ, through Christ and with Christ. If you want to change something in your life you have two possibilities open to you. You can try to will that change, you can try to redirect your life by acts of the will. I think most of us discover from our own experience that our wills are appalling weak and shockingly inconstant. There is another way: the other way is the way of total openness of the whole person. It is not the way of *in*tention but the way of *at*tention.

Being On The Way

When you start to meditate you hope that it is going to be a great help in your life. I suppose most of us then keep going because, in ways we perhaps did not imagine, it proves to be practical; it helps us. When we start to meditate, however, we should also be clear about the challenge that meditation will pose for us as we continue. At a certain point I think we are all tempted to give up. We are unsettled by the absolute nature of what appears, both of the mystery of God itself, and even by the absolute nature of the path of meditation.

In the encounter with the absolute we are tempted to hold back. We like to hang on to our familiar illusions. All of us, too, like to keep our options open. The best way to understand this inner contradiction is by reference to the ego. The ego is the father of lies, a prince of illusions. It is the ego who casts all the characters in our consciousness in their various roles. And the directing power of the ego remains unbroken as long as we are enchained to what is passing away by desire or regret which are both forms of possessiveness, forms of *being possessed*.

The Way of Unknowing

The children who come to our monastery to meditate are a marvellous witness of the naturalness of this way of meditation. They are a real example for the adults who come. They show the essentially childlike quality that we need to tread the way. 'Unless you become like little children you cannot enter the Kingdom of Heaven.'[1] It is a simple way. Its simplicity is its great challenge to us because we are trained to seek the truth, for accuracy, only in complexity. It is a simple but not necessarily easy way. It requires trust and perhaps indeed a certain recklessness to begin and it requires courage to persevere but all we have to lose are our own limitations.

Community of Love

[1] Mark 10:15

The call to meditate is an invitation to stop leading our lives on the basis of second-hand evidence. It is a call to each one of us to come to grips with our spiritual capacity and so to discover for ourselves the astonishing richness of the human capacity that is anchored in the divine reality, in the divine life-power. And it is also an invitation to be simply open to that power, to be energised by it and to be swept along by it, into the depths of the divine reality itself.

The lived process is very important. We must always beware of being intoxicated merely by the message, merely by the good news, merely by the ideas of the gospel. We must enter in, taste and see. And meditation is the process of entering in, of tasting, of seeing. Saying your mantra every day, making the time available for meditation, morning and evening, and placing your spiritual journey and the spiritual reality at the centre of your life, *that* is what is important.

That is what meditation is about – returning to your centre and finding that your centre is the gateway to the centre of All. And for that we have to stop living on the surface, we have to come to the depths.

The Heart of Creation

✿ MARCH 29

If we are to realize the full potential of the gift of life we need to see that our destiny is the same as Christ's. Our destiny is to be wholly at the service of God, to worship Him in the depth of our being, to worship Him in spirit and truth. Through such worship it is also our destiny to receive His love fully. The humble, ordinary task of saying the mantra, and saying it faithfully, is simply our way of entering this worship, of putting ourselves wholly at the disposition of God. Scripture returns again and again to the simplicity and clarity of the state of commitment and how far removed this state is from the mind-made substitutes of thought and language. It is when we learn to be simple that we enter into the absolute, the absolute commitment to the absolute love of God. To be simple is to be like Christ, an unambiguous *yes* to God.

Meditation is our total openness to the Spirit, so that in the whole of our life we say *yes* to God, say it with commitment, with generosity, absolutely.

In God we are and we know ourselves to be lovable and loved. This is the supreme reality that Jesus came to reveal, to communicate, to live and to establish. It is established in our hearts if only we will be open to it. This openness is what our meditation is about. It is only from this love and with this love that we can rightly understand ourselves and all creation. Without rootedness in love all we can see will be shadows and phantoms and we will never be able to make contact with them because they have no reality. Meditation is the invitation to journey deeply into your own heart, into your own being. What the traditional wisdom tells us is that only with such depth of experience and vision can we live our lives in real harmony with what is. This is what meditation leads us to: the understanding from our own experience simply that God *is*.

The Way of Unknowing

Meditation in this sense is a total ascesis. And ascesis is the antidote for arrogance. It is a path to ground you more and more in the strength, the 'virtue', of Christ. You thus become aware that strength comes from beyond yourself, is greater than you and contains you. Yet it is your strength. This is the mystery of the experience of prayer, that the power released in your heart is your power because it is the power of God. Learning to say the mantra is learning to receive everything from God but to receive it fully, not passively or half-heartedly. We respond in meditation with our whole being to the gift of our whole creation. Prayer realises this inherent potential for expanding in spirit, in union.

As always, we return to the mantra because to see the vision we must become still. To come into contact with God's Spirit in your heart you must come into contact with your own spirit in the simplicity of utter stillness. That is why we must go beyond all analysis, all division and observation and move into unity. And then we move from unity to union.

Word Made Flesh

Penetrate our inmost being with
your holy Spirit

Walter Hilton is a very good witness that there is no antipathy as it were between contemplative prayer, vocal prayer and liturgical prayer. He does trace a kind of progressive development through these forms but not in the sense that we ever get to a stage in our life when we have gone beyond liturgical prayer or vocal prayer. The development he really sees is a growth in the delight with which one enters into whatever form is appropriate at any time. And all these forms of prayer are, of course, complementary, provided that we know them as they really are: as entrances into the eternal prayer of Jesus which is His loving return to the Father. At all times in our lives all the various streams of prayer are coming together and binding us ever more closely to the Lord Jesus in the universal ocean of His prayer.

Christian Meditation: The Gethsemani Talks

APRIL 1

The wonderful revelation that is there for all of us to discover, if only we will set out on the path with discipline, is that our spirit is rooted in God and that each of us has an eternal destiny and an eternal significance and importance. That is a primary discovery for each of us to make, that the nature we possess has this infinite potential for development and that development can only come if we undertake this pilgrimage to our own centre. Our centre is our own heart because it is only there, in the depths of our own being, that we can discover ourselves rooted in God. Meditation is just this way of making contact with our own spirit and in that contact finding the way of integration, of finding everything in our experience coming into harmony, everything in our experience judged and aligned on God.

People ask, 'How long will this take?' or they say, 'I have been meditating every morning and every evening for six months and I'm not sure if it has made any difference yet.' The answer to that is that it doesn't matter how long it takes. All that matters is that we are truthfully on the way, on the pilgrimage, and that each day – although perhaps only by one centimetre at a time – our commitment to truth and to freedom grows. The growth is often imperceptible, but that does not matter. All that matters is that we are growing, that we have not settled for half and that we have not betrayed the gift of our own being but that we are committed to growth and to maturity.

Moment of Christ

APRIL 2

Ideals are so dangerous for all of us. There are so many who want to talk about prayer or read books on prayer or attend courses on prayer. But St Benedict advised us to say as little about prayer as possible – the monk who wants to pray has simply to enter into prayer. Because of this, monasteries have so much to offer the world as places where the turning to Christ, the conversion to Christ, is the clear basis of everything that is done in them. It is not that the monks are supermen but that they have organised their lives with an utterly clear priority. In their conversion they turn from themselves to their brethren in the community, to Christ in prayer, and to God in Christ. This is the clear Benedictine tradition and when it is fully alive in the hearts of men and women, it has the power to convert, to turn to Christ, all who come under its influence.

Letters From the Heart

93

When we sit down to meditate every morning and every evening, we respond to the task that is given to each of us to grow into that vision and into liberty of spirit, to advance in the infinite expansion of our consciousness in Christ.

St Paul speaks frequently of the evolving maturity of Christians. The call to prayer, the call to meditation is precisely a call to grow up, to leave the ego-centred irresponsibility of childishness behind and to become ourselves by finding ourselves *beyond* ourselves in union with the All. Again, understand that this requires a personal response, not just an agreeing nod, from each of us. The invitation is to see with our own eyes, to hear with our own ears and to love with our own hearts but also to do this in union with Him who is Love. Now, in practice this requires of each of us to go beyond all our personal, historical dividedness. All the dividedness within ourselves is required to be transcended. All the barriers that separate us from our true selves and from others and from God must be dismantled. And that means leaving all our images behind. Images that we have of ourselves, the images that we have of others and the images that we have of God.

The Christian vision requires us to be open to God at an imageless depth, and it is in openness there that all the false dichotomies are resolved in union, in oneness. In other words, the call is for us all together to return to a fundamental simplicity. The call of deep prayer is no less than the call to *be* to be yourself, to be in love, in trust, in total openness to what is. And it is almost meaningless to say that God is Love until we know it for ourselves, through an experience of our being in the being of God. Our call is to know it and that is what Christianity is about. Everything in Christianity must lead us to that or else we are left with a recipe for deceit.

The Way of Unknowing

Most of us start saying the mantra in the head, as we say: *Ma-ra-na-tha*. In my experience of teaching people over the years I find that most people have to say the mantra like that for some considerable time. But then, following Cassian's injunction to keep the mantra always before you – as you go to bed at night, as you wake in the morning, as you go down to your prayer, always preparing for your meditation – the mantra begins to take root. Then it begins, as it were, to *sound* in the heart and so you begin then almost to *feel* the mantra at a much more central level of your being. You could say that at this stage, the second stage you might call it, you *hear* the mantra. The third stage is when you begin to *listen* to the mantra and it's only then that your meditation is really beginning; when you are beginning to listen.

My teacher used to say this to me: 'When you get to this listening stage it's as though you are toiling up a mountainside and the mantra is sounding in the valley down below you. The higher you mount, the fainter becomes the sound of the mantra. And then there comes the day when the mantra is out of earshot altogether.'

Christian Meditation: The Gethsemani Talks

The reality of God's Spirit dwelling within us does not depend on our thinking about it. Indeed, it only becomes a personal reality for us, for each of us, when we stop thinking about it and when we enter into the living experience of it, in silence. That is why in meditation we do not think about ourselves or think about God or think about anything. Meditation is an experience of personal communion in the depths of our being. It is the capacity that each of us has if only we will learn to develop it: to be with ourselves, wholly present to ourselves, to be with God, wholly present to God. This it is that gives us the capacity to be wholly present to others.

Each of us, every one of us, is invited to discover this reality for ourselves and the way of discovery is to enter into profound silence and to stay, to remain in that silence, in humble fidelity. You must understand that meditating is very simple . . . Do not succumb to the temptation of just floating. Some people find that after saying the mantra for a few moments they become very peaceful, they become very calm, and the temptation is just to sort of possess the calm, to possess the peace. Learning to meditate is learning to be in a state of utter unpossession. Do not succumb to the temptation of finding that if an interesting thought or insight comes to your mind you follow it. Let it go.

The Door to Silence

❦ APRIL 6

We tend to think of meditation as inactivity. I think many people think of meditation as something either that prepares us for action or perhaps refreshes us after action, but the more you meditate, the more you realise that meditation is not an inactive path. It is not outside the sphere of action, rather it is at the centre of action. Meditation I think we could describe as 'pure action'. It is the highest form of human action and because it is pure action it takes us into the realm of 'pure being'. The one who follows this path rejects nothing. We reject nothing of our own selfhood and we discover ourselves integrated, all our powers, all our gifts, the total gift of our creation integrated, in harmony with the source of our being, in harmony with being.

The difficult thing for us is to be still enough and to learn to say the mantra with sufficient faith, and each of us must learn that for ourselves, but you must understand that the purpose of saying the mantra is to bring you into contact. In meditating, we come into contact with ourselves, and then journeying beyond ourselves we come into contact with pure being, with God. We have to understand that we do not belong to ourselves, that we belong to God and, therefore, we do not seek to possess ourselves. We seek only to be, to be *for* God. Listen to these words from the first Letter to the Corinthians:

> Do you not know that your body is a shrine of the indwelling Holy Spirit and the Spirit is God's gift to you? You do not belong to yourselves. You were bought at a great price. Then honour God in your body.[1]

Being On The Way

[1] 1 Cor. 6:19

It is nothing less than essential to meditate every day. Meditation is to the spirit what food and air are to the body. We must come to peacefulness, serenity and our capacity for true vision if we are to live in the light of God. Again and again the New Testament tells us that the light shines in our hearts. So we need only be open to it in humility and love. That is why we should try to the best of our ability to find a time and a place each morning and evening to turn aside from what is passing away and to be open to what is eternal. The most extraordinary mystery of our life is found in this conversion: that what is eternal is love, is God and dwells in our heart.

> What we have seen and heard we declare to you, so that you and we together may share in a common life, that life which we share with the Father and with his Son Jesus Christ. And we write this in order that the joy of us all may be complete.[1]

This is the Christian vision. It is the Christian message that we are invited to share in the light of God and in God's very being.

Word Made Flesh

[1] John 1:3–4

Meditation is a simple and natural process. It is the process that reveals our real being as a state of open-hearted receptivity to the Spirit of Jesus who dwells in our hearts. This revelation dawns when we renounce, step aside from, the external manifestations of our consciousness such as thoughts, words and images and when instead we move into the level of consciousness itself. We then become silent because we have entered silence and we are wholly turned towards the Other. In this fully conscious, fully free silence, we naturally open ourselves to the Word that proceeds from the silence. This is God's own Word, in whom we are called into being, and in which we ourselves are spoken by the Creator.

This is the living Word within us. Our faith tells us that we are wholly incorporate in this Word, but we need to know it fully, in the height, length, depth and breadth of our spirit, to know it though it is beyond knowledge. The silence brings us to this knowledge that is so simple that no thought or image could ever contain or represent it. By renouncing self we enter the silence and focus upon the Other. The truth to be revealed is the harmony of our Self with the Other. In the words of the Sufi poet: 'I saw my Lord with my heart's eye and said: "Who art Thou Lord?" "Thyself," He replied.'

Word Into Silence

As we all know we begin to meditate with all our confusion around us. We do not even quite understand why we are meditating. I think a lot of us start as very reluctant meditators. We hear about it and we begin in a half-hearted sort of way. But gradually a glimmer of light comes. We suspect that there might be something in it. The darkness is still all around us but there is just the faintest glimmer of light. When that happens the first step to take is to start meditating seriously, not with half your heart but wholeheartedly. That means to put the time aside for this way of revelation every morning and every evening. That is the first thing to do. The second step is to begin to commit yourself (and it takes time because you have to be patient) to saying your mantra for the entire time of your meditation. You should not be discouraged if you are a slow starter. It takes some of us four or five years to come to that stage. But what you will discover from your own perseverance is that saying the mantra is like a very gentle and very gradual dispelling of the dark.

Just imagine for a moment a vast, dark, empty hall. Each time you say your mantra it is like lighting a small weak candle. And I think so often it seems to us that just as we light one, the previous one gets blown out. But very gradually the dawn comes and you begin to realize that the whole hall is flooded with light. The wonder of meditation is that this revelation that the light has conquered the darkness and that Jesus is the light becomes universal in your experience. Everything and everyone is now flooded, illuminated with this light.

Moment of Christ

One of the first things we discover as we start to meditate is that we are already chock full of distractions and that it is not so easy to go beyond that surface level of distracted planning and analysis, to the depth. It is very humbling, not to say humiliating, to discover that after all our education with all the credits we have clocked up in so many clever areas of expertise, we cannot be still for more than a few moments and that our mind wanders off on the most ridiculous sidetracks. It ambles on, creating the most ridiculous fantasies with thoughts flying around at every level in our mind. We cannot be still. When you begin, and as you make that humbling discovery, you will soon face two temptations. The first is to give up completely and say, 'This is hopeless, it is not worth it, it is all beyond me.' The second temptation is to say 'Let me analyse what is happening.' The first temptation is to despair, or to evade the challenge. The second is the temptation to self-obsession, to become immoderately interested and engaged by your own mental processes.

Now the art of meditation is to teach you the discipline to continue, and to continue on a daily basis, as one who is committed to depth, to seriousness, to fullness of life. That is, to be one who rejects living at the surface as one's normal and necessary state of being. Meditation will gradually increase your discipline and your commitment will grow proportionately if you stick to it as a daily practice. Meditation will also teach you to turn away from your self, to rise above your own thoughts, to be detached from your own self-consciousness, vanities, fears and desires. It will lead you to turn naturally beyond that to something much greater than you can ever find in all the analysis or self-obsession our culture rates so highly. You have begun a journey through the undergrowth of the ego and the way through is the way of the mantra.

The Way of Unknowing

We have to learn to be content to say our mantra. Forget about all notions of progress, forget about enlightenment, forget about insight, forget about yourself and say your mantra. This is liberty of spirit. I think all of us know deep down that we have this call to liberty, that we have this capacity for liberty, and all of us know that we cannot live our lives to the full if we are always trapped in trivia, if we are always absorbed in things that are passing away. When we think of liberty we tend to think of the freedom to be able to do what we want to do. Certainly, this is an element in all living. But the liberty of spirit of which the New Testament speaks is not just freedom to *do*. It is, above all, the freedom, the liberty to *be*, to be who we are, to be one: all our potentialities joined together in a deep personal harmony.

Now we must be very careful that we are not just intoxicated by the ideas of meditation, by the theory. The theory, once we begin to encounter it in practice, in our own heart, will fill us with wonder, but encounter it personally we must. That is why our daily practice is of supreme importance. What we have to learn to do is to take our potentiality absolutely seriously, to understand that the Spirit of Him who created the universe dwells in our hearts and, in silence, is loving to all, and we have to enter our own hearts to discover that Spirit within our own spirit.

The Door to Silence

The big problem that all of us have to face is deciding what is really important in our lives and what is trivial; to learn to differentiate between what is passing away and what is enduring. The English medieval writer, John of Salisbury, wrote: 'It is not possible for one who with their whole heart seeks after truth, to cultivate what is merely empty.' I think that is the challenge that each of us has to face – not to cultivate what is empty, because with our whole heart we seek after truth, after love.

Meditation is so important for each one of us because we live in a society that is in real danger of losing its sanity. A human spirit that is healthy demands expansion. We all of us need room to breath and to expand and to fill our lungs with truth, with love. If we are healthy we know that we must cross all the frontiers to what is beyond. The spirit that is a healthy spirit is the spirit of an explorer. We are not terrified by the beyond, we are not too tired to seek what is ahead, but the spirit that is really healthy knows that there is no future for us unless we set out into it wholeheartedly.

Meditation is simply a way of coming to that basic healthiness of spirit, a state wherein our spirit has room to breathe, where it is not assailed and weighed down by trivia, by what is merely material; a state wherein, because we are open to ultimate truth and to ultimate love, we are summoned beyond all mere trivia. And we are summoned to live our lives, not out of the shallows, but to live our lives at the source, at the source of the river of life where that stream of life springs up with power and springs up in crystal clarity.

Fully Alive

Consider the saying of Jesus that whoever cares for his own safety is lost but whoever will let himself be lost 'for my sake' will find his true self.[1] To meditate is to lose yourself, to become absorbed in God, to be utterly lost in the generous immensity that we call God. None of us can ever find our true selves, we can never come into contact with full meaning or enter full understanding unless we are prepared for this way of letting ourselves be lost for the sake of the Kingdom.

None of us, in other words, can come to knowledge without faith. Fullness of knowledge is impossible without fullness of faith. And meditation is the way of faith because it is an entry into the otherness of God, and to enter on this way, to tread this path with true sincerity, we must learn to take the attention wholly off ourselves and to look only ahead. We must learn to look into pure love. The way to learn is the way of the mantra.

When you meditate day by day just say your mantra, sound it in your heart. Do not ask yourself, 'What am I getting out of this?' 'Am I enjoying this?' 'What insights am I getting?' 'How am I feeling?' All those questions can only lead us further down the blind alley of the ego. Recite your mantra and nothing else. The only problem of meditating is the simplicity of it. If only we could learn the simplicity to say our word like a child, with childlike faith, we would lose ourselves. We would lose ourselves in God and in losing ourselves we would find our way into relationship with all. We would find our way into love.

The Heart of Creation

[1] Matt. 10:39

In meditating we learn to be more and more sensitive to God's presence which we now apprehend not as something external to us, but as something interior, something which grasps us by the roots. We go on to live in his presence with absolute confidence and with a growing sense of certainty that He is the rock, the foundation, on which we are securely founded. God is the ground of being in which we are eternally rooted.

The longer we meditate the more we realise how unshakable faith is. It cannot be set aside simply because it is the very ground out of which we have learned to live. All this arises from the simple practice of saying our mantra every morning and every evening, in growing simplicity, in growing humility, in growing love, in growing wonder.

It is very easy for this to sound arrogant. It may seem extraordinarily arrogant to say that we come to know Christ as we persevere in our meditation. But I think the truth is not less than this. We do indeed come to know what it is to be in His presence. We do indeed learn, from being in His presence, to live out of the resources of that presence, thereby to communicate His goodness, His holiness to everyone we meet. We also come to understand that presence as present love, as actual compassion, as real understanding, as immediate forgiveness. The wonder of it all is that, if we live our lives rooted in these realities, as truths that are quite unshakable, we cannot be uprooted ourselves once the process is under way. Indeed, we are constantly deepening our commitment to Christ.

The Way of Unknowing

❧ APRIL 15

Meditation is so important because it is the pure consciousness of Jesus that burns away our ego. His glory is the power of a fully realised humanity, and to become engaged in a relationship with this humanity enables us to act beyond the confines of our self-perceived and often self-defined limitations. Glory is what burns away sinfulness.

The Christian way is to be centred in Christ rather than in the illusions of our egotistical self-imprisonment. We don't have to concentrate on our illusions or sinful tendencies but simply – and this does not mean easily – to allow the glory of Christ to burn them away, revealing them all as the sham they are. Glory entirely dissipates whatever is inglorious.

We need to remember today that this is what Christian prayer is about. Not the self-rejection of mock humility. Not egocentric dependence on or fear of a parental god. Not psychological games with our own minds. But transformation in glory. It is about living in harmony with the mystery of God in the depth of being. And because this is to be rooted in reality it is known by being rooted in joy and in love. Prayer is utterly realistic and the indispensable component of healthy realism. The only reality is God who is love, and the power and glory of this love are to be found within our heart – if we seek it. And if we seek if we find it. This seeking is the pilgrimage.

Word Made Flesh

APRIL 16

In contact with others we awaken to the deeper truth of our being that we are meant to see, and so we learn to travel beyond ourselves. This is why meditating regularly, whether daily or weekly, with the same group or community is such a source of healthy sustenance to our pilgrimage. We cannot maintain the delusion of an isolated pilgrimage when we are present with others. And yet, this very physical and spiritual presence recalls us to a deeper personal commitment to stillness, to silence and to fidelity.

The group or community similarly signals the end to all false heroism and self-dramatisation. Being in touch with the ordinary failings and limitations of others puts our response and fidelity into the perspective which we need for balance and harmony in our life. In the presence of others we know ourselves.

Every day I am more amazed at the range and variety of people who really hear the message of the teaching about meditation, who hear it from some deep and perhaps unsuspected stillness within themselves. And I am even more inspired that so many remain faithful to the discipline and the fidelity that makes the hearing really significant. They are people of all ages and backgrounds, educational, social and religious. But they have all discovered a common centre, Christ, who lives in their hearts and in the heart of all creation.

The Present Christ

✿ APRIL 17

St Peter tells us of the importance of holding the Lord Christ in reverence in our hearts.[1] Rooted in Him we are rooted in the principle of all life, in reality itself, and, founded in Him, nothing else has ultimate power over us, not even death itself. The challenge is to find our way to Him by finding the way to our own heart so that we can hold Him in reverence there. The way of meditation is consequently a way of learning to die to illusion to all unreality, and so it is the way of learning to rise with Christ, to rise beyond ourselves and our limitations to eternal life. It is learning to do this now, today, and not to postpone eternal life to a time when we may get to heaven. The Kingdom of Heaven is with us now and we must be open to it now because, as St Peter says, we must be alive in the Spirit and become fully alive with the life of God. As Christians we must never settle for less.

Our Christian life is not just a question of finding a way of getting through our lives. Every word of the New Testament suggests to us that it is of supreme importance that we live our lives in a state of continuous expansion, expansion of heart and expansion of Spirit, growing in love and becoming more firmly rooted in God. Each of us has to understand our potential, that we *are* an expanding universe, and so each of us possesses the potential for an energy-expansion that is not less than infinite.

Moment of Christ

[1] 1 Peter 3:15

Meditation and our daily commitment to it is simply the state of being converted, the state of living, not in imagination, not bounded by images, but the state of living rooted in the reality that is God. The simple expedient is to go beyond thought, beyond imagination, into this reality of God. That is what saying our mantra, saying our word, is about: transcending all thought and all images and being open to the supreme reality of God who is love. Our invitation as Christians, the invitation given to each one of us, is to live our lives in this state of dynamic conversion with, if you like, an *infinite* perspective: all life, all history, all time illuminated by Christ's love.

The cross is the great Christian symbol because its horizontal plane is intercepted by its vertical plane and the Christian vision is not a denial of this life, not a denial of history or of time, but an openness to the great fact of history itself, that time has been intercepted by Christ's love. This is the reality out of which we must live. We can only live out of it if we ourselves are open to it in our inmost heart – not images, not imagined illusions, however holy, however religious, but the reality, the rock that is Christ.

Being On The Way

There comes a point in time after we have begun to meditate when the self-conscious novelty of it wears thin and the ordinariness of it begins to appear. It is, ironically, at this moment when our self-consciousness is beginning to fade and the experience of wholeness begins to emerge that many people give up. The power needed to continue and to allow the mystery to dilate at the centre of our being is again what we call faith.

What the Church has always known is that faith is pure gift. The power that enables us to travel deeper into the ordinariness of meditation is fully personal. It calls forth from us a mature acceptance, but it is not our own in any possessive or self-dependent sense. We know it as the faith Jesus Himself communicates to us through His consciousness dwelling undividedly within us and among us. We receive this power from this source deep in the centre of our spirit where His Spirit dwells. We receive it too from the word of faith spoken to us in innumerable ways by both saints and sinners, the human community of the faithful.

The Present Christ

For modern people the word meditation often suggests passivity or inaction, but it is neither of these. Meditation is the way to a fulfilled state of being. Indeed it is the state of being which is prior to all action and without which all action will tend to be shallow, without the significance of permanence. All sane action in our lives must flow out of being at one with being. This means that to meditate, we begin to learn to be wholly alert; to accept oneself wholly; to love oneself; and to know oneself rooted and founded in the utter reality that we call God.

For the greater part of our life we live at the surface level, so often reacting to immediacy. But in meditation we are not reacting to external stimuli. We are learning to live out of the depths of our being, where we are finding and responding to the supreme, sole stimulus, the Creator. We are learning to be the person that we are called to be, as we align ourself in response to that source which has called us into existence. Being the person we are means enjoying the gift of our own creation before and beyond all desire, all expectations, all demands. The early monastic Fathers described this state as the state wherein we are one, and beyond all desire because we are utterly filled with the fullness of God. Being one is being whole. We have all we need for oneness, for wholeness, for passing beyond all desire. Desire is undesirable because it can only complicate and divide what is meant to be simple and unified.

The experience of meditation is therefore the experience of simplification, learning to become ever more and utterly simple. This is the secret of all happiness; to enjoy what is. Being is the primal experience of us all. Prior to all having, prior to all doing, *being* is enduring. It is the eternal in each of us.

The Way of Unknowing

The experience of prayer, the entry into the silence of Jesus, is first presented to us as an invitation that it takes nerve to accept. There will always be many reasons at hand for declining or postponing the invitation. But once it has been decided to accept it, the first moment of prayer and the first self-abandoning step requires every ounce of faith we have been given. The eternal silence of God that is so attractive in poetry or theology breaks upon us in such unfamiliar otherness that it takes much love, much being loved, to continue into the silence. Our encouragement, however, is this: whatever degree of faith we have been given is sufficient to begin, and once we have begun, the love we need floods our inmost heart.

Letters From the Heart

APRIL 22

The fullness of the life that Christ offers each of us is eternal life – life without limit. The mystery is that that fullness of life is offered to us now. All of us have to learn as we live our lives that there must be constant development. The invitation we have is to grow, to develop, to mature. One of the elements of that maturity is our growing capacity to enter the present moment more and more fully, more and more perfectly, more and more generously. That is why it is so important that we continue to meditate every day, faithfully, every morning and every evening.

Each time we meditate and each time we say our mantra we are entering into that process of development, deepening our capacity to be wholly in the now. The invitation that we have is to build our lives on the eternal rock that is Christ. It is so easy for us for our lives to pass before our eyes in some sort of haphazard kaleidoscope. It is so easy for us to live our lives being tossed around by waves of mere fortune, never knowing where we will be landing up next or how long we will be there.

The challenge for all of us is to find the rock who is Christ, to find Him in our hearts and then to respond to our lives, rooted in the knowledge that is love.

The Door to Silence

Concerning prayer, the tradition teaches us that Christianity is not basically a theology or an ideology. It does not have its fullest life in the mind. It is, most truly, a personal and total openness to the person of Jesus. In that openness we are taken by Him to the Father. Christianity is the religion of transcendence which sees us transcending our own limited life and entering the limitless life of God.

We teach meditation in a tradition of prayer that unites John Cassian and the Desert Fathers to *The Cloud of Unknowing* in the fourteenth century and, for example, Abbot John Chapman in the twentieth century. It teaches that the essential way to respond to the basic Christian truth is to be fully open to the reality of the life of Jesus within us, deeper than thoughts or words can reach. It teaches us that the way to this depth is a spiritual discipleship. We must learn to be disciplined. The essential discipline is nothing less than leaving self behind. This means leaving behind those limitations with which we so often identify ourselves and learning to be open to the limitless being of God. This teaching enshrines an astonishing Christian doctrine.

> Indeed, it is for your sake that all things are ordered, so that, as the abounding grace of God is shared by more and more, the greater may be the cause of thanksgiving that ascends to the glory of God.[1]

Word Made Flesh

[1] 2 Cor. 4:15

✥ APRIL 24

In meditation we turn the searchlight of consciousness off ourselves and that means off a self-centred analysis of our own unworthiness. 'If memories of past actions keep coming between you and God', says the author of *The Cloud of Unknowing*, 'you are resolutely to step over them because of your deep love for God.'[1] In prayer we come to a deeper awareness of God in Christ. Our way is the way of silence. The way to silence is the way of the mantra.

Time and again the practical advice of masters of prayer is summed up in the simple injunction: 'Say your mantra; use this little word.' *The Cloud of Unknowing* advises, 'and pray not in many words but in a little word of one syllable. Fix this word fast to your heart so that it is always there, come what may. With this word you will suppress all thoughts.'[2]

Abbot Chapman, in his famous letter of Michaelmas 1920 from Downside, describes the simple, faithful use of a mantra which he had discovered more from his own courageous perseverance in prayer than from teachers. He had rediscovered a simple enduring tradition of prayer that entered the West through Monasticism, and first entered Western Monasticism through John Cassian in the late fourth century. Cassian himself received it from the holy men of the desert who placed its origin back beyond living memory to Apostolic times.

Ward Into Silence

[1] *The Cloud of Unknowing*, ch. 6   [2] *The Cloud of Unknowing* ch. 7, 39

Meditation is experientially concerned with two important things: the presence of God, and becoming attentive to that presence. These concerns are as ancient and as modern as human consciousness itself, and no life can claim to be fully human that does not incorporate some training and attention to them. To ignore or postpone them is the foolishness of sin. Wisdom is different:

> If it is your wish, my son, you can be trained. If you give your mind to it you can become knowledgeable; if you enjoy listening, you will learn; if you become attentive, you will become wise.[1]

The purpose of meditation is that we listen and that we become attentive. We become attentive to the presence of God, who described Himself in the definitive Old Testament revelation as *I Am Who I Am*. Isaiah, who gives us the name of the Messiah, calls him Emmanuel, *God with us*. Over and over in the biblical revelation we read of how God reveals Himself to those who walk with Him, to those who live 'in confidence in His sight'. Again this is what our meditation is essentially about: *being with God* who is with us and making the journey of transformation confidently in his care. Meditation is a pilgrimage in which we journey to our own heart, there to find Jesus – the revealer and embodier of God. Finding His Spirit is the first stage of our pilgrimage. Then we continue our pilgrimage with Jesus to the Father.

The Way of Unknowing

[1] S1. 6:32–4

It sometimes happens that as you are meditating, particularly when you are beginning, a great feeling of peacefulness overtakes you. Then you say to yourself. 'This is rather marvellous. Where is this going to lead me? What is this about? Let me experience this.' You stop saying your mantra and the great likelihood is that as soon as you do it, the sense of peace has gone or becomes a memory. But there is usually worse to come because, having lost the sense of peace, you are determined to try and recapture it again. So you start saying your mantra more loudly or more intensely, more self-consciously to try to possess once more that feeling of peace.

But meditation, as St John of the Cross described it, is a way of dispossession. You are not trying to possess peace or God, or to get him to give graces, consolation, or a high of some kind. We are not asking for *anything*. We are meditating because it is necessary that we should meditate and so we meditate without demands, renouncing every sort of materialistic objective. The only true motive for meditation is the ultimate one – that we meditate to *be*. To be the person we are called to be in the Christian vision is a very wonderful vocation. The person we are called to be is a free person accepting fully and responding fully to the gift of our own creation.

The Heart of Creation

Meditating is utter simplicity. There is absolutely nothing complicated about it at all. It is a oneness of body and spirit and when we sit down to meditate we sit down as a whole person. We do not sit down to engage in some spiritual activity so that ten minutes later we can engage more productively in some secular activity. We sit down as the entire, the whole person that we are – body and spirit – and the purpose of meditation is that, by entering into that unity of our own being, we cease to live life on two, three, four or more levels. We live our life out of the one reality that we are. In this way the religious person can see meditation as a process of sanctification by the Holy Spirit whose gift is unity, who *is* the unity of the Tri-personal God. We are called to be holy as God is holy. This means to be one as God is one, to be unified in relationship.

In the Christian vision each of us is on a pilgrimage to discover that the wonder of our own creation is that we are created by God for an eternal destiny, for an infinite expansion of spirit. What we have to learn when we meditate is some glimmer of an insight into our own value and importance.

If God has sent His Son, Jesus, to reveal both His greatness and our potential, this is the basis of seeing our infinite value. Seeing it is the perception of faith and we learn in meditation that the source of faith is the Spirit of Jesus dwelling in our heart. Now, we know these propositions as statements of theological theory, but if we want to live the fullness of our life in the fullness of Christian faith, which is one and the same, then we have to uncover these truths as existent realities in our heart. And that is what meditation is about: uncovering the truth that reveals reality.

The Way of Unknowing

St Augustine's memorable sentence speaks freshly to every generation of Christians: 'My heart is restless until it rests in Thee.' It is the universal and perennial human search to find that rest and to realize that to find rest is to face the challenge of coming down to reality. We need to find the really solid base out of which we live. So much of life is passing away. The business of living is like sand running through an hourglass. But as we see the sand falling through we all know that this cannot be all there is. We know that there must be something more solid and enduring.

We know something else too. We know that we are not meant only to find and look at this rocklike base of reality but we are summoned to live fully from that base. This is the experience of liberty as described in the New Testament. Having been rooted and grounded in the solid rock that is Christ, we then live 'in Christ' so that our lives and their horizon begin to expand. This is the Christian experience. Our invitation is to live not just our own isolated lives, but to live out of the infinity of God – or, rather, *into* the infinity of God. The experience of meditation is about this rooted living in Christ. We find ourselves within His mystery and we lose ourselves within it.

Word Made Flesh

Meditating is absolute simplicity.

Now what happens? Basically speaking, it does not matter what happens. All that matters is that you say your mantra and you continue to say it for the entire time of your meditation. I think it is the experience of a large number of meditators, particularly beginners, that it will often seem that the half an hour you spend in meditating in the morning and in the evening will often seem a complete and utter waste of time. You will get up from your meditation and you will say, 'Now what did I get out of that?' 'Nothing.' 'What happened?' 'Nothing.' That is where meditating is an act of faith.

When we meditate, when we sit down to meditate, we put ourselves in touch with a great, a glorious physician. As we join men and women who throughout the ages have understood that the greatest wisdom is to leave self behind, men and women who have understood the words of Jesus: 'Unless you leave self behind, you cannot be my disciples'. These men and women have set out on this path to absolute liberty of spirit – the path whereby we leave behind all our own limitations and enter into the infinite generosity of God's love.

The Door to Silence

The central message of the New Testament is that there is really only one prayer and that is the prayer of Christ. It is a prayer that continues in our hearts day and night. It is the stream of love that flows constantly between Jesus and His Father. It is the Holy Spirit.

It is the most important task of any fully human life to become as open as possible to this stream of love. We have to allow this prayer to become *our* prayer, to enter into the experience of being swept beyond ourselves into this wonderful prayer of Jesus – this great cosmic river of love.

In order for us to do this we must learn a most demanding discipline that is a way of silence and stillness. It is as though we have to create a space within ourselves that will allow the consciousness of the prayer of Jesus to envelop us in this powerful mystery.

Moment of Christ

❀ MAY 1

There are no half measures. You can't decide to do a bit of meditation. The option is to meditate and to root your life in reality. The reality is the reality of liberty – that you are freed to be, and to be fully, every moment of your life. As far as I can understand it, that is what the Gospel is about. That is what Christian prayer is about. A commitment to life, a commitment to *eternal* life. Jesus taught that the Kingdom of Heaven is here and now. What we have to do is to be open to it, which is to be committed to it. Listen to Jesus's words in the Gospel of Matthew:

> The kingdom of Heaven is like treasure lying buried in a field. The man who found it buried it again; and for sheer joy went and sold everything he had, and bought that field.
>
> Here is another picture of the Kingdom of Heaven: A merchant, looking out for the pearls, found one of very special value, so he went and sold everything he had and bought it.[1]

This is the sort of commitment that we need – the commitment to meditate every day and in our meditation, to say the mantra from the beginning to the end.

Moment of Christ

[1] Matt. 13:44–6

❧ MAY 2

Meditation is our way of a total entry into the present moment. All of us have a tendency to live in the past or perhaps to live in the future. Do not live either in the past or in the future. Learn to be present wholly to the present moment, to the *now*, to the now that we can describe as the eternal now of God. Unhappiness comes largely from our refusal to be in the now. Even suffering has its meaning and unless we accept it fully in its moment we had the experience but missed the meaning. So what we have to learn to do in our meditation is to listen to the mantra with total attention. It is a narrowing down of our consciousness to a single point: the pointedness of the single sound of the mantra. That is what we have to learn to do: to say the mantra ma-ra-na-tha, to listen to it with a total and deepening attention – ma-ra-na-tha – and to do so in a growing simplicity and humility.

In The Beginning

✿ MAY 3

The journey is a simple one. It requires a certain vision of its importance, a certain humility to begin, and a certain fidelity and courage to persevere – the willingness, above all, to be led into fullness. These are all essentially human qualities, the qualities needed for any fruitful contact with life, and the journey is an ordinary one. We don't follow it to sensationalise life but to see life – every aspect of it as well as its inner harmony and direction – as the mystery it is. The greatest danger and temptation is to complicate. As far as I can see, if we are actually on the journey – if the poverty of the mantra is the rich core of our lives – then we grow more and more simple. Increasingly, we see the utter simplicity of the call Jesus addresses uniquely to each one of us, to leave all things and self behind and to follow Him into the infinite freedom of His union with the Father.

Letters From the Heart

I have often found when I have talked to people about meditation that it is the non-Christian, even the person with no religion, who first understands what meditation is about. To many ordinary churchgoers and many priests, monks and sisters, the mantra seems at first a suspiciously new-fangled technique of prayer or like some exotic trick-method, or some kind of therapy that may help you to relax, but has no claim to be called Christian. This is a desperately sad state of affairs. So many Christians have lost touch with their own tradition of prayer. We no longer benefit as we should from the wisdom and experienced counsel of the great masters of prayer.

All these masters have agreed that in prayer it is not we ourselves who are talking the initiative. We are not talking to God. We are listening to His word within us. We are not looking for Him, it is He who has found us. Walter Hilton expressed it very simply in the fourteenth century. He wrote: 'You, yourself, do nothing, you simply allow Him to work in your soul.'[1] The advice of St Theresa was in tune with this. She reminds us that all we can do in prayer is to dispose ourselves; the rest is in the power of the Spirit who leads us.

Word Into Silence

---

[1] *The Scale of Perfection*, Bk II, ch. 24

Language is so weak in explaining the fullness of the mystery. That is why the absolute silence of meditation is so supremely important. We do not try to think of God, talk to God or imagine God. We stay in that awesome silence open to the eternal silence of God. We discover in meditation, through practice and taught daily by experience, that this is the natural ambience for all of us. We are created for this and our being flourishes and expands in that eternal silence.

'Silence' as a word, however, already falsifies the experience and perhaps deters many people, because it suggests some negative experience, the deprivation of sound or language. People fear that the silence of meditation is regressive. But experience and tradition teach us that the silence of prayer is not the pre-linguistic but the post-linguistic state, in which language has completed its task of pointing us through and beyond itself and the whole realm of mental consciousness.

The eternal silence is not deprived of anything nor does it deprive us of anything. It is the silence of love, of unqualified and unconditional acceptance. We rest there with our Father who invites us to be there, who loves us to be there and who has created us to be there.

Word Made Flesh

✿ MAY 6

One of the aspects of meditation we have to come to terms with is to learn to approach it, not with seeking to gain something, to possess something. We have to try to approach it much more in terms of total devotion beyond ourselves. Spinoza wrote this: 'Blessedness is not the reward of virtue. It is virtue itself. We do not find joy in virtue because we control our lusts, but contrariwise: because we find joy in virtue, we are able to control our lusts.' Christians have often approached their spiritual life in terms of reward or possession. The enemy of all spiritual value is desire, seeking reward, seeking to possess. The wisdom that unlocks the spiritual treasure is the spirit of poverty, a spirit of non-possession. Indeed, in meditation we learn to be dis-possessed.

The spiritual path is a path that leads away from self to the other. As you know from your present experience of meditation, we must tread it in faith and with courage. To learn to say the mantra so that we dispossess ourselves of all thought, of all self-consciousness, requires devotion. It leads us to absolute liberty because we have left behind all the second-rate values: success, wealth, possession, power, whatever it may be.

Fully Alive

To learn to meditate we have to be prepared to enter into the whole truth and that is the challenge of it. The truth about ourselves, the truth about others and the ultimate truth of all reality. We have to learn that to meditate it is necessary that our meditation be unconditional. We cannot lay down any conditions whatsoever. Our commitment is to the whole truth. It would be a great mistake to start meditating unless we were ready to at least begin to launch out into this readiness to face the truth. For much of our life we keep in place all sorts of filters that filter the truth as we allow it to come in and as we allow it to go out. Probably these filters are necessary for most of us as long as we are living our lives at the surface, as long as we are trying by the expanding of much energy to protect our own image of ourselves and to project our own image of ourselves.

In meditating we commit ourselves to living our lives not at the level of image or at the shallow level of half-reality. We commit ourselves to reality as it is and we do this by a steady process, a daily process – and that is why it is important to meditate every day – a steady process of re-directing all our energy from defensive and protective channels into the creativity that leads us not to seek to protect our own image of ourselves, but urges us to set out on the road to discovery.

The Door to Silence

The challenge that each of us must face if we would live our lives to the full, if we would respond profoundly to our own humanity, the challenge that we must face is to make contact with this power–source within our own hearts. The call is a call to maturity, to fullness of life, and each of us, as we approach that maturity, must learn to accept our own personal responsibility for this work, for this journey and it is not something that we can avoid, any one of us. Either we become pilgrims and follow the pilgrimage or we do not. We cannot, as it were, pay someone else, pay some substitute to make the pilgrimage for us. The challenge that Christ addresses to each of us is a personal challenge: remain in My love. The second rule for the pilgrim arises from the fact that we do not make the journey alone. The invitation to oneness, to fullness of life is given to all.

The road may indeed be narrow but our vision must be all-embracing and must be extended to infinity. It is not just 'my' pilgrimage. It is always 'the' pilgrimage. It is never just 'my perfection' or 'my holiness'. The call that each of us has, that every one of us has is to become one with the all-holy God. It is the universality of this call and the response to it that is the basis of all true community. When we share the silence of our meditation together, each of us is transformed as we travel within and beyond ourselves and we each of us and all of us become one in Him. All our cultural, social, educational, religious barriers are transcended in the power of His love.

Being On The Way

The way that our tradition teaches us to approach this self-revelation of God is not to think, to analyse or to reason but to learn to be like a little child to learn to be humble. This we do by the simple and constant repetition of our word. So to meditate we need to sit still and to sit upright. To begin with you will want to scratch your nose or your ear but you must go through that. Just sit still. Then you must learn to say your word.

You will find as you go on that you can be saying your mantra at one level while at another level there are thoughts going on below and at another level above, at another on one side, at another on the other side. Ignore them all. Say your mantra. That is the art of meditating: to say your word in the silent eye of the storm.

The mystery of meditation is that you are led to the experience of stillness of unity, by the mantra which is just like God's harmonic sounding in your heart. It leads you into an experience of unity – unity within yourself, body and spirit, unity with all creation. As you sit meditating you are in your place in the universe and meditation leads you into the personal experience that God is the centre of the universe. This is what the daily practice – the daily practice is essential – will lead you to, in all gentleness.

You can't learn to meditate by reading books about meditation or by listening to talks on meditation. You can only learn to meditate by meditating, every day, every morning and every evening. Do not let yourself be discouraged. To begin with you will find that you miss a morning or an evening (or a day or a week or a month). But if you have understood, even dimly, what is involved in the practice of meditation you will return to it to learn how essential it is to enter into that depth of your spirit every single day of your life. Meditation is about freedom, liberty of spirit, expansion of spirit. But the way is, to us as modern people, surprising because it is a way of discipline.

The Way of Unknowing

When you begin to meditate you have to have some motivation. You have to have an objective to get you going, a push as it were to start you on the road. There is no better incentive than to achieve this state of inner and outer harmony. Peace is a noble objective and a unifying one. In many of the sacred scriptures of both the eastern and western traditions this goal is described as the state of *blessedness*, of *glory* of *salvation* or simply of *life*. The sense is of being fully, humanly alive. So, if you want a motivation to meditate that would be as good a reason as any. But once you start to meditate on a regular daily basis in your life you will begin to realize that soon meditation operates by its own dynamic.

Once you start to meditate you realize that you come to it with a decreasing amount of demands and without looking for any pay-off. We mediate simply because this is the clearest way that we can find to lead us to the sense of wholeness, of oneness, which is beyond our control or possession and which can only be enjoyed once we accept its nature as gift. In meditation we discover that the acceptance of this gift is what life is given to us for, to be whole, to be one, and thus to activate all the potential that is freely ours for life, for happiness, for being. Meditating is to the spirit just what breathing is to the body.

The Heart of Creation

❦ MAY 11

Her [Mary's] silence possesses a radiant creativity and consciousness because it is so clearly the positive, affirmative silence of other-centredness. She is not retreating from reality into a private netherworld but is attendant upon the emergence of the grand design of her life and the full revelation of its meaning. Her transcendence of self is the archetypal other-centredness of a mother's love for her child: a relationship that captured the Jewish religious imagination, both as an expression of God's unfailing love for human beings and of their dependence on God. The reality of such a relationship is only revealed in silence. And it is only in silence and through silence that we can interiorize what is beyond our comprehension and apprehend the power of a design larger than ourselves: it is the medium of *transcendence*.

Community of Love

🎇 MAY 12

It is necessary to meditate every day and that too is hard for people of our society: to undertake such a discipline that is not concerned with what we are going to get out of it, but *simply* concerned with being. Being the person you have been created to be is to be rooted in your own deepest spiritual centre. The cultivation of growth is simply the daily return, every morning and every evening, to the practice. Saying your word, sounding your word, and thereby entering into greater and greater simplicity. Aristotle defined eternity as a 'perpetual now'. The power of meditating is that we seek to be fully in this present moment, not thinking about the past, not regretting the past, weeping over it, analysing it. Not planning for the future. God is. God is love. God is now.

One of the difficulties we face in learning to meditate is that it is very difficult for us to imagine that thought is not the highest and essential activity of the human being. It seems almost scandalous to a group of people who are hearing about meditation for the first time – especially if they are a religious group – when I say to them, 'You must learn not to think about God.' And if I say to them, 'Prayer is in essence not imaginatively talking to or thinking about God,' the group is likely to be shocked. But it is true. We have to understand that each of us possesses a much greater potential than mere thought.

The Way of Unknowing

🎇 MAY 13

If you are patient and if you are faithful (and meditation will teach you to be both patient and faithful), then meditation will bring you into deeper and deeper realms of silence. It is in the silence that we are led into the mystery of the eternal silence of God. This is what St Paul says when writing to the Ephesians and telling the ordinary people of Ephesus, people who are not that different from us – what is the promise of the Christian life:

> So He came and proclaimed the good news: peace to you who were far off and peace to those who were nearby; for through Him, we both alike have access to the Father in the one Spirit.[1]

That is what meditation is about – access to the Father in the one Spirit, the Spirit who dwells in your heart and in mine, the Spirit who is the Spirit of God. Christian meditation is simply openness to that Spirit, in the depth of our being, in all simplicity, in all humility, in all love.

Moment of Christ

[1] Eph. 2:17

The teaching of Jesus on prayer in the gospel is the basic teaching underlying meditation. For example, the spirit of faithful trust implicit in the mantra is what we find in His injunction to 'Set your mind on God's kingdom and His justice before everything else and all the rest will come to you as well.'[1] Today especially, I think, many people are perplexed as to what is involved in the spiritual option in life presented in these words and accepted in meditation. You can't help, in our very materialistic society, but say what is there in this for me? If I follow the spiritual path, what am I going to get out of it? Just consider the basic concepts of life that we have in our society. The basic model we operate on is an essentially mechanistic one and life can easily become a mechanical operation. We think we are learning to deal with life by mastering the procedures and as a result we miss the vitality of experience.

Meditation is important because we must free ourselves from this mechanistic view of ourselves and of society. Spiritually it is of supreme importance because it is the most practical step that any one can take to rediscover oneself not as a machine or as a mechanistic cog in some vast assembly line, but in knowing ourselves as possessing an infinite depth of mystery. It is of supreme importance that every one of us make this discovery for ourselves. We can't take someone else's word for it. It is something that each of us must know, and know fully and clearly, from our own experience. Once we do know it, everything else follows from it in right order.

The Way of Unknowing

[1] Matt. 6:33

The Christian life is the ever deeper exploration of the truth that God loves us and that Jesus dwells in our hearts, in the deep centre of our being. Even more astonishing is to know that we dwell in His heart, 'in Him'. The mind cannot comprehend this. Only the heart can know it because it is the knowledge that arises only in love.

We know ourselves loved and so we love. Meditation is concerned with completing this cycle of love. By our openness to the Spirit who dwells in our hearts, and who in silence is loving to all, we begin the journey of faith. We end in faith because there is always a new beginning to the eternal dance of being-in-love.

Faith and love engender hope. Christian hope is the supreme confidence in the truthfulness of Jesus and in the reality of His love. This confidence enables us to say the mantra. We let go of everything that we want, everything we know and by which we know that we are. We let it go in the abandon of poverty; and we are then free to launch out into the depths of the mystery that is love, faith and supreme confidence.

> Because I live, you too will live; then you will know that I am in my Father, and you in me and I in you.[1]

This is why we leave all words behind and learn to be still: still in body, still in mind, still in spirit. Rooted in our word, rooted in Jesus and rooted in love – for one another and in Him.

Word Made Flesh

[1] John 14:20

We come to our meditation not looking for experiences, even the experience of light or enlightenment. We come to it because we have come to understand that each of us, in our lives, must make contact with what is essential. We come to meditation because we know that we cannot any longer live our lives with meaning unless we set out, in all seriousness, and with discipline, to be open to the source of meaning, to be found within out own deepest self. All of us who have even the slightest inkling of what the Christian gospel is about, all of us know that we have been created by love, for love. We know that or at least we suspect that. But we know too that love cannot be demanded. Love cannot be earned, love is given, and in Jesus it is revealed to each of us how great is the extent of God's love for each one of us personally. Jesus Himself has told us that He has placed His love within our hearts and by meditating we do not set out to earn God's love or to deserve God's love, we simply set out to be open to what is given, to what is.

In The Beginning

✿ MAY 17

Our lives are not only busy, they are usually noisy. But if our life is to be charged with meaning, to have depth and to be a true growth in consciousness, we have to be rooted in silence, rooted in the spirit, in the mystery whose depth can never be plumbed and whose meaning is found only in the consummation of union. We are each called to enter with wonder into this mystery with our whole being, in the total immediacy of the present moment which is the eternal moment of God. To be touched with this wonder is to be made reverent and so to know in the absolute certainty that belongs to our own experience that the energy of creation, the power of love, dwells in the human heart in silence and in the stillness of pure consciousness.

The Present Christ

All of us know, I think, what George Herbert expressed in his poem, 'Prayer is the soul's blood'. We know that by the experience of transcendence we are vitalized and we find our place. But what is the milieu in which we pray? Until fairly recent times we tended to think of prayer as a somewhat individual activity and our involvement with the community we saw as something else. But in the New Testament there is one central unifying reality and that is the reality of love: love of God, love of neighbour, love of ourselves.

Jesus is the revelation of God and in the New Testament He is God's love made visible in the world and His vision is a vision of a community; and Christianity, in the vision of Jesus, is a fraternity of brothers and sisters who respond together to the same reality that is beyond them and yet contains them and constantly expands them. In our meditation we seek to be, to be who we are and to come into the presence of God who is as He is and above all we know that in our prayer we are not trying to possess God or to change Him. We are trying to be one with Him as He is. I think it is true to say that there is a new and wonderful dimension added to prayer when we can find others with whom we can share this experience. In sharing our meditation together we similarly accept one another as we are.

The Door to Silence

❀ MAY 19

To understand what it means to meditate you have to begin to appreciate the fact that the essence of meditation is not thinking, but *presence*. Each of us has to learn to be wholly present in the moment that we have. So much of our time we spend thinking what we will do in the future or about what we have done in the past. So for much of our time our minds can easily become distracted with memories and with plans. In meditating we have to learn to become wholly inserted into the **now** of the present moment. To meditate we have to learn to say our word, our meditation word, our mantra, with pure attention and when we meditate together in a few minutes, each of us has to learn to say our word with a growing and deepening attention and we deepen that attention by listening to the word as we say it.

The Door to Silence

This is from the gospel of Matthew:

> No one is worthy of me who does not take up their cross and walk in
> my footsteps. By gaining one's life, a person will lose it. By losing one's
> life for my sake, they will gain it.[1] And later in the same gospel: 'Jesus
> then said to his disciples: 'If anyone wishes to be a follower of mine
> they must leave self behind. They must take up their cross and come
> with me. Whoever cares for their own safety is lost. But if one will let
> oneself be lost for my sake, they will find their true self. What will
> anyone gain by winning the whole world at the cost of one's own true
> self. For what can one give that will buy that self back?[2]

I think all of us have read the gospel and all of us who have tried to
open our hearts to the call of Jesus can sense the truth in those words: the
paradox that Jesus puts before us, that to find our life we must lose it.
That paradox we know at a deep level of our being is true and the challenge
that each one of us faces is this: How are we going to lose our life, to lay
down our life, so that we can follow Jesus, not just at the limit of our life
but at the centre, not just at the periphery but at the depth of our own
being? He himself was the great example. As we know from the gospels,
He often withdrew from his disciples to be alone with His Father. That is
exactly the invitation: that we have to leave the surface, to leave the
periphery and at the centre to be at one with Jesus, to be with Him in
the Father.

Fully Alive

[1] Matt. 10:38–39   [2] Matt. 16:24–26

❦ MAY 21

Unfortunately in our complex and self-conscious society we think of meditation as something extraordinary. Yet it is something for which each of us was created: to be simple, to be one and to flourish in the state of absolute oneness and peace. Meditation is that most ordinary part of our daily life when we are most our self. In stillness we are simply ourselves, neither remembering our past selves nor straining to become any other self. In stillness we are more and more deeply rooted in God, the creator–source and the supreme self, the 'great I am'. At these times of supreme ordinariness we are living out of the depths of that eternal selfhood, not the shallows of our ego-identities. The power of our being is ours in God.

One of the mysteries we have lost contact with in Christianity in recent times is the fullness of this power bestowed as a gift on each of us.

> I thank God for all the enrichment that has come to you in Christ. You possess full knowledge and you can give full expression to it, because in you the evidence for the truth of Christ has found confirmation . . . It is God Himself who called you to share in the life of His Son Jesus Christ our Lord; and God keeps faith.[1]

Word Made Flesh

[1] 1 Cor. 1:5–6, 9

❀ MAY 22

Meditation is, in some ways, like a mining operation and we have to go down deep into our hearts, and in the Christian vision, this descent into the depths of our being is so we can uncover the great treasure that each one of us possesses, the Spirit of God, in the depths of our own being. Now it is useful if you can meditate early in the morning and early in the evening. Everyone has to find in the circumstances of their life the times that suit them best and are possible for them. But if you can, meditate first thing in the morning and in the early evening. It is good, I think, to come to your meditation purified, to wash at least your face and hands so that you can wash away the dust of the day or the drowsiness of the night. This washing prepares the body to be alert for the purity of meditation.

Then we prepare our spirit by regular, calm, deep breathing. This sets the scene for the serious work that we are entering into. Remember that meditation is entering into the presence of the One who is and it is in His presence, in the presence of the One who is that each one of us learns to *be*, to be the person we are called to be. To meditate we must pass beyond all images and above all, the image that we have of ourselves. So that when we begin to meditate we divest ourselves of all our masks. We, as it were, set them down on the ground beside us and we begin to become the real person we are in absolute simplicity and then we begin to say our mantra – ma-ra-na-tha. Remember, we are saying our mantra not to impress anyone or to create any further image of ourselves, even a spiritual image. We are saying our mantra in order to leave all images, all words behind so that we can be in utter simplicity and we must stay still.

The Door to Silence

❀ 143 ❀

You might find it helpful at times, especially when you meditate in a group with others, to prepare for the meditation period with some suitable music, the purpose of which is to forget all the preceding words, to forget the ideas, to empty your mind of anxious concerns. It can prepare you to say your word gently. You should say your word with the simplicity of a child. Do not ask yourself, 'What am I getting out of this? Is this philosophically sound?' Put all those questions aside at the time. Say the mantra from the depth of your being, in all simplicity. For the rest, if we can make ourselves available, if we can be there, everything else is given. Everything is gift beyond that. What is necessary for us is to be there. And meditation is the simple way of being there. We are realizing the new era which Jesus has inaugurated:

> His divine power has bestowed on us everything that makes for life and true religion, enabling us to know the One who called us by His own splendour and light. And through this might and splendour He has given us His promises, great beyond all price, and through them you may escape the corruption with which lust has infected the world, and you may come to share in the very being of God.[1]

This is the spiritual reality within which we have our being: *sharing in the very being of God*. The way to realize this reality is the way of discipline and seriousness of purpose, of daily return to the discipline. It is the way of simplicity, of fidelity and, as you will find, it is the way of love.

The Way of Unknowing

[1] 2 Peter 1:3–4

MAY 24

We cannot, strictly speaking, achieve or acquire concentration. As St Paul said, we do not know how to pray.[1] There are no tricks or devices that will get quick results, no instant mysticism, or at least none that will not overload an unprepared and undisciplined psyche. But there is a way for us to prepare ourselves for the emergence, in a natural process which is itself the gift of God, of the light of the Spirit. The mantra stills the mind and summons all our faculties to the resolution of a single point; that point we know as the condition of complete simplicity which demands not less than everything.

Meditation is not a technique of prayer. It is, though, an incredibly simple means of leading us into an integral awareness of the nature of our own being and of the central, authenticating fact of our being which is the Spirit praying 'Abba, Father' in our heart. I say 'simple', not 'easy'. The way of simplicity soon becomes a pilgrimage in which we will experience the difficulty of laying down our lives. But we are not alone on the pilgrimage. We have both the community of the faithful in persevering, and the guidance of the Spirit in our heart. To the degree that we lay ourselves down, to the same degree and a hundredfold will we be restored to ourselves. The fruit of the radical simplicity of the mantra is a joy beyond description and a peace beyond understanding.

Word Into Silence

[1] Rom. 8:26

What Jesus tells us is that there is nothing worse than being half awake (or half asleep). When you sleep, sleep fully and when you are awake, come to full wakefulness. And that is what our meditation leads us to. By becoming wholly present in *this* moment, in the moment when we say our mantra, we enter into the Eternal Now of God. The principal criticism one might have of contemporary Christians is that we are and have been so slow to understand the full, present magnificence of the invitation that we have to be wholly open to Christ. St Paul writing to the Corinthians of this invitation to life says, 'It is God Himself who has called you to share in the life of His Son Jesus Christ Our Lord; and God keeps faith.'[1]

The tradition tells us that the life, the power of God, the power of His love is to be found in our own hearts. Finding that power requires that we be totally present to it. The tradition also tells us that our call is to become wholly awake to this mystery and to awaken to it as a mystery of wholeness. We discover ourselves by losing ourselves in the Other, and only then can we discover our essential place in the total mystery of Reality.

Moment of Christ

[1] 1 Cor. 1:9

The essential message of Christianity is that our call and our potential is to enter into the life of God through Jesus, through His Spirit present in our heart. We do this, not by analysing God or analysing Jesus, not by thinking about God or thinking about Jesus, but by being silent and still and, in His Spirit's presence, opening our hearts to His love. We do so in the steady rhythm of our daily meditation.

There is a great paradox to face. People looking at meditation from the outside see it as dull repetition. They see the saying of the mantra as something so repetitive as to be almost impossible. But if you really learn to say the mantra, that is, if you really learn to meditate, you will find that the mantra can never become mere repetition. It never becomes boring, because it is always, in new depths, taking you beyond yourself. It is always opening your spirit to what is beyond, to more of the infinity of God.

But these are only words. You can only learn this from your own experience. And you can learn it, if only you can learn to say your mantra, not thinking about yourself, not surveying yourself in the silence of meditation but by letting go of thought and all self-concern. Say the word with the simplicity of a child. As St Paul says elsewhere, the secret of life is Christ because in Christ lie hidden all the treasures of God's wisdom and knowledge. The astonishing thing is that Christ Himself is to be found in our own hearts. Learning to say your mantra is simply setting out on this pilgrimage to your own heart, there to find all the treasures of wisdom and knowledge.

The Way of Unknowing

Meditation is so simple that this is part of the difficulty. People in our sort of complex society are trained only to give their faith to what is complex. That is why it is probably helpful for people to go along to meditation groups several weeks in a row and to share again and again the simplicity involved in meditation. They can learn the essentials of simplicity and hear some of the ordinary things that make it easier to be simple – taking off your shoes, perhaps, not wearing tight clothing, sitting upright.

Meditation is a discipline of simplicity. Our world needs to learn it urgently. It is a discipline whereby you direct all your powers of consciousness to God. Instead of being at the mercy of your mind with its myriad thoughts and imaginations you bring your mind, your consciousness, to silence. In that silence you quite naturally become open to God and God's power. It is an utterly benevolent power which we can only describe with the word '*love*'.

Word Made Flesh

❧ MAY 28

There is nothing that our modern world needs more urgently than men and women who are rooted in themselves, confident of their own being, confident in their own capacity for goodness, their own capacity for loving and for being loved, and for that confidence we need that sense of being wholly at one with ourselves and sitting still every morning and every evening. Once we are rooted, once we are still, then we begin our next great task of learning to be attentive to the mystery at the heart of creation and learning to live our lives in harmony with the mystery.

What does it mean to be alive? Surely, it is our awareness of being and that awareness is intensified by our awareness of the being of others, by our awareness of the being of all creation, by our awareness of the being of God. And our life begins to reach its fully human point, its point of profundity when we begin to realize that being is love. Each one of us is filled to our capacity for love and for being loved, and meditation is simply the process whereby we enter fully into that mystery of love.

The Door to Silence

The advice that I would give you is, try, to the very best of your ability, to just keep saying the mantra. It seems much more difficult than it is. It is like swimming or riding a bicycle. You know when you see a bicycle for the first time as a child you look at it in awe and you think it is impossible, no one could possibly stay on those two wheels and keep going. I am bound to fall off. And you get on the thing and tense every muscle in your body and – you fall off. So you say, there you are, what did I tell you, it's impossible. It is the same with meditating. We tend to approach it from a very tense starting-point. But if you can only stay there, the gentleness and the compassion and the peace and the love of God will overwhelm you.

You need not be at all concerned about your distractions. They are only a cause for humility. It is an extraordinary thing – here we are, living in the most sophisticated, complex culture that has been known on the face of the earth – with all the advantages we have of education, and every kind of book at our fingertips – and we cannot sit still for ten seconds! So it should make us humble.

Just persevere with that encounter with humility and say your mantra. You have to be gentle when you start. But what I would suggest is, if you do find that you have to give up, say in the first week of meditating, well, maybe you had better give up. But in the second week, out of the seven days, only give up on six, not on all seven, and gradually try to extend it. Do not give up because you do not achieve perfection. Perfection is relative. You are perfect if you reach the potential you have at this moment. To be perfect means encountering our limits and gradually pushing them back.

The Way of Unknowing

Meditating is in many ways a sacrificial act. We lay ourselves on the line, we offer ourselves to God abandoning everything that we are and we simply say our mantra. That is both the challenge of it and the power of it. It requires trust, absolute trust, and you cannot be a Christian unless you learn to trust absolutely. What every one of us can find out from our own experience is that at the moment of trust the trickle of life becomes a torrent and the reason is that this act of trust starts the process of breaking down the barriers of our own ego. Again, as we all discover on the pilgrimage itself, this is a mere beginning. As St Paul says, 'We start out in faith, we continue in faith and we arrive in faith.'

Our Christian life, the power of the life of Christ within us, is something that is constantly expanding, constantly growing in our hearts. Meditation is an entrance into the nearness of God. He is to be found in our own hearts. Also, it is an entrance into His infinite space. As each of us must discover for ourselves, it is entry into this vast, silent space that is the real power of meditation. From that silence God answers our questions, God answers the yearnings of our heart with the simple answer of love. His love is our hope, our unshakable confidence that, whatever the difficulty, whatever the challenge, we can meet it out of the infinite resources He gives us. He does all this within us in silence, if only we will allow the mystery to encompass us.

Being On The Way

People often ask. 'What is the experience of prayer like?' By that they mean, 'What happens?' In the silence – peace. In the silence – presence. And deeper silence. The way into that silence requires great patience, great fidelity and it requires in our tradition of meditation that we learn to say our mantra. As John Cassian said, the mantra contains all the human mind can express and all the human heart can feel. That one little word conveys and leads us into the silence which is the silence of creative energy. How long this takes us is of no concern to us. 'To the Lord a thousand years are as a day.'[1] The only thing that matters is that we are on the way and that means the simplicity of our daily meditations, every morning, every evening.

The wonder of the way is caught in these words of St Paul writing to the Romans:

> Therefore, I implore you by God's mercy to offer your very selves to Him: a living sacrifice, dedicated and fit for His acceptance, the worship offered by mind and heart. Adapt yourselves no longer to the pattern of this present world, but let your minds be remade and your whole nature thus transformed. Then you will be able to discern the will of God, and to know what is good, acceptable, and perfect.[2]
>
> *Moment of Christ*

[1] 2 Pet. 3:8
[2] Rom. 12:1–2

❀ JUNE 1

The purpose of meditating is to advance along the way to the fullness of your own humanity. Meditating is simply accepting the gift of our creation and developing the potential we have to respond to the gift fully. We are not people who have to live on the surface, or people who are condemned to live lives of shallow emotion. Meditating is leaving the shallows, leaving the surface and entering into the depths of your own being.

The reason why, in the Christian tradition, we meditate, is that we believe that Jesus has sent his Spirit into these depths to dwell in our heart. Or, to use other words, the Spirit of God, the Spirit of the Creator of the universe dwells in our hearts and in silence is loving to all. In the Christian tradition, meditating is simply being open to the Spirit of Love, the Spirit of God.

One of the things we learn through meditation as we mature, as we go further along the path, is to be equally content with either form of silence: with the infinite sense of his presence or with the finite sense of his absence. It is harder for us at the beginning because when we start to meditate we haven't learned much detachment. We haven't reached the stage where we can be equally content with absence as with presence, and anyway we are always looking for our meditation to satisfy us.

We are always looking to prove to ourselves that it works, that now we know God, now we have learned to live in his presence. But the purpose of the second form of silence, his absence, is to purify us so that we learn to love God selflessly as He loves us (and Himself). He teaches us to be strong in love, strong in fidelity and to ensure that we love God *for* Himself and *in* Himself and not only for any manifestation of His presence that satisfies us.

The Way of Unknowing

🎞 JUNE 2

We had a dear Irish lady come to one of our groups a few months ago and I explained to them briefly what had to be done. And I told them that the mantra that I recommend is 'Maranatha'. I recommend it because it is in Aramaic, the language Jesus himself spoke, and because it's probably the most ancient prayer in the Church: St Paul ends Corinthians with it, John ends Revelation with it, it can be found in the Didache. Throughout the *Cloud of Unknowing* the author urges us to choose a word that is full of meaning; but that once you have chosen it, to turn from the meaning and associations and to listen to it as a sound. 'Maranatha' is a perfect mantra from that point of view. Anyway, this good lady listened to all this and then we went in and meditated. And when we came out she said, 'Oh, Father, a dreadful thing happened once I got into the meditation room: didn't I forget the mantra!' And she said: 'I sat there and I thought, how can I meditate if I hadn't the mantra? But, Father, God is good; didn't I remember it after a few minutes: Macooshla, Macooshla!'

Christian Meditation: The Gethsemani Talks

✿ JUNE 3

A group of Christians who meet together to meditate, to pray, to worship is not, then, just a mere social gathering. It is a group aware of its power: a power that arises from the transcendent reality of the presence of the Lord Jesus in their midst. The purpose of their meeting is, before anything else, to attend to the reality of this presence, to deepen their silent receptivity to it, to make it (what it already is) the supreme reality of their lives. So, each member of the group is other-centered, turned away from him or herself towards the living Lord. And the group then becomes truly a community – like that described to us at the end of the second chapter of Acts: 'A sense of awe was everywhere ... all whose faith had drawn them together held everything in common ... with unaffected joy.'[1]

Letters From the Heart

[1] Acts 2:43–4

Meditation is important for us because it is the process whereby we keep our contact with the creative centre of our being, not just open but in a constant and continuous state of expansion. So meditation is a process whereby creative energy is released within us. In our modern secular world we easily forget that we have a divine origin, a divine source, that the incandescent energy of our own spirit emanates from the Spirit of God. We forget that God is our Creator and in the forgetting we lose contact with our own essential nature and because we lose this sense and contact with our divine origin we ourselves become de-humanised.

The great task that confronts each one of us is to discover our own inner spiritual capacity. That is to say: to discover within ourselves our own potential for creativity, our potential to respond fully to the gift of our own life and to the lives of others and to the gift of the whole of creation.

The Door to Silence

🎋 JUNE 5

The early Church was utterly clear that our call is to enter into the very life of God. No other objective compared with this in priority. The early Christians also knew that the way we come to this is through the human consciousness of Jesus which is to be found in the deep centre of our being. Meditation is simply the pilgrimage to the heart where we find the Spirit of Jesus worshipping the Father in love. Christian meditation is simply to be open to that love which is the Spirit.

This is the plan of the universe: the purposeful call to share in the life of God in Jesus. Our tradition teaches that this call is given to everyone, not to specialists. We have only to listen to it. Anyone who takes the time to be silent will hear it in their heart. Then we respond to it simply by being wholly open to it. Cleansing our hearts and minds of everything foreign to it is the way to purity of heart. Letting go of everything that blocks it is poverty of spirit.

Meditation is the way to poverty and purity of heart. It is necessary to meditate every day and to be faithful in constancy to the mantra. That is how we leave our egoism, distraction and fear behind us. Meditation then gradually brings us to that discipline whereby we can be wholly free, wholly open to God and at one with love. Nothing could be more ordinary.

Word Made Flesh

There is no doubt of the absolute demand of the mantra. In essence it is our acceptance of the absoluteness of God's love flooding our heart through the Spirit of the risen Jesus. Our death consists in the relentless simplicity of the mantra and the absolute renunciation of thought and language at the time of our meditation.

This is not an esoteric doctrine or method. The mantra has been in the Christian tradition of prayer from the beginning and the understanding that prayer is beyond the operations of the mind is to be found in every authoritative statement. St Bonaventure wrote that, 'if this passover is to be perfect, we must set aside all discursive operations of the intellect and turn the very apex of our soul to God to be entirely transformed in Him.'[1]

I do not wish to imply that meditation is the only way, but rather that it is the only way I have found. In my own experience it is the way of pure simplicity that enables us to become fully, integrally aware of the Spirit Jesus has sent into our heart; and this is the recorded experience of the mainstream of the Christian tradition from Apostolic times down to our own day.

Word Into Silence

[1] Journey of the Soul to God VII

I am sure you have reflected on what it is that brings each of us to meditate. People must have a pretty strong desire to meditate to come out to talks on meditation on cold winter nights and then to undertake a new spiritual discipline that they, with difficulty, begin to incorporate into their already overcrowded lives. I think it is that some instinct in us tells us that we must go deeper. We can never be content just to live at the usual surface level of activities and distractions. Some spiritual instinct tells us that there is a great wealth and a great power to be found if only we can learn to be still and mindful.

The great interest in meditation in our society is symptomatic of the self-evident limitations of material things to bestow any ultimate satisfaction or meaning. More and more people in our busy, shallow society are discovering that they must find how to live their lives at a deeper and at a richer level. We are beginning to understand how urgent it is that we do not allow ourselves to be trivialised. We must refuse to be conditioned to be content to live at the surface. We must insist on the need to make contact with the depth of our being.

The Way of Unknowing

✿ JUNE 8

Meditation is in no way isolated from the meaning of our ordinary activity. Our set times of meditation, our fidelity to the saying of our mantra from the beginning to the end of these times, constitute the essence of our activities because meditation is our realization of Being, of pure action. Meditation is pure activity. It is action in the sense that it is the positive, purposeful deployment of energy, an ordering and focusing of all the energies that make up the mystery of our personhood. It cannot be a merely passive state, because what is both energetic and still is at the highest point of action, energy incandescent – consciousness. We know this in very immediate experience, the experience of persevering in our journey up the mountainside. The faith demanded of us by the pilgrimage requires the quite unpassive qualities of courage, perseverance and commitment.

The Present Christ

Meditation is learning to be sensitive to, and to be aware of, His presence within us. It is His presence within us that teaches us that each one of us is made whole by the power of His love and if we can make contact with those depths within us we discover that we are not just isolated persons. Each of us, in this mystery of Christ dwelling in our hearts, each of us is called to love and to be loved beyond all division. Now why meditation? The key to all this is the essential principle of harmony to be found within us and that principle is the Spirit, the Spirit of Christ, and meditation is simply the way of focusing – not just our attention, but our lives – on that principle of harmony, of unity, of love.

It is essential, in order to take the journey seriously, to meditate every morning and every evening. There are no short cuts. There is no instant mysticism but there is the reality of the pilgrimage to your own heart and in meditation you are not asked to accept someone else's experience second-hand, not even the testimony of the apostles or St Paul. Each of us is invited to plumb these depths, to make contact with the Spirit of Christ ourselves, out of our own experience, and in that process to become wholly real, wholly the person you are called to be. In that process, living out of the power of Christ, all division is transcended.

In The Beginning

To begin to meditate requires nothing more than the determination to begin. To begin to discover our roots, to begin to discover our potential, to begin to return to our source. And God is our source. In the simplicity of meditation beyond all thought and imagination we begin to discover in utter simplicity that we are in God; we begin to understand that we are in God in whom we live and move and have our being. We try to describe this growing awareness that we discover in the silence and daily commitment as 'undivided consciousness'.

Meditation is just this state of simplicity that is the fully mature development of our original innocence. As St Catherine of Genoa expressed it. 'My me is God. Nor do I know myself save in Him.' The wonder of the proclamation of Christianity is that everyone of us is invited into this same state of simple, loving union with God. This is what Jesus came both to proclaim and to achieve. This is what each of us is invited to be open to. 'My me is God. Nor do I know myself save in Him.'

As we all know from our own sad experience we are so easily distracted. God's love is given to each of us freely and generously and universally. God's love flows in our hearts in a mighty stream. But, like Martha in the gospel story, we are all of us so busy about so many things.

All of us must therefore address our own lack of discipline. We must bring our restless wandering minds to stillness. It is one of the first great lessons in humility we learn, when we realise that we come to wisdom and stillness, and we pass beyond distraction, only through the gift of God. His prayer is His gift to us and all we have to do is to dispose ourselves, and this we can do by becoming silent. Silence is the essential human response to the mystery of God, to the infinity of God. We learn to be silent by being content to say our mantra in humble fidelity.

Moment of Christ

The gift of His Spirit that is given to each one of us is infinite. It is the gift of the totality of God pouring out His Spirit into each of us and our response has to mirror that generosity and totality. It is a call to Christians *not* to respond mindlessly, half-heartedly, occasionally. The call is to respond generously with everything we are, with everything we have at this moment. And we have much to bring. We have our hearts, our minds, our lives, all of which, when we meditate, are integrated, concentrated and aligned on Christ. Everything that we are comes into a harmony with His being, with His love. Nothing is excluded and that is why we have to learn to say the mantra with such total fidelity, total generosity, total attention.

The gift *is* given. All we have to do, each one of us, is to be open to it, to realise it. But we must approach our task and follow our way with simplicity, with humility and with gentleness. We must learn to be very gentle with ourselves as we learn to root the mantra in our heart. Only the smallest effort is required. Everything is given to us and basically what is asked of us is only that we are faithful to the daily pilgrimage and that we give the pilgrimage first place in our lives. Fidelity leads us to realise that the gift *is being* given. Then, as each morning and evening we turn faithfully to our meditation and during our meditation remain faithful to the mantra, the gift reaches us, the cycle is completed.

The Way of Unknowing

JUNE 12

We all need to be encouraged to tread the way faithfully day by day as we return to our morning and evening meditation. We don't need to be encouraged in the progress we are making. That would be altogether too self-conscious an approach to prayer and far too egotistical. Yet we need to take heart constantly and to be encouraged by reflecting on what God has accomplished in Jesus. Looked at from His point of view it is His glory that matters. From our perspective (as long as this is separate) it is our faith, not our progress, that matters. We should, in the great poverty of the mantra leave even our progress behind. The way of faith is also the way of humility.

> Humble yourselves then under God's mighty hand, and He will lift you up in due time.[1]

This faithful humility and humble fidelity is the way of meditation. Every time we sit down to meditate we humbly leave everything behind and make ourselves as fully available as we can to the power of God released in our hearts. We must learn to be awake, to be alert. Not, as usual, alert only to ourselves, our ideas, fears and desires, but alert to God.

Christian prayer is not only attention to God but it is coming to fullness of being in God. This is our invitation and our invitation is our destiny, given to us in Jesus. Do not be discouraged, then, and do not try to rate yourself. Measuring your progress has no significance whatever. The only significant measure is the infinite power of Christ in your heart.

Meditation is the way of being, being in God, being-in-love. All that is necessary to know is that we are on the pilgrimage and that we are continuing to be faithful. Continuing to say our mantra as best we can, day by day, with growing simplicity, deepening poverty.

Word Made Flesh

[1] 1 Pet. 5:6

One of the things that Jesus says to us is: 'The truth will set you free.' Meditation is our way to perfect liberty of spirit and this is a call that each one of us has to respond fully to – the gift of our creation – and to respond in the depths of our own being so that we may attain to this perfect liberty of spirit. When we are beginning to meditate, we must be very clear in our minds that we understand it as a discipline. There is no liberty unless we undertake the discipline and beginning to meditate is a commitment to that discipline. Meditation is nothing whatever to do with some magical technique. It involves the fullest human response from each one of us, a response to a daily discipline, to a lifetime discipline that leads us to this absolute liberty of spirit.

The Door to Silence

❀ JUNE 14

Maranatha means 'Come, Lord'. You can use another mantra but the word, the mantra, that I recommend you to use is *maranatha* to begin with. I think it is important to use it, if you can.

The essence of the mantra, as I have suggested to you, is that it brings you to silence. It is not a magic word. It is not a word that has any esoteric properties to it or anything like that. It is simply a word that is sacred in our tradition. *Maranatha* is possibly the oldest Christian prayer there is after the Our Father. It is a word that brings us to great peacefulness, to rest and calm. Certainly to begin with I would recommend you use a word that has at least an open vowel sound in it. I think that everything considered the best word you could use to start with is *maranatha*.

The best time to meditate varies very much according to the body chemistry of the individual. The best time for most is probably early in the morning, before breakfast, when you are at your freshest. Perhaps a cold shower might be part of the prescription. And then in the evening. I think probably the best time is before your evening meal. That isn't always possible for everybody, especially if you are coming home from work and your family has got the meal ready or a guest arrives. It depends very much on the circumstances of your life. Those are probably the optimum times but what is of supreme importance is that you do meditate every morning and every evening. It can be done. The busiest people often find the time that the less busy say they cannot find.

The Way of Unknowing

We have come to think of prayer largely as our movement to God, as an activity that we are responsible for, a duty we perform to please God or to appease Him. There can be an element of charm, of childish sincerity in this, but true prayer eschews the sentimental. We have been summoned to a spiritual maturity in which, as St Peter tells us, we are 'alive with the life of God'.[1] Now if he, St Paul, and the New Testament as a whole deserve to be taken seriously, we are led to say that prayer is something greater than our talking to God, or imagining God, or imagining holy thoughts. Indeed, as St Paul said, this cannot be a real explanation of prayer if it is true that we do not even know how to pray. But as he goes on to say, 'the Spirit is pleading for us in our inmost being beyond words, beyond thoughts, beyond images, with sighs too deep for words.'[2]

Prayer then, is the life of the Spirit of Jesus within our human heart: the Spirit through whose anointing we are incorporate in the Body of Christ and by which, in turn, we are returning fully awakened to the Father. We are praying when we are awakening to the presence of this Spirit in our heart. If this is so, there can be no forms or methods of prayer.

There is only one prayer, the stream of love between the Spirit of the risen Jesus and His Father, in which we are incorporate. If this is so, there is no part-time or partial prayer as if the Spirit were not always alive in our heart. But there are times, our twice-daily meditation, when we make a complete turn of consciousness towards this ever-present reality. There comes a level of awakening to which St Paul was clearly directing the Thessalonians when he told them to 'pray without ceasing',[3] when our awareness of this reality is constant throughout the most diverse activities or concerns.

Word Into Silence

[1] I Pet. 4:6   [2] Rom. 8:26   [3] I Thess. 5:17

If you want to learn to meditate it is necessary for you to meditate every day, every morning and every evening. That means that we avoid all the business of rating ourselves in terms of success or failure, in terms of progression or regression. Meditating is the way of learning just to *be*, to be who you are, in the presence of God, to be who you are in complete simplicity and that is what the mantra leads us to when we learn to be faithful to it. I think it is true to say that the gospel calls us, not to analysis but to synthesis, the synthesis that is knowledge. To know another requires commitment to the other.

In the language of classical antiquity, it was said you could never know another until you loved the other. This in turn required the simplicity to let go of everything else so that you might love. Then we come to the heart of the mystery: the knowledge that the New Testament speaks of is not so much *our* knowledge, which in any case is always limited, but it is the knowledge by which we are known and that is our invitation: to so open our heart and minds that we know with the knowledge of God, and the call of the New Testament is a call to union. We must be unified in ourselves in order to find our union with God.

The Door to Silence

✿ JUNE 17

By being wholly still we become wholly open. Open to our own wholeness, the mantra brings us to a depth and wonder of attention that eventually transcends distraction. The purpose of the word is to bring us to this point of stillness and openness which is beyond all division and disharmony. Do not therefore be discouraged if the stillness and peace do not become an immediate and constant reality. There will be glimpses of this reality. But do not linger over them or try to possess them.

When you encounter the division and disharmony within yourself continue saying the word, open and faithful to the prayer of the Spirit in your heart. The weekly meditation group is a real grace to help you to persevere and to continue deepening your journey. Indeed it is a grace that we should be seeking to be open to the supreme reality that is God, that is love. The way – it cannot be said too often – is the way of simplicity. Say your word like a child and you will realize the dimensions and wisdom of this simplicity. Do not try to unravel the mystery but allow God to unfold His mystery in your heart. God will do so within the simple union of love you have in the deep centre of your being. It will be a personal, unique unravelling which makes a unique contribution to the universe as a whole and to the whole design of creation.

Sit down, close your eyes and say your mantra.

Word Made Flesh

Christian prayer, then, has the essentially dynamic quality of the mystery of Jesus himself because it is an encounter and entry into the person of Jesus, who is the way to the Father. The Christian pilgrimage is a turning, a conversion, a following of Christ and a journey with Christ. It is never complacent or self-satisfied. And its essential insight is that our full meaning lies beyond ourselves. Salvation, within this terminology, is *being on the Way*, being turned toward the dynamic power of Jesus and being taken up in him to the Father. Salvation is entering the kingdom of heaven that is within us.

One of the great perils of the pilgrimage is that we talk so much about it and so cleverly *imagine* ourselves on it that we actually fail to tread it, to put one foot in front of the other. I have spoken to you of this danger often enough. It is the *pax perniciosa*, mere religiosity or 'body floating.' We are all in continuous need of that quality that St Paul speaks of in I Thessalonians[1], the quality of *hippomone*, sometimes translated as patience, sometimes as endurance, but best of all, it seems to me, as fortitude. This is the courage to keep on the Way with growing fidelity to our twice daily meditation – times in the day when we quite explicitly put everything aside so that we may enter the journey of the Lord with our full attention.

Letters From the Heart

---

[1] Thess. 1:3–8

❀ JUNE 19

Scripture is a continual source of understanding and inspiration for the Christian pilgrimage and for the way of meditation that makes that pilgrimage a single-minded and unified journey. Consider these words from the Book of Revelation in the light of your daily meditation.

> I heard a loud voice, proclaiming from the throne: Now at last, God has His dwelling among the human race! He will dwell among them and they shall be His people, and God Himself will be with them. He will wipe away every tear from their eyes; there shall be an end to death and to mourning and crying and pain; for the old order has passed away.[1]

We are led to meditate because we are convinced that the old order has passed away and because we are convinced that God does dwell among us. In faith we are convinced that God dwells in our hearts. And if only we will take the trouble and the time, each of us is invited to *find* God in our hearts. Everyone is invited to undertake the journey and then all that is required is that we stay on it.

The Way of Unknowing

[1] Rev. 21:3–4

The way of meditation is not a way of escape. Above all, it is not a way of illusion. We neither try to escape the real world of untidy ends and chaotic beginnings, nor do we try to construct an alternative, illusory reality of our own. What Jesus promises us is that if we do hold Him in reverence in our hearts, if we believe in Him and believe in the one who sent Him, His Father and our Father, then all the chaos and all the confusion in the world can have no ultimate power over us.

The stresses, the strains, the challenges, all remain but they are powerless to defeat us when we have founded our lives on the rock who is Christ. This is the real task. This is the real challenge that each of us must face, to enter into the reality that is Christ, the rock on whom we can build our lives with the absolute assurance that He will love us through all our mistakes, through all our changes of heart and mind and through every moment of our lives until the last moment of our life, because He is supreme love.

The love of Jesus has made us one with Him. By becoming open through silence to His reality we become open in wonder to the reality of God. That is why the way of prayer is a way of ever deeper, ever more generous silence. It is not enough just to think about silence or to talk about silence – we must embrace it! To learn this silence, to be open to the gift of it, we must learn to say our mantra.

Our regular times of meditation immerse us in this silence and we emerge from the silence refreshed, renewed and re-baptized in the power of the Spirit. What each of us discovers in our prayer is that simply to *be* in His presence is all sufficing. In that presence we are healed. In that presence we find the courage to live our lives through Him, with Him, in Him and for Him. Once we begin to be open to this power, everything in our lives is charged with meaning. The meaning comes out of the silence. All our talking, all our living, all our loving find meaning from this silence and flow back into it.

Moment of Christ

Why meditation is important for all of us is that, in order to enter this all-important process of conversion, to change our angle of vision and learn to love, we have to make certain significant readjustments. We have to adjust to the fact that God is the ground and centre of all being. We have to adjust to God as the centre of *our* being and so we have to accept that we can only be truly ourselves in Him.

There is no human being who does not need to learn that we have to abandon all the compromises we have made with the truth, and to see and know that our destiny is to come into the full light of His love. Only in that light will we ever be able to know who we are, what reality is, who God is. It is the primary destiny of each of us to come to that knowledge, to come to that self-authenticating truth, the liberating truth about ourselves, about Him, about all that is.

Meditation is of such supreme importance because it is in the power of His presence that we learn that we have nothing to fear in coming to the truth about ourselves. We have nothing at all to fear from past or future events. In coming to the truth about all reality we learn that we have nothing to fear in coming to the truth about God, for we learn that God is truth itself and is unfailing compassion, almighty gentleness, rectifying forgiveness. Meditation is the traditional and simple process whereby we learn to leave all fears behind because they are cast out by a truth-filled love.

And meditation is a pure opening of the heart, a *being energized* by God's infinite love.

The Way of Unknowing

More and more thinkers in our society who reflect on the large questions determining our common future are coming to realise that the basic social problems are essentially spiritual. The basic problem – it is also the basic opportunity – for each person is to know who we are, what our potential is and then to realise that potential in the love of God.

Meditation meets these basic questions of life for each person. Because of our commitment to its practice, meditation means we do not have to be content living at one remove from spiritual reality, merely reading about it or listening to others talking about it. The social importance of meditation is rooted in this personal dimension of spiritual experience.

The supreme Christian insight is that God is *love*. The supreme Christian experience, which cannot be separated from authentic insight, is to know this love in your own heart. All this is mere words – sounding brass and tinkling cymbals – unless we take practical steps to be open to the reality to which the words point.

Word Made Flesh

Some more fortunate people might start to meditate while still in the stage of innocence, but most begin with a sense of having lost something that they must recover. Often we have an urgent sense that our essential survival depends on our finding our way back to that innocence. The marvel of the journey within, however, is that we recover something much greater than what was lost.

The wonder of the Christian message and its vision of the journey is its proclamation that we recover not just our own lost innocence, but the innocence of Christ. Our new innocence is what He recovered for all mankind, through the cross, through the resurrection. The path back to the spring of eternal life may be demanding but on the way we follow the stream that flows directly from the spring. And so, even on the journey itself we are given all the refreshment and all the guidance we need.

Meditation is our way onto the path. The Spirit is the stream flowing within our hearts. The mantra is the implement that clears the way through the impenetrable forest. We must simply stay on the journey and we must be faithful to the recitation of the mantra. We must never settle for half clarity, for half enlightenment. Our call is to come into the full light of Christ, and it is a call given to each one of us to grow to that maturity and full stature which is nothing less than the full, immortal life of Christ. As St Paul says:

> So shall we all at last attain to the unity inherent in our faith and our knowledge of the Son of God – to mature manhood, measured by nothing less than the full stature of Christ.[1]

The Way of Unknowing

[1] Eph. 4:13

Two sayings of Jesus are of great importance when we are beginning to meditate. The first is: 'Unless you become like a little child, you cannot enter the Kingdom of heaven.'[1] To learn to meditate we have to learn to be very simple. We have to re-learn how to be childlike. We have to learn, as a child learns, by accepting the teaching on faith and by devoting ourselves to its practice. We have to learn to rediscover the capacity for wonder which comes with faith and practice combined. We so easily lose that as we lose our early simplicity. Meditating is a returning to innocence and a sign of it is a returning to a state of wonder.

The second helpful phrase of Jesus is: 'No one can be a follower of mine unless he leaves self behind.'[2] In saying your mantra you have to let go of your own thoughts, your own theories and ideas, your imagination, fears and daydreams, and simply be there, listening to the sound of the mantra. Whatever you do, do not think about yourself. If you find, as all of us do, that it is difficult to sustain this, as soon as you discover that you are distracted, or that you are again thinking about yourself, return very gently and very humbly to the mantra. The mantra is a great teacher of humility.

The Heart of Creation

---

[1] Matt. 18:3   [2] Luke 9:23

❀ JUNE 25

What I would recommend you to do when you are starting is to start with a morning and an evening meditation. When you have got that absolutely, regularly built in, then if you want to and if the circumstances of your life permit, put in a midday meditation. I think that would be good, but I wouldn't expect most people to come to that for maybe a couple of years or so. One has to start very gently, being very compassionate towards oneself. All of us I think find that we start, we give up, we start again, we give up and so on. You have to be very gentle, prudent and have self-understanding. What I think you will find is that the experience itself is self-authenticating. Experience teaches.

You will simply find that the longer you have been meditating for, the more your day seems to come into shape and the more purpose you have in your life. Then the more you begin to see the meaning in everything and the more you will find that love grows in your heart. Now it may be that there is a good deal of meanness there as well, but the love is growing. And that is the real test of meditation. But you cannot put any sort of materialistic test to meditation. More does not necessarily mean better. The real test is the love growing in your heart.

The Way of Unknowing

Now to tread the spiritual path we must learn to be silent. What is required of us is a journey into profound silence. Part of the problem of the weakening of religion in our times is that religion uses words for its prayers and rituals, but those words have to be charged with meaning and they must be charged with sufficient meaning to move our hearts, to set us out in new directions and to change our lives. They can only be charged with this degree of meaning if they spring from spirit, and spirit requires silence. We all need to use words, but to use them with power we all need to be silent. We all need religion, we all need the Spirit.

Meditation is the way to silence because it is the way *of* silence. It is the way of the mantra, the word that leads us to such a silence that it ultimately charges all words with meaning. Now we don't need to be too abstract about this. We all know that we can often come to know another person most profoundly in silence. To be silent with another person is a deep expression of trust and confidence and it is only when we are unconfident that we feel compelled to talk. To be silent with another person is truly to *be* with that other person. Nothing is so powerful in building mutual confidence between people than a silence which is easeful and creative. Nothing reveals inauthenticity more dramatically than silence that is not creative but fearful.

Moment of Christ

And so we have to understand, to begin with, that the Kingdom of God is not a place but rather an experience. Because our understanding of the nature of prayer is so often distorted by our imagination this is not always an easy insight to hold on to. But it is vital. Our childhood education about heaven as a 'place we go to after we die' and about prayer as 'telling God what we want' has enormous and enduring influence on us. But we have to awaken to the major limitations of this education, designed, as it was, for children. So often our spiritual maturity falls far behind our other levels of growth and development.

The experience of prayer is the experience of the liberating consequences of transcendence. It is, as I have said, transcendence realized. What happens in prayer is that the love of Christ is set free in our hearts. All the illusions and images that restrict or distort it are transcended. It is a work of finding and realizing our own human freedom, our freedom from desire, from sin, from illusion. Only if we are free and so restored to our divine likeness can we know the love of Christ. Our freedom is the condition of our being real, being in harmonious contact with the ground of our being, our source and origin. The ground of our being is reached only by the movement of other-centredness, of transcendence. Following that movement, led by the Spirit, we enter the experience of becoming wholly real within God's own free-flowing and all-embracing reality.

Community of Love

Meditation is pure action that purifies all our other activities. It is pure because it is selfless, wholly other-centred. Most of our activities, our hopes and plans are carried out with a predominant concern for results, for their material worthwhileness. At its worst this concern is mere self-interest, egoism at its most intense. But any concern for results, for the fruit of action, betrays a possessiveness or attachment which disturbs the harmony of the energies deployed in the activity. In meditating day by day, however, humbly and ordinarily, we set out into the mystery of selfless, other-centred activity.

We may indeed begin meditating with a superficial concern for results, trying to estimate if our investment of time and energy is justified by returns in knowledge or 'extraordinary' experience. Perhaps anyone formed by our society is conditioned to begin in this way. But the ordinary practice of meditation purifies us of this spiritual materialism, and as we enter into the direct experience of Being, of pure action, we find all our other activities progressively, radically, purified of egoism. To put this more simply – because meditation leads us into the experience of love at the centre of our being, it makes us in our ordinary lives and relationships more loving persons. Meditation teaches us what theology alone could not convince us of, that Being is Love.

The Present Christ

✿ JUNE 29

Be absolutely clear in your mind about the sheer simplicity of the way. It is also necessary to be very humble about the way, to accept it and not to try to change it around, to water it down, to make it suit you. This is the way of meditation: to take your mantra, your word, and to recite it. However peaceful you are feeling, recite it. However drowsy you are feeling, recite it. However difficult it is for you, recite it. However much you are getting out of it, or however little you are getting out of it, recite your word. If you can understand that, you have understood almost all there is to understand ... to say your mantra from beginning to end. You must also meditate every morning and every evening. If you seriously want to set out on the path that the tradition puts before us, then you must make that time available every morning and every evening. Everything beyond that is more or less obvious. You must learn to sit absolutely still. You must learn to enter into the experience of a total stillness of body and spirit.

In The Beginning

The author of *The Cloud of Unknowing* speaks of meditation as the way to heal the wound of sin in us at its root. This is the work of meditation, the work of healing, a work of growing and it is a journey in which we leave behind all dividedness, and leaving the perception of reality as divided we travel in faith into the unity of God. In Genesis we read that after the fall Adam hid himself when he heard the Lord God walking in the garden in the cool of the evening. The basis of our dividedness is fear and meditation is the way of discovering infinite love in your own heart, infinite love that casts out all fear.

Ego is essentially the image we have of ourselves, the image of ourselves that we try to project. Adam's image of himself, once the ego was unleashed in him, suddenly required clothes so that he could present himself in the right light, but all illusions, all false perceptions of ourself and others and of God are the offspring of the ego. The ego is like a demonic prism: the light of reality passing through it is refracted and split up. The pure shaft of light is split up into component parts and then deflected from its true course.

Meditation leads us to smash that prism and it reunites the pure beam of light by shattering the prism to pieces. It enables us to enjoy the gift of our being as a whole and it enables us to be fully open to the wonder of God's oneness and all this is His free gift. That oneness we now enjoy, not by observing its facets from outside but by entering into its centre. The ego always calls us to self-preservation but the true self is created for self-transcendence. Meditation takes us beyond dividedness into unity.

The Door to Silence

❧ JULY 1

One of the most difficult things for Westerners to understand is that meditation is not about trying to make anything happen. But all of us are so tied into the mentality of techniques and production that we inevitably first think that we are trying to engineer an event, a happening. According to our imagination or predispositions, we may have different ideas of what should happen. For some it is visions, voices or flashes of light. For others, deep insights and understanding. For others again, better control over their daily lives and problems.

The first thing to understand, however, is that meditation is nothing to do with making anything happen. The basic aim of meditation is indeed quite the contrary, simply to learn to become fully aware of what *is*. The great challenge of meditation is to learn directly from the reality that sustains us.

Don't neglect the discipline of stillness of body when you meditate. Remind yourself of it periodically in case you have started to get a little indulgent with your fidgeting. In saying the mantra you can breathe it in in one breath and breathe out silently. Then, in saying your mantra, it is as if you are accepting God's Spirit, which is your life. You breathe it in. And breathing out in silence is like returning your life to God in absolute faith and with absolute love, ready to receive it from Him again should He give it back to you. Our breath shows how meditation is firmly anchored in the essential axis of the Christian revelation: death and resurrection. We die to everything that is passing away. Life is into the infinite God.

Word Made Flesh

This is from the Letter of St Paul to the Colossians:

> May He strengthen you in His glorious might with ample power to meet whatever comes with fortitude, patience and joy and to give thanks to the Father who has made you fit to share the heritage of God's people in the realm of light.[1]

Just pay attention to the language that St Paul uses. He invites us to be strengthened in His glorious might and with His ample power. We must constantly remind ourselves that this is what Christianity is about, learning to live out of this ample power of God, not looking at our lives just in terms of what we can do ourselves but looking at our lives realising that there is a power–source available to us that is infinite. The call that we have St Paul describes as sharing the heritage of God in the realm of light. Now all this is undoubtedly the most extraordinary language, describing what can only be called an extraordinary experience: the 'glorious might' and the 'ample power' of God are offered to each one of us to enable us to meet whatever comes with fortitude, that is, courage, with patience, with the capacity to stay with it, and with joy, the capacity to expand our hearts.

The Door to Silence

[1] Col. 1:11–12

Meditation is a powerful way if you can learn to say the mantra continually, ceaselessly, because that is the way in prayer to leave self behind, to lay down our life so as to be absorbed in the infinite mystery of God. People ask, 'What is the experience of prayer?' The experience of prayer is of going utterly beyond ourselves, going beyond any words that we could possibly use to describe the experience. St Paul describes it as the entry into the glory of God. But in saying our mantra we leave behind all the words, because they limit the experience. They make the experience self-reflective. The experience is one of infinity, and no finite word can possibly encompass the experience.

But again let me stress for you the way is the way of simplicity and childlikeness. 'Unless you become like children'[1] means unless you find again in your own heart the capacity for wonder, for innocent wonder, an innocence we all lose so easily and so carelessly. But we must find it again. The way we find it is to enter into silence, to *be*, to be open to God's glory, to the wonder of his being. That is why our mantra is of such supreme importance. That is why daydreaming is such a dreadful loss of opportunity, such a dreadful encapsulation in time. Whereas all of us are called into that eternal moment when we lose ourselves in God.

Moment of Christ

[1] Matt. 18:3

It is difficult for us to meditate because we are so hyper self-conscious. We cannot help, as it were, looking at the little television monitor serviced by the ego and seeing ourselves, thinking about ourselves, analysing ourselves. But meditation is concerned with a definitive silencing of that monitor screen. Meditation is a time of poverty, of silence, of self-forgetfulness. It is not a time for analysing ourselves, for thinking about our motives or imagining ourselves to be spiritual or sinful, but a time to be absolutely still in mind as well as body.

The way to it is a very simple way, it is the way of silence, the way of faithfulness, the way of poverty of spirit. A generous poverty is a joyful one in which we surrender all our thoughts, all our imagination, all our words and stay with the one word, the mantra. When you begin you have to take this on faith; you have to say your word beyond all reason. And then you have to come back to your meditation every morning and every evening. You have to give up the categories that we are conditioned to using of success or failure, whether it is working or not working, and to go on simply, in childlike faith, to say your mantra. Say your word. The wonderful power of it is that the very exercise of this childlike faith brings us back to our innocence and the freedom of innonence. We learn to be in the presence of Being. Simple, still, loving and utterly free: in meditation and in daily life, in mind and body.

The Way of Unknowing

Learning to meditate is learning to become a really harmonious person. There is nothing life-denying or self-rejecting about meditation. It is simply the way to get every aspect of our life into a harmonious relationship with every other aspect. If we were to try to achieve this by thought alone we would be defeated by the enormous complexity of it, but prayer is deeper and more powerful than thought. Our intellect and our emotions need not compete with one another and prayer harmonises them so that they work together in peaceful complementarity. Every time we sit down to meditate we enter into a state of oneness where the whole of our life gently shakes together in the presence of God. God is one and He calls us to be one.

There is a real point therefore in *The Cloud of Unknowing* calling meditation the process of one-ing, becoming one. By analysis it is possible to discover and endlessly to uncover all the disparate elements in our life and personal history. However in meditation we tread a path of synthesis whereby all the various, happy and unhappy, elements are bound together in the knowledge that we are one with God. It is a discovery that each of us is invited to make personally. Each one of us accepts a personal responsibility for meditating, for sitting down, morning and evening, and for saying our mantra. Accepting and fulfilling this responsibility is a powerful factor in our developing into full personhood.

The Heart of Creation

✿ JULY 6

In its essential significance, the aim of meditation is just this: the realisation of our total incorporation in Jesus Christ, in the cycle of His utterance by, and return to, the Father. The qualities we need in this fundamental encounter between ourselves and the ground of our being are attentiveness and receptivity. In order to realize our complete incorporation with the Word, we have not only to listen to its silence, the silence within us, but also to allow the cycle of its life to be completed in us and to lead us into the depth of its silence. There in the silence of the Word we share His experience of hearing Himself eternally spoken by the Father.

This is why the life of Jesus is of such meaning and why Scripture's record of His life is of such value. The experience of Jesus of Nazareth in awakening to Himself, entering the spheres of silence within Himself, finding His own Spirit and the source of His Spirit, is the experience of every person reborn in spirit. And it is, within the unimaginable design of the Father, the self-same experience. The wonder of creation is found, not in a succession of awakenings, but in the single all-inclusive awakening of Jesus, the Son, to the Father.

Word Into Silence

The purpose of saying the mantra is that it becomes the focus of your attention. We are not thinking of anything nor are we pursuing any insights that may come to us as we say the mantra. Let them all fall away as you come to an ever deeper silence in which the only sound in your mind is the mantra. The mantra itself will teach you the patience needed to say it. It will also teach you the humility needed. In meditating we are not seeking to possess God or to arrive at a profound insight about God. We are seeking simply to accept the gift of our own creation as fully as we presently can and to respond to it as generously as we can. To do this we learn to be still, to be silent and to be truly humble.

In commonday language, the essence of meditation is to leave the ego behind. We are not trying to see with the ego what is happening. Ego-vision is limited by its own self-centredness. The eye with which we see without limit is the eye that cannot see itself. The paradox of meditation is that once we give up trying to see and to possess, then we see all and all things are ours.

Word Made Flesh

A great deal of the interest in the spiritual life in our time has a psycho-logical origin. People are often interested in what prayer and what meditation can teach them about themselves. It is very easy for people of our generation to see everything in terms of self-improvement, self-understanding and so forth. In fact, of course, this fascination that we have for looking at ourselves can be disastrous for the spiritual journey.

There is a real danger that if we take up meditation and then do begin to see that we are understanding ourselves better and then begin to follow this line of discovery, we quickly find that we have left the pilgrimage of meditation, which is a pilgrimage into unlimited knowledge and wisdom. And we find that we end up stuck in the limited knowledge of isolation, our own isolation, and there is a very real danger for us that we can become, as it were, entranced with ourselves, by our own mental operations. We can become so entranced that we forget that we are on a pilgrimage into the mystery of God. The essence of the gospel message and the essence of the experience of meditation is not self-analysis but self-transcendence.

The Door to Silence

The ultimate meaning of God does not arise from what society says we are – that would be to 'prefer human approval to the approval of God', as Jesus put it. When St Thomas More was imprisoned in the Tower of London for preferring his conscience to the approval of the king, his public role was destroyed and he became a common criminal. Yet his integrity was not destroyed. He knew who he was not only in the eyes of the world, or even his own eyes, but in the eyes of God. He enjoyed a profound confidence arising from the true depth of self-knowledge which let him know who he was eternally – created by God, redeemed by Jesus and a temple of the Holy Spirit.

We must be as radical, in our own way, as Thomas More in order to fulfil this purpose. Everyone around him tried to dissuade him from his integrity. And we live in a society that does not recognize the crucial value of spiritual practice because it has forgotten the spiritual reality.

Meditation is a practice that enables us each day to root our lives in the spiritual reality of God. It is a positive way, even though our current materialistic and outer-directed values may dismiss it as a waste of time or as unproductive introversion. Yet in meditation we do not reject the world or construct any false opposition to it. We wish to live fully in the world but we know we can only arrive at that fullness and wholeheartedness if we are truly rooted in God.

Word Made Flesh

Our daily meditation is an entry into the supreme conviction that God has revealed himself in Jesus and that Jesus reveals himself to us in our hearts. If only we will pay attention, if only we will be silent, if only we will be simple, humble, obedient. In order to learn that obedience, simplicity and humility, we say our word. Our hope is rooted in the supreme goodness of God. And the hope is made personally real in the supreme goodness he has given to each one of us in Jesus.

Meditation is a time of profound joy. It is the peace beyond all understanding, beyond all words, concepts or analysis. Let me remind you again what is involved.

Firstly, a daily commitment and a commitment that goes totally beyond what we feel. We do not meditate when we feel like it or not meditate when we do not feel like it. We accept the discipline of the daily meditation and the daily return to it. Then we accept the discipline of the word of the mantra, the recitation of it from beginning to end. And all because of the glory of God revealed in Jesus. All because of the supreme conviction that Jesus is Lord and that we are able to say that He is Lord because He has given us the Holy Spirit.

Moment of Christ

JULY 11

Greetings in the Lord. Today we have been celebrating the Feast of St Benedict and it seems a suitable date to send this letter out to so many of you who share with us his vision and achievement. His understanding of the Christian life as a commitment to ordinary reality rooted in the contemplative experience has inspired, and continues to inspire, people in many different walks of life and following different vocations to the one God. I remember some years ago hearing an old monk quoting a description of monastic generosity that seemed to be wonderfully apt: 'on things of no account an unaccountable zeal bestowing'. It is the particular that reveals the universal, and a commitment to perfection in all we do for its own sake that enables us to leave ourselves behind.

The genius of Benedict's vision is that whereas this approach could so easily become fanatical, he renders it humane, compassionate and tolerant – truly Christian. The enduring power of this vision is its humanity. So often a religious vision of life can lose its human focus, but for Benedict it was through the humanity of Jesus and our own humanity that we enter the divine mystery.

The Present Christ

Those who follow the Rule of St Benedict and the spirit of the Rule are those who humbly search for the way to realise their potentiality in God. It seems to me that the supreme importance of the monastic life, both for the Church and for the world, is that it is a sign of the reality of God's presence in our midst. The message that the monk has to give to the world arises not in the first place from his words but from his life itself. His life has its priorities arranged very simply. And in the first place is his whole-hearted search for God. The effectiveness of the message that he has to give arises from the depth of the personal commitment with which this search is pursued.

And that is the power of the Rule of St Benedict for all of us, whether we are in the monastic order or whether we associate ourselves with the monastic order. The message that those who follow St Benedict's vision have is the message, *Lift up your hearts. Open your eyes to what is eternally real, the new creation, and seek the purity of heart that will open your eyes.* What the Benedictine vision has to say above all is *know from your own heart, from your own experience that you were created for infinite expansion of spirit.*

Community of Love

Meditation is the step away from self-centredness to God-centredness. In taking that step we find our own place in the world, where we should be and where we truly are. All our relationships are consequently put into a right order: our relationships with one another, with the environment and all creation, our relationship with God. Then we discover, and it is vital for our health that each of us does discover it, that we do have an essential place in God's plan. It is perhaps the most important thing for people in our society today to discover the dignity of responding to the unique gift of our own creation.

How can we set about doing this? Meditation is the discipline of doing it. Its discipline is that we learn to stand back and to focus our attention, our whole being, on God. We have to begin somewhere. We have to begin with ourselves and by learning to be silent within ourselves. This means simply learning to be, to be ourselves, rather than defining ourselves by what we do or what we think. As an art and a practice, meditation brings us towards this state of simple being through the still, silent repetition of the mantra.

Word Made Flesh

❀ JULY 14

To those of you who have recently begun to meditate I would like to send you especially much love and encouragement. The commitment this journey calls from us at first is unfamiliar. It requires faith, perhaps a certain recklessness to begin. But once we have begun, it is the nature of God, the nature of love to sweep us along, teaching us by experience that our commitment is to reality, that our discipline is the springboard to freedom.

The journey to our own heart is a journey into every heart. And in the first light of reality we see that this is the kingdom Jesus was born to establish and in which He is born again in every human heart to realise. What we have left behind is loneliness, confusion, isolation. What we have found is communion, sureness, love. Our way is simplicity and fidelity. The simplicity of the mantra. Our fidelity to our daily meditation. As we travel this way we are drawn closer together by the same power of love that unites us.

The Present Christ

The meditative journey is one, therefore, that has to involve our total being, and it is the challenge that everybody who starts out on this journey should realise at the beginning. Every part of our personality, every aspect of our life, must be brought into this exercise and then every part of our personality, every part of our life, has to be transcended as we journey from the periphery to the centre. Our family life, all our relationships, our work, our recreation – everything in our life – is brought into harmony, because in the process of meditation everything in our life is aligned on the centre.

A profound commitment to the spiritual reality has repercussions in our total life. We have, of course, to begin, and we have to begin with confidence. We have to begin knowing that the demand is profound, because the journey is profound. The journey might seem to demand courage, energy and dedication. And it demands all those three. But what we have to do is to commit ourselves to the first step.

The way to the centre is the way of our daily meditation, the time we set aside every morning and every evening of our life. As Christians, we believe that the source of all energy, of all harmony is to be found in our hearts. The practice of meditation is simply the way to be open to this presence, to this energy, to this harmony, and to be open to it ever more profoundly.

In The Beginning

JULY 16

We have to realize that when we talk about 'our prayer' we are really talking about our disposing ourselves for the full liberation of the life of the Spirit within us, which is the prayer of Jesus and His vital connection with the Father. This is why we pray to the degree that we turn away from ourselves, from the possessive self-consciousness and trivial distractedness of everything we sum up as ego. That this really does mean everything is the demand it makes. It is summed up in the old monastic saying, 'A monk is only truly praying when he does not know that he is praying.' If this sounds like annihilation, it is only because it is a description of the unified consciousness of transcendence – a condition of complete simplicity that demands no less than everything.

The difference between childlikeness and childishness is the essential challenge. We have also to realize that the 'Kingdom' which the childlike enter is one that demands the *ascesis* of deepening simplicity at the core of our being, where, far from being annihilated, we are fully, wonderfully restored to ourselves. For the first time in our lives we know the wonder of our being, the beauty of life, the centrality of love.

Letters From the Heart

As Jesus puts it, 'If anyone would be a follower of mine they must leave self behind.'[1] There is no doubt that there is something arduous and demanding about this journey. It requires nerve to take the attention off yourself, to let go of your ideas and to gaze wholeheartedly ahead. The person meditating is like the eye that can see but cannot see itself. So this is a journey that requires faith – that is, commitment – and the commitment is to what is beyond yourself, what is greater than yourself. And so the journey requires humility, a humility to stop thinking about yourself. And what this means is that as we advance on the journey we must continually let go of what we think we have achieved. The problem is that when we start we are always concerned with our progress, with how perfectly we are fulfilling the techniques and so forth, but we must learn that we have to let go. This is the challenge and it is the challenge that in classical terms requires us to keep saying the mantra from the beginning of our meditation until the end. That is something that you must understand absolutely clearly.

The Door to Silence

[1] Matt. 16:24

Perhaps the reason too why people so often misunderstand this way of simplicity is because of the patience that is required. We need patiently, day after day, to return to this path of selflessness and silence. It may take people months, even years, just to come to a clear point of beginning, that first degree of unconditional commitment which starts the journey. Yet once you have begun you will find that your daily meditation becomes the great integrating power in your life. It will give depth and perspective to everything you are and everything you do. The simple reason for this is that you are beginning to live from the prime source of integrity, of wholeness, the God who alone is holy. You begin to live out of the power of this love of God that is one, that is the creative origin of all that is and that unifies all with itself.

This power in all its immensity and simplicity is present in our hearts in the consciousness of Jesus. The integrating power of meditation affects every part of our life. Every part is reconciled to the whole. All our life is aligned on Christ, and His presence makes itself felt in every part. The way to this is the way of humility and self-knowledge, of simplicity and silence, the way of the mantra.

> Be humble always and gentle, and patient too. Be forbearing with one another and charitable. Spare no effort to make fast with bonds of peace the unity which the Spirit gives.[1]

Word Made Flesh

[1] Eph. 4:3

As you know, Dame Julian of Norwich, in the fourteenth century in England, described prayer as a way of complete simplicity, demanding not less than everything. That is what we have to understand: that the invitation that God gives to each of us is to enter into the fullness of His life, which means that He gives us everything but in order to enter that fullness, in order to receive that gift we ourselves have to be equally generous. Everything is given both by God and by ourselves. When we begin to understand the scale of it, you can get nervous. There is no need for nervousness because it is given to you and to me to give. The power that we require to be generous is given to us and it is given to us in the silence and that is why our commitment to the silence is of such supreme importance. The silence that you will encounter is not just the silence of quiet but it is the silence of energy.

Being On The Way

✛ JULY 20

Meditation has always been seen as this way of vision. It has often been described as the process whereby we open the eyes of our heart and learn to see with love and the best analogy for it is the analogy of falling in love. The beloved still seems the same to everyone else, but when we love someone deeply and unreservedly we see them in a new light and their slightest gesture can convey to us what no one else can see. Falling in love is such an important and profound experience for all of us because it takes us out of and beyond ourselves into the reality of the other; and profound meditation is of the same order.

We abandon our isolated view of life and we learn in the silence and discipline of our daily meditation to travel beyond our own limitations into the limitless ocean of God's love. By our entry into silence, by our opening of the eyes of the heart to the light of infinity, we begin to see with a new vision and we see with a sharpness and acuity of vision that is startling and with a profundity that is intoxicating.

The Door to Silence

Let me end by reminding you that nothing can be said about prayer that can at the same time describe its utter fullness and its utter simplicity. I suggest that you now forget most of what I have said to you except the two words 'simplicity' and 'faith' – and both of these are summed up in the practice of the mantra, which will allow the Spirit to guide you. I do not suggest that the simplicity is easy to reach or the faith easy to maintain.

But let me remind you again that our wholehearted openness to love is the condition to which you and I and every human being is called. It is the meaning and purpose of our lives. It demands a great deal, but in the end we will find that all we have lost are our limitations.

Letters From the Heart

Biblically, conversion had two aspects. There was the ritual, exterior conversion typified, for example, by putting on ashes and rending garments. But the constant theme of the prophets and throughout biblical history is that this external conversion is of no use unless it is inspired and springs from an inner conversion of heart. The prophet Isaiah cries, therefore, 'this people honours me with their lips but their heart is far from me.'[1]

Meditation is about deep conversion of heart. Religion is meaningless if it is confined to external and ritual acts of worship. Liturgy and ritual only have meaning when they are inspired by conversion of heart. This is what we are turning to as we learn to be still. In stillness an awareness matures that God has revealed Himself to humanity in Jesus and that Jesus reveals Himself to us, in our heart, by His Spirit which He has sent to dwell within us. Our life, no less than liturgy, finds meaning when we are as fully open as we can be to this Spirit.

Word Made Flesh

[1] Isa. 29:13

The mantra is a device of such importance. As we learn to root it in our consciousness, the mantra becomes like a key that opens the door to the secret chamber of our heart. At first, in the set times of our meditation, both morning and evening, saying the mantra is work. We have to learn to become thoroughly familiar with it. But as we progress, as we begin to sound it and to listen to it, then, each and every time we recite it, we enter into and remain in our heart. Thus, by merely calling the mantra to mind at other times of the day, we enter straight away into the presence of the Creator who dwells within us; 'I am with you always,' says the Lord.[1]

Learning to pray is learning to live as fully as possible in the present moment. In meditation we seek to enter as fully as we can into the now, and in entering into the now to live as fully as possible with the now-risen and ever-loving Lord Jesus. To be thus fully committed to the present moment is to find ourselves, to enter into ourselves, to dwell within ourselves; and this we do by renouncing thought and image. In meditation we are not thinking about the past, neither our own past nor anyone else's, nor are we thinking about the future, our own nor anyone else's.

In meditation we are wholly inserted into the present, and there we live to the fullness of our capability, our consciousness expanding as we entertain the Lord of Life. The experience of this being wholly conscious is an experience of unity and simplicity.

Word Into Silence

[1] Matt. 28:20

Truth is about body *and* spirit and so the first thing we have to learn when we begin to meditate is to sit.still. As Westerners we can become technically over-concerned with posture. We may like the image of ourselves in certain stereotyped poses. Posture is *not* about posing and the only essential rules about posture are that the spine is as upright as possible and that you sit as still as possible. But this reveals a discipline that every one of us must learn. We are not used to sitting still. We are not used to being mentally still. But the spirit must come to stillness in a profound unity with the body that rests in profound stillness.

You will find out from your own experience that bodily stillness is not the most difficult form of stillness. More demanding is the stillness of mind involved in our going beyond imagining, reasoning, comparing, analysing and judging. One of the greatest hazards we face in meditation is as a result of our over-intellectualist education. In meditating we are not thinking about God or analysing reality. We are being still and learning to know His essence, learning, that is, how to learn. We come to see that He is love and, in a true sense, meditating is simply uncovering the love that is God in our own hearts.

The Way of Unknowing

Our meditation is always concerned with another step deeper into the present moment, another step into the eternal now of God. Every time we meditate, we take a step further into the divine life, wholly present and yet wholly expansive and expanding. Like all growth, this involves pain. It is the pain of maturing, of ripening and it means leaving earlier stages of development behind. Part of the difficulty is that we have to learn to leave behind not just part of ourselves but the whole of ourselves that was the past.

We can only become fully present to the now of this moment if we can leave the past behind. What we try to do instead is to maintain observation, points, base camps, along every stage of our growth. At each of these observation points we are loath to let go of any part of ourselves in favour of the new stage of growth. It becomes simpler, and even easier, if we recognise that it is not part of ourselves we need to be concerned about leaving, but our whole self. If we refuse this, opting instead for piecemeal surrenders, then instead of life being an experience of growth we find our lives contracting.

At each stage of growth we have to leave all of ourselves behind in order to go forward, becoming an ever new creation. This is precisely what we do every time we meditate. Each occasion we sit down to meditate, everything we have done until that moment, including everything we have been until that moment, is simply abandoned. The more fully the past is abandoned, the more fully renewed we are as we return to our present day. So meditation is a continuous breakthrough into the present moment, into the present moment of God.

The Heart of Creation

The word 'meditation' comes from the Latin *meditare* which breaks down into the roots *stare in medio* – to remain in the centre. The word 'contemplation' suggests the same. The word contemplation does not mean looking at anything – God or anyone else. Contemplation is 'being in the temple' with God. The temple is your own heart, the depths of your own being.

By meditating we leave the shallow levels of our life behind and enter into something that is profound. By meditating we leave behind the passing, ephemeral things of life and enter into what is eternal. The ultimate goal of all religion is a *re-linking* and it is essentially the re-linking with our own deep centre. To be re-linked to our own centre is the purpose of all religion. We know from the Christian revelation that the Spirit of God dwells in our own centre, in the depths of our own spirit. The truth we discover from our own experience, if only we will tread the pilgrimage to that place of holiness, is that there is only one centre and that that centre is everywhere.

The way is the way of unlearning. The way is the way of dispossession. The way is the way of simplicity. We unlearn and we dispossess ourselves by turning aside from all our own words and thoughts and staying solely with the mantra. That is what takes us to the depths. What all of us must understand is that you can't just do a bit of meditation. If you want to meditate then you have to place it in a central position in your life.

Moment of Christ

What all of us have to understand about meditation is that we are not meditating in order to make something happen. We are not meditating in order to get some sort of insight. In fact, we are not meditating to gain any possession whatsoever. Quite the reverse. We are meditating so that we can dispossess ourselves – not just of our ideas and insights but to dispossess ourselves of our very selves. The essence of Christian meditation is that we become absorbed in God, where we lose all sense of ourselves and find ourselves only in God.

As the great woman mystic St Catherine of Genoa wrote, 'I know myself only in God.' Now that is a very difficult concept for us to come to terms with, because we are all brought up to be such materialists. We are all brought up to be such controllers, such possessors and to sit down and to voluntarily make ourselves poor – dispossess ourselves as we enter into the presence of God – is a real challenge for us.

The Door to Silence

The only other thing you need to know is that it is essential to say your mantra every day of your life, every morning and every evening. This again is difficult to understand because we have so little understanding of spiritual discipline. But we *need* to put aside about half an hour every morning and half an hour every evening, to be still, to be simple and, in the language of the very early monastic fathers, to rest in the Lord. An honoured word they used to describe their meditation was *quies*, rest, being quiet, being still. At that moment of *quies* you are not concerned about what you will do; you are wholly concerned about being.

Meditation will teach you that living fully means expanding, crossing the frontiers of your own limitations. Crossing the frontier of your own being you find yourself in God. So do not think that stillness is static or that *quies* is passive. In peace we find the God who conceives and sustains a cosmos.

Remember, meditation is not about making something happen. It has all happened. Each day every one of us has the potential within ourselves, along with the means, to become fully the person we are called to be. That potential and the means is nothing less than the presence of Jesus Christ in our hearts. Meditation is simply being open to that.

The Way of Unknowing

❄️ JULY 29

Meditation is sometimes called the prayer of faith because during our time of meditation we let go of everything by which we know that we are and everything that we think we are. We simply let it go. There is no need to count the cost and no advantage in trying to salvage anything from the bankruptcy.

Glory follows this great poverty. St Peter describes it as the utter freedom of spirit that sweeps us into the presence of God's timeless and spaceless glory. We are summoned to this, according to the New Testament, now, in this life. It is not just a future glory. Enlightenment with the light of Christ is a present reality, a new way of living in this world. During the time of meditation we are absorbing the knowledge of faith that we are not obliged to live merely on the material level of reality. We learned from the faith and generosity of Christ, according to St Paul, that every one of us is summoned to the new, eternal level of reality called Spirit.

Word Made Flesh

More and more people are aware that somehow or other, in modern life, we have lost contact with what is essential. Contact is lost with our own essential being, our own centre. The problem we face, as a consequence, is that we have ceased to look upon our religious practice or our spiritual practice in terms of a discipline. More often we look upon our religious or spiritual commitment in terms of what we get out of it. We had a young man from London staying with us last year and as we were talking one day he said something to this effect: 'You know, Father John, you'll be shocked when you hear this, but I gave up religion because I wasn't getting anything out of it. Blimey, when I think of it now I wake up in the night and cold shivers run down my spine. Imagine, *I* was thinking what *I* was going to get out of it.' He had begun to remake contact.

I imagine all of us have adopted this ego-centred approach to our religious or spiritual practice at some time. We too need to examine the true nature of our religious life to find a way to begin decreasing the egotistical element in it. We need to be grasped by the truth that religious values are not to be exploited or experimented with because they – and the sacred they represent – call on us for commitment. As soon as we have begun to commit ourselves we have begun a journey. It is a journey that asks for discipline, and the challenge to us is that it is a journey away from our own egoism.

The Way of Unknowing

Saying the mantra is like unlocking the door of our heart. The mantra is like the key unlocking the door to allow the pure light of love to flood in. Although powerful, it is a gentle process. Do not expect dramatic miracles. In fact, do not expect anything. Be humbly content every morning and evening, to return simply to the practice. In the practice itself you will find the powers of gentleness, forgiveness and compassion, all revealing themselves. Do not fear their power to change you.

When you begin you may have many questions about the technique, the technical aspects of meditating. How should you say your mantra? Should you, for example, say it to your breathing? Or should you say it to your heartbeat? My recommendation is, when you begin, begin as simply as you possibly can. Just say it. If it is natural for you to say it to your heartbeat, say it to your heartbeat. If it is natural for you to say it to your breathing, say it to your breathing. If it does not seem that you say it to either, say it as you can. The technical questions are secondary and many will be answered naturally through the experience gained by the practice itself.

The Heart of Creation

Meditation is our availability to the eternal moment. In it, during the chronological time of our meditation, we are, in so far as we can be, wholly present to the God who is. From our point of view, in our meditation we are with *Him. God with us.* Jesus, reveals the glory of the Father to us in our own hearts. Purifying our hearts for the reflection of this glory is the whole purpose of the mantra. The mantra trains us to listen and so brings us to fullness of being, to God, in the present moment as we leave the past entirely behind and place the future in the hands of God. In our meditation we are not thinking about the past nor planning for the future because we are open to the eternal moment, the eternal now of God. Here is the importance of the mantra, in that it puts an end to thinking of the past, of the future, and leaves us wholly open to the presence of the God who is.

Meditation is therefore a way of renunciation. Being so, it is also a way of discipline, an ascetical path. All this, renunciation, discipline, ascesis is caught up and combined in the act of faith that is the mantra, as we say it with ever deeper fidelity.

The Way of Unknowing

Meditation makes demands on us. It is a discipline. It isn't good enough just to read books about it or follow courses on it. You have to practise it. In the practice, you find your place. But to find your place you have to reduce yourself constantly until you become just a point. We all know that there is nothing worse than self-importance. There is nothing worse than selfishness. The purpose of meditation is to enter into our central point which is the experience of self-transcendence, a going forward. We leave self utterly behind and our ego is reduced and reduced and reduced until we have our place but no magnitude.

Coming to that point at the centre of our own being is like adjusting the aperture of a camera. When we have reduced ourself to that one-pointedness and when we are still, the light shines into us, into our hearts. That is the light of God, the light that enlightens and illuminates our entire being. Once we have achieved that pointedness and stillness the light shines in our heart for all eternity. Don't misunderstand me. To tread this path you do not require any special characteristics or special talents except the ordinary talent of knowing that we must go beyond self-importance and self-centredness. And it does not take much ingenuity to realize that. We must root ourselves not in self-love but in universal love. We become persons, not for ourselves, but for others, for all, for *the* all.

Moment of Christ

In entering into our own silence, we risk everything, for we risk our very being: 'So I said to my soul. "Be still." ' The stillness of mind and body to which the mantra guides us is a preparation for entering this silence. It prepares us for our progression through the spheres of silence to see with wonder the light of our own spirit, and to know that light as something beyond our spirit and yet the source of it. This is a pilgrimage through our spheres of silence that we undertake in faith, putting our entire trust in what is only a dim apprehension of the authentic, the real, yet confident in doing so because it is authentic.

In saying the mantra, we lay down our life for the sake of Him we have not yet seen.[1] Blessed are they who believe and act on their belief though they have not yet seen. In saying the mantra we are plunged into a silence that explores our infinite poverty of mind and spirit, revealing our absolute dependence on another. We are led from depth to depth of purifying simplification until, having contacted the very ground of our being, we find the life we laid down and the self we surrendered in the Other.

Word Into Silence

[1] 1 Pet. 1:8

❧ AUGUST 4

The journey into the God who is Love cannot be followed in isolation – we cannot determine the itinerary of our own pilgrimage or the conditions of our own commitment. Indeed, when we find ourselves 'planning' our own inner journey, steering our course so as to catch the sights on the way, it is a sure sign that we have yet to take our hand off the wheel. We must let the God-motivated direction reveal itself – we have not, to put it another way, placed our centre of consciousness outside of ourselves.

The community is the context in which we learn the truth and power of other-centredness. And our fidelity to the community – our loving openness and freedom with others – is, as it were, the complement to our fidelity to the mantra – our generous and magnanimous poverty of spirit.

The way of meditation is the way of love: 'this work of love,' as *The Cloud of Unknowing* calls it. And so it is real, not theoretical; incarnate, not abstract; practical, not just a matter of words or ideas. To act upon this vision and really to begin the journey requires a decisive and open commitment. There is, though, no commitment without the simplicity of spirit that allows us to say an unambiguous 'yes' to the invitation to journey to reality.

Letters From the Heart

✻ AUGUST 5

In the language of prayer, people are sometimes worried by the negativity of the language: surrender, annihilation. What is surrendered is what is worthless; what is annihilated is what is unreal. The essential experience of prayer is the surge of power of God's creative love and it is this surge of power that brings us into the kingdom of God, because that is what the kingdom of God is: simply, the power of divine love released into every fibre of our being. 'The kingdom of God is within you.'[1] The kingdom is an experience that must be known from within. It is the knowing of it that harmonises us, that integrates us. This knowing can only be known through the power of divine love. It can only be known by opening our hearts and minds to the heart and mind of Jesus. It can only be known by opening our consciousness to his.

What we need for this journey is silence and attention. The overcoming of self-consciousness is the work of pure attention. The state of prayer, to which we are all summoned, is a state of utter purity of heart and in this state we are wholly open, wholly attentive to reality in its purist and most intimate manifestation. We are open to the Spirit who is creative love, present in the depths of our own spirit.

The Door to Silence

[1] Luke 17:21

❦ AUGUST 6

Looked at from the outside, meditation can be thought of as a static condition, one in which you had closed down the doors of perception. But from actual experience meditation is known to be far from a static state and is far better understood as a dynamic awakening to the fullness of your own potential for development. The expansion of our spirit in the love of Jesus is this fullness. Simplicity, childlike trust and wonder are the ways to realise it.

We are not looking for anything to happen, for any insights or wisdom. We are not analysing any superficial or external phenomena. All this is trivia compared with the knowledge of the Spirit dwelling within us that arises when we turn our minds aside from what is temporal and passing and instead open our hearts to what is enduring: God and God's love for each of us. This is how we discover our love for all our brothers and sisters, knowing that we are loved.

Word Made Flesh

I first started to meditate like this about thirty years ago. I suppose that I was as crass as anyone of my age because I was always saying to the man who taught me: 'How long is this going to take? I can't sit around here saying this word forever, you know.' He would look at me with a rather pained look, and either he would just look straight through me or else he would say, 'Say your mantra.' Thirty years later I am still astonished at the wisdom of that teaching. As I say, you have to take it on faith when you begin. Nothing that I can say or, I suppose, that anyone can say will be very significant for you in comparison with the persuasive power of your own experience. You will enter into profounder and profounder silence. You will enter into clearer and clearer simplicity.

The author of *The Cloud of Unknowing*, who teaches this doctrine from fourteenth-century England, said that very often he got objections to his teaching from learned people and from theologians. But, he said, rarely do objections come from simple people. The most frequent objections are that this is a complex, esoteric doctrine. But it is not. It is a doctrine of utter simplicity. It requires no more than faith.

The Way of Unknowing

❧ AUGUST 8

In the silence of meditation, when you go beyond thought and imagination, you begin to experience and later to understand that *being* is what life is about and that in meditation you are learning to *be*. To be is to live as the person you are, without trying to justify your existence or make excuses for your personality. Just to be, as you are. The wonder of it is that the more simple you become, the more you are able to enjoy to the full the gift of your being. But when you begin you have to begin in faith. You cannot come to meditation saying, 'If I can get something out of this I will do it for a trial run for three or six months.' You cannot come to it with demands.

As St John of the Cross described it, 'The way to possession is the way of dispossession.' You have to let go of your thoughts, of your ideas, of your conscious and hidden ambitions and you have to *be*. The way to do it is to say your word. If all your attention is directed to saying your word and if you are neither lazy nor impatient, then gradually you are unhooked from all the thoughts and words and ideas and hopes and fears. You are free.

The Heart of Creation

❊ AUGUST 9

The extraordinary revelation of the gospel is the absolute value of the ordinary and the potential of the ordinary, to be transfigured by the divine power, the universal energy of love. A life that is structured within the discipline of our morning and evening meditation is rooted in the reality of this power and so is always being transformed and penetrated by it.

What we might at first seem to 'lose', by sacrificing the time for meditation in the course of a demanding day, is not worth comparing with what we gain. We indeed regain even what we lose, because of the sense of clarity and order which meditation gives us in our ordinary decision-making, and because of the sharpened sense of the value of time and our growing incapacity to waste or use it trivially. But above and beyond this, a light is shed on our life and radiates through it, that reveals it in its true meaning and sacredness. Our meditation deepens our appreciation of the Eucharist because it refines our perception of our own life as a sacrament of the love of God.

The Present Christ

Do not lose sight of the way. The way is the way of silence. It is the way of the mantra and the power of the mantra is precisely this: that if we are faithful to it, if we approach our meditation each morning and each evening and in sincerity of heart, then everything in our lives, everything about our lives must come into harmony with that supreme harmonising force: the power of God, the divine energy, the divine love. Perhaps the quality that we need more than any other is to be patient with ourselves on the way because we have to be gentle.

It is not always possible to get that profound silence, that profound togetherness, in the first stages of our pilgrimage. That is why it is so important to learn to say the mantra. And the mantra is just like the sculptor with the large block of granite. He chips away and each time we say our mantra, the form that God has for us is being formed. We may think of ourselves as slow, even as unworthy. We may even give up saying our mantra. But the form is there and the energy to create it is there, and that energy is the divine energy and all we need is to return to our practice, to our silence, to our faithfulness; and as the energy flows more strongly in our own heart, the silence is more profound and the interior and exterior life come into harmony.

Being On The Way

The experience of prayer is the experience of coming into full union with the energy that created the universe. What Christianity has to proclaim to the world is that that energy is love and it is the well-spring out of which all creation flows. It is the well-spring that gives each one of us the creative power to be the person we are called to be – a person rooted and founded in love.

Our tradition tells us all that but it tells us still more. It tells us too that this is not just poetry. Our practice of meditation tells us that this is the *experience* to which each of us is summoned. The way to it is the way of simplicity and of faithfulness. What our tradition teaches is that to enter this mystery we must learn to be silent. Meditation is entry into profound silence.

To meditate means to live out of the centre of our being, that profound centre we find when we determine not to be shallow, not to be content to rest on the surface but to live out of the depths of our being. We must opt for this, because it is in the depths of our being that the union with Christ is continuously taking place. The path to follow is a path of almost incredible simplicity and this is perhaps a good part of the difficulty for us as men and women of the twentieth century. To enter into the simplicity of it demands courage. To meditate, each of us must learn to be very simple, to be very quiet, to learn to say our word.

Moment of Christ

A step that each of us has to take as we follow a Christian way of prayer, the first step, is to find ourselves. As St Augustine puts it, 'We must first be restored to ourself and then making of ourself, as it were, a stepping stone, we rise thence to God.' That is, each of us is invited to discover our own inner reality, our own essential being. This is the first step. To many in our society this might seem to be the ultimate goal. But in the experience of prayer, once this first step is taken we are swept beyond ourselves into the infinite mystery that is God. If you consider it, it is hardly surprising. All that is required is that we be ourselves, that we be who we are, and for this what is required is honesty and integrity. And this is simply the essential prerequisite: for the journey beyond, the journey into the otherness of the Other.

His absolute integrity can only be encountered by our own integrity. This is of supreme importance because religion can so easily keep honesty at bay. We can be so busy with our rituals, with our rites, that we never take that first step into honesty, integrity, openness. But how can we do this? How can we – weak, fallible creatures that we are – come to this absolute integrity? As we already know, the power, the energy necessary for this journey of discovery is given to us and is to be found within our own hearts. What the practice of Christian prayer teaches us is that we are summoned to the centre and we are summoned from the centre, by the centre.

The Door to Silence

Perhaps the greatest tragedy of all is that we should complete our life without ever having made full contact with our own spirit. This contact means discovering the harmony of our being, our potential for growth, our wholeness – everything that the New Testament, and Jesus Himself, called 'fullness of life'.

So often we live our life at five per cent of our full potential. But of course there is no measure to our potential; the Christian tradition tells us it is infinite. If only we will turn from *self* to *other* our expansion of spirit becomes boundless. It is all-turning: what the New Testament calls conversion.

We are invited to unlock the shackles of limitation, to be freed from being prisoners within our self-limiting egos. Conversion is just this liberation and expansion arising when we turn from ourselves to the infinite God. It is also learning to love God, just as in turning to God we learn to love one another. In loving we are enriched beyond measure. We learn to live out of the infinite riches of God.

Word Made Flesh

❀ AUGUST 14

The great test whether your meditation is working or whether you are making progress (I do not advise you to rate yourself), is: Are you growing in love? Are you growing in patience? Are you growing in understanding and compassion? That is the effect of our meditation. For some of us it takes longer, with some of us the end of egoism requires a big struggle and sometimes we are carried more or less kicking and screaming into the Kingdom of Heaven.

But the important thing is not to bother how long it takes. It does not matter how long it takes. The only thing that matters and the thing that I wish I could communicate to every one of you here this evening – the only thing that matters is that we are on the journey. The journey is a journey away from self, away from egoism, away from selfishness, away from isolation and it is a journey into the infinite love of God. Jesus says, 'Unless you become like a little child you cannot enter the Kingdom of Heaven.'[1] Saying our mantra every morning and every evening is just this entry into a childlike state where we place our full confidence and trust in God. Whatever gift He gives us we receive with simplicity and joy. Whatever barrenness He leads us through we accept with the same simplicity and joy.

The Door to Silence

[1] Matt. 18:3

Whatever you are doing put your whole heart into it, as if you were doing it for the Lord and not for others, knowing that there is a Master who will give you your heritage as a reward for your service.[1]

Put your whole heart into it. Meditation calls us to the deepest and clearest level of understanding. Once we begin to meditate, once we have taken the first step, we soon realise that we can no longer remain in the shallows. The call we have responded to is for a complete reorientation of our being, a radical conversion. The call is, above all else, to enter the mystery itself, to learn what cannot be learned anywhere else or in any other way. For this call to be answered, every part of our being has to be involved because the knowledge we come to in meditation is not of a partial or quantative type. It is not that we know more and more *about* God, or that we know God to be all good, all holy, all just, all merciful and so on.

On the contrary, in meditation we come to realise that we know as a consequence of being known. This is not easy either to believe or to understand at first, but we need only remember that in meditation we are entering into the basic relationship of our life. God, our Creator and our Father, calls us into an intimacy with Him that arises because God first knows and loves us. And, in this act of knowing and loving us, God invites us to come into a relationship of knowing and loving Him.

The Way of Unknowing

[1] Col. 3:23–4

Meditation is an entry into divinisation through Jesus. Through Him we become one with God. With Him we utterly transcend ourselves, leaving the whole of ourselves behind and becoming a new creation in Him. In Him, meditation is itself the process of self-transcendence. To the degree that we are transcending ourselves we are sharers in the divine nature because we are learning to be one with the power of love. Our growth in meditation cannot be seen in the accumulation of experiences but rather in the transcending of all experience. What we so often call an experience is only a memory. But in the eternal act of creation which is the life of the trinitarian God everything is present. Each of us by our own little self-transcendence is nevertheless empowered to become one with God. This is what we must never forget.

Each time we sit down to meditate we enter into that oneness, the oneness of God who is now, the oneness of God who is love. We cannot adequately conceptualise all this. It is too simple for our mind to comprehend. But what we can do is to sit down and say our mantra with humility, with fidelity and with absolute trust in the goodness of God who calls us beyond our every limitation. He calls us, such is the marvel of the Christian revelation, to expand into infinity with Him. The more we do contemplate the wonder of our vocation the more humble we must become, the more poor in spirit. We become humble, we become poor in spirit, by our fidelity to our mantra. As we progress we have to become *more* faithful.

The Heart of Creation

By opening our hearts to love at the deepest and most silent level of our being, we are not repressing human knowledge or rejecting human values or relationships. On the contrary, all of these are enlightened, that is, we see them in a new light, in a transcendent light. The extraordinary thing about the Christian message is that this light is not less than the light of Christ, the light who is Christ. The call to us to enter this light is for each of us to know from our own experience, with St Peter and St Paul and St John, that we are not just reading poetry to each other or designing religious scenarios for dreamtime 'walkabouts'. They were trying to communicate to us the fact, the supreme and redeeming fact, that Christ's light shines in our heart and that the first task of our life is to be open to it, to be bathed in it, to be made whole in it and to see with it.

Meditation is our journey to that light. To come to it we have to learn how to be humble, to be patient and to be faithful. By faithfully returning to your meditation every morning and every evening you will learn all this. Reciting the mantra from the beginning to the end of your meditation you will learn humility. By the gift of God you will then learn of your own lovableness as you learn that the light shines *for you*.

The Way of Unknowing

How do we learn commitment? What does Jesus tell us? He tells us to *worship*. The Hebrew word for worship derives from the root word, to *serve*. Jesus teaches us that 'The worshippers whom the Father wants must worship in spirit and truth.'[1] The worshipper is one who serves, that is one who is absolutely at the disposition of his Lord. Absolutely. We must serve in spirit, that is from the depth of our being, not at the surface, not using other people's insights, but worshipping from the ground of our own experience, our own unique being. We must serve in truth, beyond all illusion, wholly accepting the reality of God and the reality of ourself as we are.

The theological basis of Christian meditation is that the essential reality of prayer is the prayer of Jesus. In the same way that there is only one essential Christian prayer, the prayer of Christ Himself, so there is only one Christian worship, the communion we have through Christ in the Trinitarian love. Each member of the Trinity wholly *at the service* of the other. Entry into this worship can only be found at the heart of creation, that is through the human worship of Christ, wholly at the disposition of the Father and receiving the Father's love, absolutely.

The Heart of Creation

[1] John 4:24

In the overall course of our life's pilgrimage we do not reject thought, we do not reject emotion, but we recognise that if the pilgrimage is to bring us to the fulfilment of God's pure Being, we must transcend them by a discipline that becomes, like the burden, sweet and light. Our meditation is that discipline. We do not think about God; we do not analyse our feelings about him when we are meditating. We say our mantra with absolute confidence, with absolute faith because we are in the presence of absolute Love. As a result, in our meditation thought is clarified because it is founded on the rock who is Christ and not on our egos. Our emotion, too, is purified and pacified by His gentleness, by His forgiveness, by His love.

I think the importance of all this is that this clarity and purity free us for the greatest act of neighbourly love of our life which is to lead others to this purity of consciousness, to this clarity of vision. Nothing that any of us could do for our neighbour could be greater than this service of leading them to realise their enormous potential, if only they can clarify their consciousness in Christ's. If only they can purify their emotion in the warmth of His love.

The Way of Unknowing

The stages of our progress in meditation will come about in their own time. God's own time. We in fact only hinder this progression by becoming too self-conscious about our stage of development. This is where a teacher is of immense help for keeping you on a straight course. But basically your teacher has only one instruction to give you and that is: to say your mantra. More than this is simply encouragement and comfort until the mantra is rooted in your consciousness. The path of enlightenment is one we tread for ourselves. Each person wins wisdom for himself. The teacher is there to keep you steadily going forward. The word 'guru' itself, dispeller of darkness, means the one who is steady.

The greatest temptation of all is to complicate ourselves. 'Unless you become like little children . . .' Meditation simplifies us, simplifies us to the point where we can receive the fullness of truth and the fullness of love. It prepares us and enables us to listen with childlike attention to the Spirit of Jesus within us. As we persevere in meditation, we enter ever more deeply into relationship with this Spirit, with God who is love dwelling in our hearts, enlightening us and vitalising us.

Word Into Silence

If you want to meditate, the first thing you require is to be serious about it. Not solemn. But serious. To see this as a serious invitation will lead you to the deepest personal actualisation of your potential. If you want to learn to meditate, you must put aside the time for it every day of your life. Ideally you should find a time every morning and every evening. The morning time of meditation sets the tone for the day and prepares you to set out on your daily pilgrimage knowing better who you are. Then your evening meditation brings together all the various strands of the day's activities, and unifies them through your own concentration. So you must understand that the daily discipline is of immense importance.

You cannot make the journey by just admiring the spiritual realities from a distance. You must enter. You must taste and see. The time I recommend you to spend in meditation is a minimum of twenty minutes and an optimum time of half an hour, every morning and every evening.

The Way of Unknowing

Meditation is the way to the most profound openness to power, light and glory of which we are capable in this life. But anyone interested in meditation should understand from the outset that once this power begins to have its way and this light begins to shine undimmed in our hearts, we are transformed. In becoming ourselves we are never the same again. Life is itself transfigured because we begin to live from the vitalising power of the supreme glory of Jesus which is His love.

We could say that the glory of Jesus is the result of His pure receptivity and total openness to the love of the Father. It is our destiny to be receptive to His love and so to return with Him to the Father. The dimensions of this destiny escape our minds. And words are only words. Yet the words have the limited value of calling us to be open to all this, not as words or concepts but as reality. Such radical and simple openness requires discipline and fidelity: the kind of faithful discipline we practise each day in returning to our word.

Word Made Flesh

Meditation is openness to a reality that we can only discover and only encounter in the depths of our own being. So we have to learn to be silent and to be profoundly silent. The extraordinary thing is that, in spite of all the distractions of the modern world, this silence is perfectly possible for all of us. To descend into this silence we have to devote time, energy and love. The first thing you have to understand about meditating is that you have to devote the time to it. It is necessary to meditate every morning and every evening.

In the Christian vision we are led to this source of our being by a guide, and our guide is Jesus, the fully realised person, the person wholly open to God. As we meditate each day we may not recognize our guide. That is why the Christian journey is always a journey of faith. But as we approach the centre of our being, as we enter our heart, we find that we are greeted by our guide, greeted by the one who has led us. We are welcomed by the person who calls each one of us into personal fullness of being. The consequences or results of meditation are just this fullness of life – harmony, oneness and energy, a divine energy that we find in our own heart, in our own spirit. That energy is the energy of all creation. As Jesus tells us, it is the energy that is love.

Moment of Christ

This other-centredness of the awakened Christian is not, strictly speaking, just the condition *for* prayer. It is essentially the condition *of* prayer, the state of prayer itself. It will always be accompanied by a personal commitment to the *daily experience of prayer* as a total turning of the whole person towards God, aside from all distraction and all activity, everything that is not concentrated solely upon God. Such a Christian is fulfilling St Paul's injunction to 'pray without ceasing'.[1] Because the inner eye of his or her consciousness has been opened by redemptive contact with Christ's love and is permanently attentive to his indwelling presence. Thus every Christian is called to be a person of prayer.

Community of Love

---

[1] Eph. 6:18

Meditation is concerned not so much with thinking as with being. And in contemplative prayer we seek to become the person we are called to be: not by thinking about God but by being with Him. Simply to be in His presence is all-sufficing. Simply to be with Him is to be drawn into being the person He calls us to be. This is the message of Jesus's injunction to seek the kingdom first and then all else will be given. But this is no easy task for those of us reared in our contemporary Western culture. We have all been conditioned by this culture's excessive regard for cerebral activity. And we have defined ourselves far too narrowly as 'rational creatures'. It seems to me that this is one of the principal reasons for the impoverishment of our prayer life. The response of the *whole person* to God has been shattered and only the cerebral, verbal splinters are active in our very much attenuated understanding of prayer.

Our aim in Christian prayer is to allow God's mysterious and silent presence within us to become more and more not only a reality, one of several to which we give what Cardinal Newman called 'notional assent', but *the* reality which gives meaning, shape and purpose to everything we do, to everything we are. And so, prayer is not the time for words, however beautifully and sincerely phrased. All our words are wholly ineffective when we enter into mysterious communion with God whose Word is before and after all other words.

Christian Meditation: The Gethsemani Talks

In his gospel St John teaches that the person of faith must be 'of the truth'[1] and truth is conceived of as something growing and dynamic. It is not enough to think of accepting the faith once and for all. Faith is not a static condition. The indwelling Spirit of Truth continually influences and forms us. The importance of our daily return to meditation is that it deepens our openness and responsiveness to the Spirit's vivifying and enlightening presence.

In meditation we are constantly being refreshed by the power of the Spirit as it teaches us how to commit ourselves and dedicate ourselves to the truth. This is the truth that God is, that God is one and that our meaning is to be one with Him. John describes Jesus telling us that only the person who abides in the Word can fulfil this meaning and come to a genuine knowledge.

Word Made Flesh

[1] John 4:24

❀ AUGUST 27

Success and failure give way to what we come to know to be true through our own experience of meditation: death and resurrection. Every time we sit down to meditate we die to self and we rise beyond our own limitations to new life in Christ. We know that it is His life within us, His indwelling Spirit in our hearts, which is real and the essential energy of our *growth*. We also know that we can only come to our full potential if we are rooted in that reality, rooted in that love and living out of its power.

We have to learn to say our mantra. We have to learn to say it from the beginning of our meditation until the end. We have to understand that it is the daily discipline of our meditation that finally unmasks the ego. Unmasked, it disappears. We must not be impatient or despondent. We must say our mantra, with faith, day after day. Success or failure will then have no significance. The only thing that is significant is the reality of God, the reality of His presence in our heart, and our own reality as we respond to that presence. The discipline we first of all learn from our physical stillness. This is why we have to learn to sit still throughout our meditation, and then we learn the discipline from the faithful repetition of our mantra.

The Way of Unknowing

The Cloud of Unknowing calls it the 'one little word'. Reciting the word will teach you many things. Humility. Poverty. Fidelity. Hope. In surrendering all the richness of words and all ideas you can be open to the supreme reality, the infinity of God which cannot be captured in any concept but can be encountered in your own heart. Learning to pray is not a matter of listening to talks or reading books on prayer. It can only happen if you pray and all we can do in prayer is to dispose ourselves.

The gift is given, the Spirit is in the heart. All prayer is the pure gift of God given to us with infinite generosity. God can only give in an infinitely generous way. Meditating is a small token of our reciprocal generosity in our openness to His gift. I recommend you, therefore, to see those two daily periods of meditation as God's times, not your own. Approaching it in this way, rather than thinking of it as a way to get something out of it, will help you to build up your fidelity.

In faithfulness we learn faith. We learn to go into the dark, that expanse of consciousness which lies beyond the little island lit by our ego. We learn to go into the silence where there is no sound and to go ever deeper into the silence of the mystery of God. In meditation we learn the courage to launch out into the deep. From those depths come the power and the glory of the resurrection. Here is the new life given back to Jesus by His Father that places Him in the divine aura of glory for ever. His new life, glory and power – all words struggling to express the dimensions of love – are ours. The mystery that renews our hold on life once we enter it is that we, very ordinary people, are to be transformed in Christ. We have only to be mindful and so to realise from our own experience everything that has been achieved for us by Jesus.

Word Made Flesh

How do we enter into the tradition? It is no good just reading the accounts of the great spiritual men and women of the past. We have to do what they did and basically, that challenge to us is to let go of our own ideas and that means letting go of our ideas about meditation, about the spiritual path, about God and letting go of all our concepts, ideas, images in our minds. We have to learn to be still, to be silent. What each of us can learn, if we have the courage to enter into this silence, is that it is in the silence that we really begin to learn. It is in the silence that we really begin to enter the experience of what it means to *be*.

When you begin it is essential to understand that meditation is something utterly ordinary. It is just of the same sort of order as breathing, and meditation is to the spirit what breathing is to the body. Basically, we have to learn to be who we are now and with great simplicity. Do not imagine that anything should happen when you meditate. Do not imagine that your meditation is *successful* if something happens, or a failure if nothing happens.

The Door to Silence

One of the things we have to keep in mind in meditating is that we are moving towards greater and greater simplicity. It is useful, therefore, to have very clear in your minds at all time the simplicity that the teaching gives us: to say your mantra, to say your word, from the beginning to the end, and stillness and silence are of great importance. Meditate every morning and every evening, beginning your day out of the power of the mystery of God and completing your day in the power of His love. Listen to this reading from St John's gospel:

> It is my Father's will that everyone who looks upon the Son and puts his faith in Him shall possess eternal life.[1]

Everyone who looks upon the Son of God . . . that is what our meditation is. It is forgetting self, leaving self behind and becoming totally absorbed in the mystery, the wonder of God's revelation in Jesus. The great gift of God to us in Jesus is precisely 'eternal' life. That is the gift we are all offered: the definitive sharing in the being of God Himself and the gift we are given is to share in His unlimited capacity for life, for living, for love.

Being On The Way

[1] John 3:36

Meditation does call us to a maturing of love and so it is a great way of purification. We are purified of our egoism and possessiveness. An ancient word that the Desert Fathers used to describe this process is *apatheia*. It is difficult to translate *apatheia* but it is something like 'indifference'. It is like the attitude that Job eventually had: 'The Lord gives, the Lord takes away. Blessed be the name of the Lord. If we have received good things from his hands must we not also be prepared to receive evil things?'[1] The purpose of it all is that as we grow in fidelity, we grow in maturity and arrive at loving God because of who He is. We love God as God is in Himself. We love Him, not because He gives us good gifts, but because He is God. We love God because He is Himself: Love.

To mature at any level we have to grow through all the difficulties produced by change or loss, all the feelings, emotions and thoughts so generated and learn to love God simply and strongly. Part of the discipline of saying the mantra is that it teaches us to stay in that love, come what may. Nothing will shake us from our conviction that God is, that God is Love and that His love dwells in our hearts. If we are committed to the journey then the sense of absence will indeed deepen and strengthen our conviction of God's existence, making Him more familiar, teaching us to know Him more fully. At this depth of faith we are indifferent to whether we have a sense of His close presence or a sense of His absence.

The Way of Unknowing

[1] Job 1:21

SEPTEMBER 1

Meditation is practised in solitude but it is the great way to learn to be in relationship. The reason for this paradox is that, having contacted our own reality, we have the existential confidence to go out to others, to meet them at their real level, and so the solitary element in meditation is mysteriously the true antidote to loneliness. Having contacted our conformity with reality, we are no longer threatened by the otherness of others. We are not always looking for an affirmation of ourselves. We are making love's search, looking for the reality of the other. In the experience of encountering the reality of the other, we discover our own existence enriched and deepened.

Meditation is demanding. We must learn to meditate whether we feel like it or not, whether it is raining or snowing, or the sun is shining and whatever is on television or whatever kind of day we have had. In the Christian vision of meditation, a perspective gained from the words of Jesus, we find the reality of the great paradox He teaches: if we want to find our lives we have to be prepared to lose them. In meditating, that is exactly what we do. We find ourselves because we are prepared to let go of ourselves, to launch ourselves out into the depths which soon appear to be the depths of God. The essential message of Christianity is that God is present in the depths of each human being. That is why we must learn humility. That is why we must learn silence; because we must enter those depths of our self to encounter the otherness of God and in that encounter, to discover our essential self in union with God.

The Heart of Creation

Meditation is a discipline. It is the discipline of the disciple open to the Master, alert, present and reverent as we come into his presence. Meditation is becoming wholly present in the now, that is, the eternal moment of God. Meditation is simply the full acceptance of that reality in discipline, in faithfulness and in love.

And so, whether you are meditating on your own at home or with a group, be still. Be as still as you can be. Be open to God's gift to you. The gift of your own being and the gift of His Spirit who dwells in your heart. St Paul wrote to Timothy:

> Never be ashamed of your testimony to our Lord, nor of me His prisoner, but take your share of suffering for the sake of the gospel, in the strength that comes from God. It is He who brought us salvation and called us to a dedicated life, not for any merit of ours but of His own purpose and His own grace, which was granted to us in Christ Jesus from all eternity, but has now at length been brought fully into view, by the appearance on earth of our Saviour Jesus Christ. For He has broken the power of death and brought life and immortality to light, through the gospel.[1]

This is the context within which we meditate today. In the light and life of Jesus.

The Way of Unknowing

[1] 2 Tim. 1:8–10

As you begin to meditate all sorts of questions will arise in your mind. Is this for me? What does it mean? Should I be doing this? Am I getting anything out of it? and so forth. All these questions you must leave behind. You must transcend all self-questioning, and you must come to your meditation with childlike simplicity. Unless you become like little children, you *cannot* enter the Kingdom of Heaven.[1]

So my advice to you is, say your word, be content to say your word and allow the gift to be given by God. Don't demand it. We should come to our meditation with no demands and no expectations, but with just that generosity of spirit that allows us to be as present as we can to ourselves and to God. Meditating is very, very simple. Don't complicate it. As you meditate you should become more and more simple, not more and more complicated. As you know, nothing in this life that is really worth having can be had without a considerable amount of self-transcendence. It is the real loss of self that brings us the joy. And meditating is having the nerve to take the attention off yourself and to put it forward, to put it forward on God, to look ahead.

Moment of Christ

[1] Matt. 18:3

We, however, possess the mind of Christ.[1]

The ongoing pilgrimage of meditation leads us to an ever-deeper encounter with the essential theology of prayer. What does St Paul mean when he says we possess the mind of Christ? We know from the doctrine of the indwelling of the Holy Spirit that the fullness of God is to be found in our own hearts. We know that the full life of the Trinity is lived in our hearts. This is because Jesus Christ dwells in our hearts. His human consciousness is to be found within each of us. The journey of prayer is simply to find the way to open our human consciousness to His human consciousness and to become, on that way, fully conscious ourselves. The way passes beyond all dividedness, for there is no longer any subject or object, there is only full consciousness containing both.

This is the wonder of the doctrine of the Incarnation. Jesus being man and possessing a human consciousness, is our way to the Father. Humanly it is possible for us to open our human consciousness to His. That is the marvel, indeed the perfection, of the Christian revelation, that He is the Way, and He is the One Way because His love embraces all human ways. He is the universal redeemer and the universal sanctifier. He can be so for us because His human consciousness is fully open to the Father in the Spirit of love. When in the silence of prayer, and the concentration of our meditation, we open our human consciousness to Him, we go beyond Him, to the Father. We go beyond Him by *His* power of self-transcending love.

The Way of Unknowing

---

[1] 1 Cor. 2:16

SEPTEMBER 5

In responding to the gift of God in meditation we place ourselves wholly at His disposition. We do not even think any of our own thoughts. We do not even tell God of our own thoughts. We are simply and totally at His disposition by responding totally to the gift, body and mind, in absolute silence.

The silence of meditation could be described as the *eternal* silence of God. So when people ask, 'How long will it take?' the answer is that it takes no time at all, or it takes the time of your morning meditation and your evening meditation. The gift is given. The Spirit is poured into the hearts of each one of us. All we have to do is to *realise* what is given to us by God in Jesus, through the Spirit. It is the task of our daily meditation to go beyond time in a way that transforms time by the gift of the Spirit.

In your meditation at the beginning of each day you stand on the day's threshold holding the gift in open hands. You do not know what the day will bring. But you approach it in absolute faith and confidence because you approach it from the eternity of God. The beginning of every day is rooted in faith in God and in His goodness, His mercy, His compassion, and His love. That is how you start your day – not only thinking about these ideas but by entering into their reality in Jesus.

That is the Christian vision: that Jesus lives in your hearts beyond ideas. The Spirit is poured into each of us in silence. And so that is the way you start the day, in faith, and by discovering that faith in the Spirit's silence of your own heart. When each day begins in this way, the goodness, compassion and love of Christ bless and fortify the work of the day with His active presence in our action and thoughts.

The Heart of Creation

❧ SEPTEMBER 6

The impersonal and materialistic assumptions our society creates in our attitude to life have done great harm to our understanding of the reality of prayer and to our capacity to pray. Above all they have replaced the value of *presence* with the idea of *function* – it is not what a person is but what he does that counts. The truth is that the value of action consists in the quality of being. Our experience of love is always contradicting the false assumptions, but they remain deep-rooted attitudes of the modern consciousness. Meditation challenges it at root, because when we meditate we are not trying to do anything: we are simply attending to the reality of the divine Presence and learning to be in that Presence.

We learn a little each step we take, each time we meditate, every morning and evening. More deeply we discover that to *be* is not to be isolated, but to be realized *in communion*. The Presence of Christ is eternally present to us and we grow in our capacity to be present to Him. In that realisation of mutual presence, of communion, the divine transcendence occurs and we are swept away from the netherworld of self-centredness into the infinite energy and complete fulfilment of the reality who is Love.

The Present Christ

❧ SEPTEMBER 7

Perhaps you have been meditating for long enough to realise that nothing anyone can say about meditation is ever very satisfactory. If so, you will also know that the only ultimately important thing is that we meditate, treading the path of this pilgrimage each day of our lives.

Talking about a path of this kind can even be dangerous because, in the nature of language, it is so easy to imagine that by talking about it we know about it. Yet if we talked about it from now until the end of time we would know almost nothing about it.

The mystery is that if we can only learn the humility, patience and fidelity to say our mantra we can enter fully into everything there is. This is the present-ness of the mystery of God, who is, who is now, who is always, who is all. The time-bound structures of language and the ego-bound drives of desire and imagination perpetually fail to find the entrance to this mystery. The mantra, taking us into the present moment and beyond the ego, slips through the narrow gate into the city of God.

Word Made Flesh

In the rich tradition of Christian devotion, the figure of Mary stands out among all the 'devotions' of the Church as one of the richest and most personally identifiable signs of the real possibility of human harmony. All the aspects of the human spirit and its relationship with the corporeal dimension of our life find their fusion and perfect balance in Mary: her purity, her fertility and motherhood, her strength and humility.

It is just this balance, this inner harmony of our human spirit and our human facilities that is the condition for prayer – and, in a real sense, too, the condition *of* prayer. It is this condition of prayer which leads to that full and undistorted awareness of our union with the Spirit of Jesus that the early Church Fathers knew and called the 'real knowledge of God' – conversion, the 'enlightenment of the eye of the heart'.

Mary's motherhood is a sign, a sacrament of her full interiority. If Mary became so valuable a symbol of prayer for the early Church Fathers it was because they were inspired by their own experience of the interiority of the Christian mystery. In Mary they saw a reflection, indeed the ideal, of their own experience. They responded so warmly to Mary, the mother of Jesus, because they knew that every Christian is called to bring Jesus to birth within him or her; that, as Jesus was conceived and grew in bodily reality within Mary, so no less really He is conceived by the power of the Spirit and grows to full stature with the power of love within every responsive human heart. Just as the essential condition for Mary's reception of Jesus was her openness and her simplicity – what the gospel calls 'purity of heart' – so also, purity of heart is necessary for every Christian.

Community of Love

To learn to meditate it is necessary to meditate every day: every morning and every evening. Learning is a discipline and we have to be generous with our time, with our energy, with our attention. We have to be generous. We can never learn to enter into the supreme self-giving generous love of God without that generous commitment to the Way and to the discipline of the Way.

It is not good enough to talk or read about religion or spirituality. It is not good enough to study or have a spiritual director. We must enter personally into the basic Christian experience and we can only do so with childlike simplicity. This connection between simplicity and discipline explains why it is important to say your word from the beginning to the end. All of us have such an appalling hunger for self-analysis, for self-preoccupation which often masquerades as spirituality, that if we used the time of meditation to satisfy this desire it would be entirely counter-productive. We would fail to meet our deepest need which is for unity. The essence of meditation is taking the attention off ourselves and looking forward, beyond ourselves, into the mystery of God; of travelling beyond ourselves into His love, into union.

So let me stress to you the importance of saying the word. Do not think about God, do not think about yourself. Do not analyse God, do not analyse yourself. Be silent. Be still and be with Him, in His presence.

The Way of Unknowing

❦ SEPTEMBER 10

To meditate you must learn to be still. Meditation is perfect stillness of body and spirit. In that stillness we open our hearts to the eternal silence of God, to be swept out of ourselves, beyond ourselves, by the power of that silence. So the first thing to learn is to sit completely still and the only essential rule of posture is that your spine is as upright as possible. Take a couple of moments at the beginning of each meditation to sit still; get a comfortable posture and sit as upright as you can. Your eyes should be lightly closed. And then interiorly, silently, in your heart, begin to say your word, your mantra. The word I recommend is *maranatha*. And that is all you have to do. Don't think about God, don't work up in yourself any holy feelings about God.

Christian meditation is far more than thinking or feeling about God. It is being with Him, living not just in His presence but from the resources of His presence. We are able to live with His power, while being united to His power and His power is the basic energy of all creation, the power of love. That power is a mighty river flowing in and through our hearts and in meditating what we do is to open our hearts to the pure reality of that stream of love. Where are we when we meditate? We are in God. Where is God? He is in us. Quite simply, this is the great conviction of the early Church, of all Christ's disciples. The presence in our heart is that of the living Christ, and the supreme task of every life that would be fully human is to be open to that presence.

The Way of Unknowing

SEPTEMBER 11

When you come to your evening meditation, the whole of the day is gathered together. It is summed up in Jesus and in His presence in your heart. All the tensions, worries, as well as the joys, everything good and ill, is brought together in Jesus. But this is all dependent on practice. There is no way anyone can learn to meditate by reading books about meditation or by listening to talks on meditation. The only way we can learn is by meditating. That is why it is essential to meditate every day, each morning and evening. It is a considerable demand but one that leads us into the wonder of everything the gospel reveals. We discover in the experience of truly silent prayer what Jesus has achieved and what He has given to each one of us.

The secret of meditation is to be relaxed and alert, silent and simple. If you want to know why, then read St Paul writing to the Colossians where he speaks about the essence of the Christian message. This core-teaching is what meditation is about and in coming to understand the essence of Christianity in your own experience you find God in your own heart.

The Heart of Creation

❧ SEPTEMBER 12

What we know from the words of Jesus and from the actions of Jesus is that God is wholly turned to us in Jesus and in our meditation, and in taking our meditation absolutely seriously, in making it the fundamental axis of our life, we turn wholly to God in Jesus. That is what our meditation is about: turning our lives around so that they are wholly focused within the consciousness of Jesus, and this is what it is to enter eternal life. The astonishing thing about the gospel is that it is our destiny to enter this now, *today*, if only we can listen, if only we can turn, if only we can take the words of Jesus seriously. Then we can understand the wonderful destiny that we have and to enter into His consciousness, to open to it fully, is to pass beyond all limitations, all the limitations imposed on us by our thought patterns, our cultural patterns, our capacity for delusion and fantasy; to open to His consciousness is to travel beyond all that into the mystery of his unlimited life.

What we must understand is that every one of us not only has this call but has this capacity to transcend the limitations that we impose on ourselves by our own egoism, to transcend the limitations we impose ourselves by illusion, by desire. To enter the eternal life by opening our human consciousness to the human consciousness of Jesus is to enter now, in this life, into unlimited life, unlimited peace, unlimited joy: a peace that is way beyond all understanding.

Being On The Way

🎖 SEPTEMBER 13

This is a scene from the life of Jesus in the Gospel of St Luke:

> They even brought babies for him to touch, but when the disciples
> saw them they scolded them for it. But Jesus called for the children
> and said, 'Let the little ones come to me. Do not try to stop them. For
> the Kingdom of God belongs to such as these. I tell you that whoever
> does not accept the Kingdom of God like a child will never enter it.'[1]

Learning to meditate is learning to unlearn. The big problem that faces
anyone who starts to meditate is the simplicity of it. God is One. And
Christian prayer has been described as the way of one-ing, becoming one,
becoming one with the One who is One. The problem we face is to leave
complexity behind. We are used to complexity because we are brought up
to believe that the more perfect the technique, the more stunning will be the
result. The perfecting of techniques increases complexity. The perfecting of
a discipline leads to simplicity. And Jesus tells us to become simple, to
become childlike. Meditation is the way of rediscovering our innate, childlike sense of wonder. Christian prayer is a state of innocence.

When we meditate we go beyond desire, beyond possessiveness, beyond
self-importance, beyond all sources of guilt and complexity. So the first
thing you must learn when you set out on the pilgrimage of meditation is
to listen to the message with the simplicity of a child. God is One. And the
extraordinary thing about the Christian proclamation is that our vocation is
to be one with Him, in Him and through Him.

The Way of Unknowing

---

[1] Luke 18:15–17

SEPTEMBER 14

Each of us is summoned within our own personal experience, to learn to see with our own eyes, to hear with our own ears, and to love with our own heart and to do so in Him, in union with Him and at one with Him. What this means in practice is going beyond all dualism, all dividedness within ourselves and beyond ourselves. The call to each one of us is to transcend all the barriers that separate us from ourselves, from others and from God. We must go, and go definitively beyond – beyond all these false dichotomies, the false dichotomies that can only be resolved in union, in love, in God. In other words, what each of us is summoned to is to a fundamental simplicity.

Each of us must learn to *be* and this is exactly the call of deep prayer, to be in love, in trust, in total openness of heart to what *is*: to God who is love. The vision, as we open our hearts and eyes to it, the vision is so intoxicating that we must approach it with humility and we all need, each one of us, to be truly humble. That is to say, truly rooted in what is.

The Door to Silence

Stillness takes us into the silence beyond the lopsidedness of language. It restores us to the inner equilibrium from which we can then use language more precisely and truthfully. But we are still so that God may find us in our finding of Him at the deepest level of our being.

This is why faithfulness to the daily meditation and to our mantra during those meditation times is everything. We know that we must not think about God or imagine God during these all-important times, simply because He is present. He is there, not just to be found, but to be loved. Being in love we let thoughts fall away.

> I am convinced that there is nothing in death or in life, in the realm of spirits or superhuman powers, in the world as it is or the world as it shall be, in the forces of the universe, in heights or depths – nothing in all creation that can separate us from the love of God in Christ Jesus our Lord.[1]

What need then to be discouraged by our distractions?

Word Made Flesh

[1] Rom. 8:38–39

❧ SEPTEMBER 16

Meditation is the activity of total peace in an all-encompassing silence. In the silence of meditation we love all, we love *the* All. The way is the way of discipline, the way of stillness and silence, the way of the mantra. We do not seek anything except total truth, total love, because we know that we can only find fullness in God. Finding it, we are ourselves enlivened with His life and enlightened with His light. Jesus assures us that if we will listen and if we will trust we will not come up for judgment: 'He who puts his trust in Him who sent me has hold of eternal life and does not come up for judgment but has already passed from death to life.'[1] This is because in that act of trust we cannot but choose God when we know ourselves chosen by him: that is the passing from death to life.

And so, meditation is not about making something happen. What it is about, and this is the basic aim of meditation, is to become fully aware of, fully inserted into, fully grounded in *what is*. If we wanted to invent a term to describe something that precedes all language we could say that meditation is about *isness*. You remember how in Exodus God describes himself simply in the words, '*I am* . . . tell them. *I am* sent you.' *I am* is the present tense of the verb to be and God is, essentially, *present being*. Meditation is full openness to our own present being. What you can learn from meditating is that your being comes to fullness when you are wholly open to the one who is *I am*.

The Way of Unknowing

[1] John 5:24

The message *we* have been commanded to deliver, to repeat with all the freshness that the creative Spirit imbues us with, is of immense and contemporary urgency, most of all perhaps for the young. But it is a hard message, a hard saying, and it can barely be heard let alone accepted unless we ourselves are the living witnesses of its authenticity. Conceptually, we can talk about it in any number of ways – the discovery of our personhood, an encounter with the absolute, have been the terms I have been using. I think these can find responsive echoes in contemporary thought and language. But the conceptual is no substitute for the practical. And in practical terms our message is a call to the *rediscovery of prayer* and of ourselves as having the capacity for deep prayer in spirit and in truth, of prayer as the central authenticating fact of our life and personhood.

Community of Love

❧ SEPTEMBER 18

The great fact of the experience of meditating is that once we do enter into the human consciousness of Jesus we begin to see as He sees, to love as He loves, to understand as He understands and to forgive as He forgives. Our angle of vision on the whole of creation is profoundly altered. Once expanded it need never again contract, and will not, if we always remember the pre-eminence of the practice.

It is, practically, necessary to meditate every day, morning and evening. It is necessary in order to ground and root our lives in the foundational reality of Christ's living Spirit that is manifested in every aspect of human life. But it is especially characterized by its gentleness and the powerful gift of forgiveness. You may well ask, 'How will sitting to meditate bring *me* to this compassion and forgiveness; how will the mantra lead me to this love?' When you begin you have to take that on faith. There is no way of answering that question except for yourself, through the practice.

In meditation we seek to disassemble the barriers that we have set up around ourselves and that cut us off from the consciousness of the presence of Jesus within our own heart. In meditating we start the process of dismantling the ego and its persistent attempt to place ourselves at the centre. We begin to understand that God is at the centre and so our whole perspective and orientation changes. In the practice of meditation, we begin to learn what real humility is about; being ourself in our proper place.

Meditation also teaches us that we can reach God the Father, *through* the human consciousness of Jesus, the Son, because we discover by meditating in faith that Jesus is the bridge that takes us to the further shore. He is the ferry that takes us across the little tributary of egoism and launches us into the mainstream of divine love. Egoism flows into backwaters of isolation. Meditation leads us through this isolation into the oceanic love of God.

Word Into Silence

SEPTEMBER 19

The first step in this process of transcendence and union with God is made when we turn to prayer. This is a moment of truth. It is a moment when we are confronted with the fact of our own existence and are challenged to accept the gift of it with utter generosity and simplicity. It is a moment of silence and a moment of love. We have, in this moment of decision, to turn with a faith that allows us to turn aside from everything. This is the abandonment, the letting go of prayer. It is casting out into the depth of God as the ground of our being and allowing ourselves to fall back into our source. It can seem – because of the language we have to use to describe it – as a retrogressive movement. We call it a 'going back,' a 'returning.' And in a sense it is. It is the returning home of the prodigal son who understood that his reality was to be found at home and not in the restless pursuit of illusion abroad.

The monastic Fathers used to describe it as a wandering in a land of 'unlikeness' and a return to our real likeness as image of God. This aspect of prayer as a restoration, a returning or homecoming, is profoundly important to us. It emphasises the humanity of the journey we are all called to make and it suggests some of the tenderest and most intimate reasons that God is known to us, and described by Jesus to us as 'Father.'

Letters From the Heart

❀ SEPTEMBER 20

Why I believe that meditation is so important for all of us is that it teaches us in our own hearts, right in the centre of our own being where we can know it from our own experience, that indeed God is all in all. What we must learn is that all life is energy. The humblest plant, the most complex movement of the brain, both are alive and their life consists in their vitalising energy force that keeps them alive and drives them to communicate their energy, to new life, to expansion of life. I think what each of us is invited to in our lives, as mature people, is to come into contact with, to discover, the mystery of God in our own hearts and the mystery of God is the mystery of the divine energy.

What each of us must learn from our own experience is that this divine energy that we can encounter within ourselves is limitless, infinite, self-communicating love. What we must know is that God is the ground of our being. What we must know is that God is the ground of all being and once we begin to make contact with this reality, with this truth in the depths of our own heart, we are led into the understanding of the most profound and yet most simple truth: we are all one in God.

The Door to Silence

❧ SEPTEMBER 21

The power of meditation is its simplicity and its practicality – that we take the practical steps to set out on the way leaving the books, the talks, the lectures, the ideas behind. We learn to attend in depth, to attend profoundly, learning to *be* and learning to be in the presence of God, learning from our own experience. All that is necessary for us is to be as totally as we can be in His presence. What we have to learn from our meditation – and in every generation this must be re-learnt, is to see this light and to see everything illuminated by this light and the light is the light of Christ and, as St Paul tells us, this light shines in our hearts.

This is the purpose of our meditation, this is the work of our meditation: to learn to see with this visionary dimension; and our work in this life is to prepare our hearts to expand in this light, this light which is life, which is love, which is God. What we have to learn – and this is the most astonishing thing of all, is our destiny in this life is to become this light, to lose ourselves in God, to find ourselves in God, to become one with Him.

Being On The Way

It is so important for all of us to learn to be still. In that stillness we learn to remain with the energy that arises from the contact we have made with our own spiritual nature. The phenomenon of so much contemporary 'spirituality' is not of a pilgrimage to the centre. It is more like a raid mission that descends suddenly, plunders what can be got in the form of spiritual experience or insight, and then immediately retreats behind the walls of the religious ego. There is all the difference in the world – the difference between reality and illusion – between the pilgrim and the nomads.

The pilgrim stays on the journey, steadily and selflessly, focused not on emotional or intellectual satisfaction but upon the goal, the goal that leads us, the goal who is Christ. This is true Christian conversion, the revolution that Christ taught and exemplified in His own person. It is what makes our beliefs credible – to ourselves and to others because it makes us credible. The steadiness – firmness, rootedness as St Paul described it – is the guarantee of our sanity. Our seriousness about the journey guarantees its joyfulness.

The Present Christ

The word 'meditation' has an interesting possible connection with the Latin *sto in medio* – 'I stand in the centre'. Meditation indeed means learning to live out of the centre of your being.

It is not an esoteric practice. Everyone needs to learn that rootedness in their centre so that they can be fully themselves. It is something deeply ordinary and natural. We live in a world that makes great demands on us and is continually threatening our ability to stay rooted in the centre of our being. Stress and all its related forms of dysfunction, depression, anxiety and addiction are not rare conditions in modern living. It is perhaps difficult to think of modern life at all without them.

To be stable we need to be sure of ourselves. We need to feel we are standing on firm ground and that we will not have our identity or self-respect blown away by the first storms of disappointment or conflict which we encounter. Meditation is the way to this first and basic sense of stability, rootedness in ourselves. Without it external or physical stability can degenerate into a search for security or ways of self-protection. The essential stability is the reality of our own being, and how many are in touch with that?

Word Made Flesh

❧ SEPTEMBER 24

In the Christian vision of meditation, the whole purpose of this process is to free your spirit to be open to infinity. Allow your heart and your mind, your whole being, to expand beyond all the barriers of your isolated self and to come into union with all, with God. When you start you will find all sorts of distractions in your mind.

The purpose of the mantra is to bring the mind to calm, to peace, to concentration. And the way to do it is to keep saying the mantra. When you first start, you will find that if you say the mantra, continuously, faithfully, then after about ten minutes it will probably bring you to a deep peacefulness. You will be amazed and you will say, 'I had no idea I had this capacity for peace. This is wonderful. I'm just going to hold on to this now and I'm going to stop saying the mantra?' When you do this one of two things happen. You enter into a state of reverie, just floating nowhere, and that's exactly where you are, nowhere. Or your mind is immediately filled again with all sorts of distractions.

So when you are starting, be absolutely clear in your mind that the way to meditate is to say your mantra from the beginning to the end. Don't allow any experience of wellbeing that you want to possess or hold on to or any narcissistic approach to prayer that you may be encouraged to adopt, distract you from the truth of the continuous selflessness of the mantra. This is what makes meditating *absolute* simplicity.

The Way of Unknowing

Now let me try to describe how to come to the simplicity needed for prayer. When you prepare for meditation try to find a sitting posture that is both comfortable and alert. The only essential rule of posture is a straight back. Close your eyes and start repeating your mantra without moving either lips or tongue. And say the word continuously until the end of the meditation. It is difficult for Christians when they first hear about this to understand how it could even be prayer. How can this non-thinking state be significant in the life of a Christian? Is it just a way of relaxing? Has it really any ultimate significance in the Christian vision of life? If you persevere with meditation you will discover that significance for yourself.

The significance is that the gift of God in Jesus to each one of us is an absolute gift. Meditation is our absolute, accepting response. God has given us Himself. Nothing has been kept back. He has given us the fullness of the divinity in the humanity of Jesus. A Christian life is our response to that gift and, just as the gift is absolute, so must our response be absolute and permanent.

The Heart of Creation

❦ SEPTEMBER 26

One of the greatest forces that resists life is fear and fear is largely the fear of being punished or of dying. Fear, death, life and love are the actors in the Christian drama.

> In very truth, anyone who gives heed to what I say and puts his trust in Him who sent me has hold of eternal life and does not come up for judgment but has already passed from death to life.[1]

That is the truth of the gospel that each of us is invited not just to read, but to live. The gospel of Jesus is about living. It is about life and all of us are invited to live our lives not, as it were, at fifty or sixty percent of our potential, but at a hundred percent: to live life with fullness. The witness of the gospel proclaims that this is only possible for any of us if we are fully in touch with our life-source, which is the source of all life, the Divine energy. Jesus spoke to 'anyone who gives heed to what I say'.

We have to learn to *listen* to him, to listen deeply to the invitation to live our lives to the full and so to be filled with divine power. We have to listen with the fullness of our own being, profoundly, totally. That is why the silence of meditation is so important and why each of us, through our own experience as we continue to meditate, discovers that silence is so precious a value in our lives in general. Silence also touches our common life together so that we can share a sense of the mysterious power both in our midst and beyond us.

The Way of Unknowing

[1] John 5:2

The purification that leads to purity of heart, that leads to the presence within us, is a consuming fire; and meditation is entering that fire, the fire that burns away everything that is not real, that burns away everything that is not true, that burns away everything that is not loving. And we must not be afraid of the fire. We must have absolute confidence in the fire, for the fire is the fire of love. The fire is even more. This is the great mystery of our faith. It is the fire who is love. Listen to Jesus speaking in the gospel of John:

> I am the vine, you are the branches. He who dwells in me as I dwell in him bears much fruit but apart from me you can do nothing. He who does not dwell in me is thrown away like a withered branch but if you dwell in me and my words dwell in you, ask what you will and you shall have it and this is my Father's glory: that you may bear fruit in plenty and be my disciples. As the Father has loved me so I have loved you. Dwell in my love. If you heed my commands you will dwell in my love, as I have heeded my Father's commands and dwell in His love.[1]

The Door to Silence

[1] John 15:5–10

✿ SEPTEMBER 28

The Indian mystic Sri Ramakrishna, who lived in Bengal in the nineteenth century, used to describe the mind as a mighty tree filled with monkeys, all swinging from branch to branch and all in an incessant riot of chatter and movement. When we begin to meditate we recognise that as a wonderfully apt description of the constant whirl going on in our mind. Prayer is not a matter of adding to this confusion by trying to shout it down and covering it with another lot of chatter.

The task of meditation is to bring all of this mobile and distracted mind to stillness, silence and concentration, to bring it, that is, into its proper service. This is the aim given us by the psalmist: 'Be still and know that I am God.'[1] To achieve this aim we use a very simple device. It is one that St Benedict drew to the attention of his monks as long ago as the sixth century by directing them to read the *Conferences* of John Cassian.[2]

Cassian recommended anyone who wanted to learn to pray, and to pray continually, to take a single short verse and just to repeat this verse over and over again. In his Tenth Conference, he urges this method of simple and constant repetition as the best way of casting out all distractions and monkey chatter from our mind, in order that it might rest in God.[3]

Word Into Silence

[1] Psalm 46:10
[2] *Rule of St Benedict* 42:6, 13:73, 14   [3] *Conference* 10:10

Saying the mantra is like dropping the anchor. It falls into the depths of our being; and it is there we have to go, far below the surface, however unfamiliar this transition may at first be. We are so caught up in dealing with all that is going on on the surface that we do not give the time to stand aside from these passing concerns. Stress, anxiety, depression can all be invoked as reasons for avoiding meditation because of a lack of time.

But time is what we have to give it, each morning and evening. Think of it not so much as a time for 'doing' meditation as simply a time for being. Try not to get uptight about meditation itself, if at all possible! It is time for being yourself. It is not necessary to justify or defend yourself or make yourself acceptable to God. Be practical about the time. Set aside a minimum of twenty minutes which you can gradually extend to twenty-five and up to the optimum of half an hour. During that time learn to say your mantra from the beginning to the end.

Word Made Flesh

✿ SEPTEMBER 30

I find it more difficult to meditate in the evening than in the morning. I think it is much more difficult to meditate when you are tired, when you haven't a great deal of physical energy. I certainly found, a couple of years ago when I was in hospital recovering from an operation, that particularly when I was very weak just after the operation, I would say the mantra maybe a couple of times and then I would be in a very deep and reposeful state of sleep. When I would wake up I would say it another couple of times and be asleep again. But I think that we have to be very careful that we do not rate ourselves for success. I think you have to do the very best you can in the circumstances that you are in. For example, ideally it is useful to meditate in a very quiet place so that you can be as recollected as possible. Even if your next-door neighbour starts using a steam hammer and recollection is lost, it is far preferable to keep on meditating rather than to say, 'Well, I haven't got the ideal circumstances therefore I will give up.'

For example, when I was coming home from Ireland last week on the plane I decided that the time had come to meditate. The air hostess, however, decided that it was a good time to have a chat with a passenger who seemed to be looking rather lonely or rather quiet and she came and sat down beside me so I chatted with her for a while. She was rather more than usually loquacious and it took me some time before I could politely return to my meditation. You have to do the best that you can in the circumstances and I would always advise you not to give up, even though you are tired and you haven't a lot of energy. Do your best to put in the evening meditation.

Being On The Way

One of the tensions that runs through the history of Christianity is a tension between the active and contemplative modalities. One of the tragedies of modern Christianity is that the tension has become so slack. Every Christian is called to live the contemplative dimension of the Christ-vision. Every Christian, in other words, is called to a deep *consciousness* of what it means to be created by God, of what it means to be redeemed by Jesus, of what it means to be a temple of the Holy Spirit. Whenever religious people have turned their backs on that contemplative dimension of their calling, they have become too *busy*, unreflectively active, and they usually end up by becoming busybodies.

If our life is rooted in Christ, rooted in His love and the conscious knowledge of His love, then we need have no anxiety about regulating our action. Our action will always spring from and be informed and shaped by that love. Indeed, the more active we are, the more important it is that our action springs from and is grounded in contemplation. And contemplation means deep, silent, communion; knowing who are we are by being who we are. That we are rooted and founded in Christ, the Resurrection of God, is Christian self-knowledge.

The Way of Unknowing

❧ OCTOBER 2

As St Paul puts it, 'Outwardly, our humanity is in decay, but inwardly we are being renewed, transformed from glory to glory.'[1] At the level of biological life, we all have our share in the divine flow of energy, in all its variety, in all its complexity. The wonder of the Christian understanding is that this creative flux of energy through all these different forms of matter and spirit have their guiding principle, their focal point and their end. The guiding principle, the direction of this flow, its purposefulness, is the Spirit, the Spirit which is beyond form and yet which informs all form. The focal point from which everything in creation is aligned is the Son, and the marvel of our Christian vocation is that in Him we ourselves are focused and clarified. And the end, the goal of all, the goal of this whole flow of energy, is the Father, who is the source of all.

When we sit down to meditate every morning and every evening we must do so in utter humility at the sheer marvel and wonder of our vocation and we must do so in absolute confidence that there is in the power of Jesus, a real continuity between the finite and the infinite, between the mortal and the immortal, and that Jesus lives in our hearts.

The Door to Silence

[1] 2 Cor. 4:16

❧ OCTOBER 3

The path of meditation is the path of faith and the sacrament of faith is our silence. The door to silence is the mantra. It is not then long before we begin to understand that the loss of self involved is not abnegation but empathy, not an extinction of individuality but a communion of persons. For as we become more deeply rooted in the ground of our being we have our being clarified and affirmed in the purifying silence of the mystery present to us in our heart.

We are no longer outside creation or outside God, because through the power that dwells in the open space in the centre of our being we pass beyond ourselves into fullness of being. To do this we have to be simple enough to be rooted in reality, and faithful enough to stay on our pilgrimage and to meditate each morning and evening. Then we realise our union with our point of origin. Our destination and our companion are one. 'I call you servants no longer; a servant does not know what his master is about. I have called you friends because I have disclosed to you everything I have heard from my Father.'[1] It is this that makes the pilgrimage possible for us all.

The Present Christ

[1] John 15:15

❧ OCTOBER 4

The mantra accepts the human challenge to know God, to know Him without fear and to know Him to the fullness of our capacity to know. To rise to the adventure of life, our meditation requires not part of our attention or part of our love, but the whole of our attention and the unified intention of our love. And so, we learn to say the mantra with complete fidelity and with total attention.

To learn this art of prayer, as to learn anything, we must be prepared to be patient, because to learn fidelity and full attention requires continual patience. The knowledge we come to in meditation is not merely new additions to the memory bank. The knowledge we come to is wisdom. Wisdom is to know the significance of what we know, to know in perspective and true proportion. Wisdom is simply knowing with a divine perspective; it means knowing everything we are given to know in the perspective of eternity. We know what is important when we know what it is that endures forever. Wisdom is the fruit of growth in meditation because we know with certain knowledge that God is, and that He is eternal. And that He is eternal Love.

The Way of Unknowing

It would almost be impossible for you not to feel, when you begin, 'Surely this is a great waste of time. Shouldn't I be using this marvellous mind that the Lord has given me, this wonderful intelligence that I have, and so forth, to deepen my insights, to deepen my understanding?' You have to learn to be still. You have to learn, from your own experience, what St John of the Cross meant when he wrote 'the way of possession is the way of dispossession'. The great word that the early monks used to describe the way of meditation was that it was the way of poverty. We dispossess ourselves of all our words, of all our ideas, and we learn to be utterly still.

> Out of the treasures of His glory, may He grant you strength and power through His Spirit in your inner being, that through faith Christ may dwell in your hearts in love.[1]

In The Beginning

---

[1] Eph. 3:17

❧ OCTOBER 6

Purity of heart is acuity of vision, sharp vision, and as we say our mantra, we narrow down our concentration to a single point: the mantra. That single point leads to this vision. Everything else – all distractions, all thought about ourselves, all the ego – has been put aside and our vision is concentrated wholly and completely ahead into the mystery, into the vision of God. Now the secret is learning to come down to that single point.

I do not know how many of you have had that experience – a very wonderful experience if you have had it – of polishing a brass table? A few years ago someone gave me a table made of brass. It looked as though it was made of ebony: it was black. Now if you are faced with polishing a brass table, you can try wide, broad strokes, but you will not get very far and you will use a lot of polish. The secret is to concentrate on one small, select point at a time. As we work at the one point and then out from this point, the whole brass table begins to glisten, to shine.

The teaching of Jesus is that the purity to which each one of us is called is an interior purity. It is an interior clarity. That is where we have to start, that is where we have to – as it were – sharpen our vision and then the extraordinary thing about the Christian revelation is that this interior clarity to which each of us is summoned is nothing less than His own presence, His own being, His own love.

The Door to Silence

I think it is true to say that all of us begin meditating as egoists and the first crisis we come to is when in our meditation itself we experience egoism's sterility, dryness, nothingness. All of us, I think, when we begin, come to a point when we ask ourselves 'What am I getting out of this? What is it doing for me?' or, 'Is this the same as everything else? Am I going to end up here, too, with nothing but sterility?' The temptation, of course, is to give up, to fly from this new and perhaps even deeper sterility. It is at this point that all of us have to make an act of faith. It may appear to be the faith to enter the darkness and to embrace the sterility, but there is no way we can embrace it except with total abandon. It has to be a total act of faith. In other words, we commit ourselves to meditation, and to the mantra as a way to commit ourselves, to letting go of self-consciousness. In effect, we are committing ourselves to letting go of our sterility.

Meditation is growth *and* transcendence. Just as the plant that is rooted and that we cultivate is in a constant state of self-transcendence, leaving behind its former state and being what it is now, so are we on this journey of spiritual growth. The seed is the shoot, the shoot is the stalk, the stalk is the fruit and so on. Meditating is just that flowing movement of self-transcendence that unfolds as one reality – the person we are – in God's eternal present.

In meditation we are simply as wholly and fully open to the love of this present moment as possible. If we can be faithful to it, returning every morning and every evening, our capacity for love will be in a state of constant daily growth, a constant deepening of quality and expansion of range. This is what St Paul understood as the fruit of faith in the process of living the Christian life.

> So shall we all at last attain to the unity inherent in our faith and our knowledge of the Son of God – to mature manhood – measured by nothing less than the full stature of Christ.[1]

The Way of Unknowing

[1] Eph. 4:13

❦ OCTOBER 8

It seems to me impossible to convince people about meditation by mere talk. There is very little point in arguing about it because anyone who meditates begins to meditate because they recognise the truth of it. They *respond* to it. Perhaps they even *remember* it because it is something that seems both to clarify and to *recall* their deepest sense of the meaning of life. This is simply the way reality is structured. If someone wishes to find his or her life he or she must first lose it. We know from our ordinary experience that this is the way things are. What we need to find is a practical way which will allow us to apply and to fulfil this knowledge at the deepest level of our being. In this way, at that deepest level, we become one with the very structure of reality.

In meditation we enter into harmony with the way things are. And what we learn is this – that we have to enter into the reality of the present moment we have been given before death folds up the past and the future into the eternal. That means that we must learn to die to the ego and the state of egoism that is forever slipping out of the reality of the present by regretting its past or day-dreaming about the future. To meditate is to learn to be present, to be still. *Be still and know that I am God.*[1]

Community of Love

[1] Ps. 46:10

❧ OCTOBER 9

I think you will find that as you enter into the peace of meditation and the simplicity of it and the silence of it, it is anything but boring. What I would say to anyone who does at times find it boring is to persevere, keep going. The advice that I would give anyone is 'say your mantra'. That is perhaps the most difficult thing to understand when you are beginning. Because you think you should be 'praying' or you think you should be getting great insights or you should be levitating or you should be doing something, whereas the real thing is to say your mantra and to be *content* to say it.

That is difficult in that it is particularly difficult for modern people because we are not a contented generation. We are always expecting something to happen. It seems that if we have a certain input then there will be a certain output, there will be a pay-off. But that is why I say at the beginning: meditation is the way of unlearning and you have to unlearn both your materialistic attitudes and most of your religious attitudes as well. Both have to be unlearned. We are realising what has happened and is happening eternally. The realisation is what is happening in our meditation. When we see that there is no more boredom!

The Way of Unknowing

🏵 OCTOBER 10

Our society trains us to remain childish, dependent on external stimuli and amusement, spoon-fed on the prepackaged experiences we call entertainment that have as much spiritual nutrition as the convenience foods that, like television, symbolise our culture. In discovering the existence of such a responsibility in our lives we are tempted and trained to evade it, to retreat yet again into childish distraction and dissipation. The responsibility of making a mature response seems to us like a curtailment of our freedom.

This is why meditation is so important for us all. It prepares us for the real freedom that lives and rejoices at the heart of this mystery of love within us, the movement of divine energy that is also the stillness of our pilgrimage of faith. To pray in the infinite depths of our spirit, which is the depth of God, is to be utterly free.

And our daily meditation, the deepening experience that flowers on the trellis of our discipline, teaches us the essential lesson of maturity: freedom does not consist in doing what we want but in being who we are. To be free is to have been liberated into being by a power of love greater than our own power of ego. It is to have encountered and responded to the Other in humility. The liberty is the liberty to be open to God as the ground of our being – the structure of all reality, inner and outer. It is to be redeemed by love from the slavery of self-consciousness and self-preoccupation.

Letters From the Heart

One of the earliest things we discover when we begin to meditate on a daily basis is that the practice itself begins to have results throughout our life. The harmonic sounded within us at the time of our meditation sets up sympathetic responses in every aspect of our personality and life. If it were not so – if our meditation were isolated in a spiritual vacuum – then we could be sure that the practice itself was illusory.

It is good to remind ourselves occasionally that meditation is not just another activity or interest in our life. It is so absolutely fundamental or central that we could say that it is, in a real sense, *lifegiving*. All life involves movement, growth, development. A person or an institution begins to die when their commitment to growth begins to wane. This is why our faith is, in effect, the energy that fuels the journey of meditation and, because it is a journey into God, our commitment is to a deep, divine principle of infinite growth. Our journey, like the Gospel itself, as St Paul describes it, begins in faith and ends in faith. Our daily commitment to meditation is the expression and renewal of our faith.

The Present Christ

The problem for us, as men and women of the twentieth century, is to be trusting enough, to be still enough, to be simple enough, just to be content to say our word. Remember those words of Jesus: 'Unless you become like little children you cannot enter the kingdom of Heaven.'[1] Jesus did not say, 'It will be difficult for you, it will be hard.' He said, 'Unless you become like little children you cannot enter the kingdom of Heaven.'[1] Learning to say our mantra faithfully, humbly, is our way into that childlike trust, that childlike faith. As far as we are concerned, in the tradition from which we speak as monks, the essential thing is the practice.

If you have an hour a day to devote to your spiritual life, my recommendation is that you spend a half an hour in the morning and a half an hour in the evening in meditation. Do not waste as much as five minutes on reading books about meditation. Enter into the experience yourself. When you have entered into the experience, that will be time enough to read the books. You might even understand some of them at that stage. But even at that stage, the essential thing is the practice. Half an hour every morning and the same every evening.

The Door to Silence

[1] Matt. 18:3

In meditation we do not seek to think about God nor do we seek to think about His Son, Jesus, nor do we seek to think about the Holy Spirit. We are trying rather to do something immeasurably greater. By turning aside from everything that is passing, everything that is contingent, we seek not just to think about God, but to be with God, to experience Him as the ground of our being. It is one thing to know that Jesus is the Revelation of the Father, that Jesus is our Way to the Father, but quite another to experience the presence of Jesus within us. In meditation we experience the real power of His Spirit within us and, in that experience, we are brought into the presence of His Father and our Father.

Many people today are finding that they have to face the fact that there is an all-important difference between thinking about these truths of the Christian faith and experiencing them, between believing them on hearsay and believing them from our own personal verification. Experiencing and verifying these truths is not just the work of specialists in prayer. St Paul's inspiring and exultant letters were not written to members of an enclosed religious Order, but to the ordinary butchers and bakers of Rome, Ephesus and Corinth.

These are truths that each one of us is called to know for ourself, and in meditation we seek to know them.

Word Into Silence

Walter Hilton is a very good witness that there is no antipathy as it were between contemplative prayer, vocal prayer and liturgical prayer. He does trace a kind of progressive development through these forms but not in the sense that we ever get to a stage in our life when we have *gone beyond* liturgical prayer or vocal prayer. The development he really sees is a growth in the delight with which one enters into whatever form is appropriate at any time. And all these forms of prayer are, of course, complementary, provided that we know them as they really are: as entrances into the eternal prayer of Jesus which is His loving return to the Father. At all times in our lives all the various streams of prayer are coming together and binding us ever more closely to the Lord Jesus in the universal ocean of His prayer.

Christian Meditation: The Gethsemani Talks

Coming to knowledge of Christ brings us to grasp the full meaning of our own life as well as the meaning of the lives of those we love and share life with. The greatest tragedy of a human life would be to mistake its meaning. The tragedy of Romeo was that he misread the situation at the climatic moment of the drama, thinking that Juliet was dead. So can each of us easily mistake the meaning of an event by judging it by its appearance alone. So easily can we miss the mystery of life's inner meaning.

In meditation, as we go beyond appearances, we seek to open ourselves – our deep centre – to the mystery of our creation so that we can, at depth, comprehend the gift of God in Christ. We can do so only in faith which is our capacity for self-transcendence. Faith leads us into the truth that Christ is our redeemer and that we are already redeemed. As we come to this truth we are led to be totally committed to it. This is essential in all discipleship: not to be half-hearted but fully responsive in our openness to His gift of our life and of His love in our life.

Word Made Flesh

What you can discover by persevering in meditation is that it is not just that our life has found its own inner coherence. That is, of course, a necessary first step for each one of us, but it is something even greater than that, and this is what everyone is summoned to if only we can undertake a discipline to come to it. In meditation we find our own inner resonance in God. I think that what we have to say to you as monks is that no one must be content to live their life just at ten percent of their potential. Each of us must live at one hundred percent of our potential and we must enter into that profound inner resonance in God – not just that we are called to be resonant *with* God but *in* Him. This is our call, this is our destiny: to find peace beyond ourselves in God.

The Door to Silence

❀ OCTOBER 17

Meditation leads us into the state of pure prayer. When we meditate we lay aside action, we lay aside all the operations of the mind in favour of *being*. Learning to say your mantra, learning to say it from the beginning to the end of your meditation, is your way into that state of being. We leave thinking behind because we can only think of God the Creator, the God who is just, God who is good. But what we have to learn in meditation is that our God is the God who is, who is 'pure being' and what we have to learn is that in the light of His reality, all reality is made real. In the light of His being, all goodness is made good and we have to pay attention, and to pay attention with the totality of our own being, open to the being of God. To meditate is to be in a state of empathy with God, to be in a state of union with Him.

Being On The Way

🎋 OCTOBER 18

Especially when you are starting to meditate it is extremely important to approach meditation with absolute clarity as to what is involved. When I learned to meditate I had a teacher who put it before me with crystal clarity. His teaching was summed up in three words: say your mantra. In the last thirty years I have been increasingly impressed by the extraordinary wisdom of his teaching. Saying the mantra is the first thing to understand. It may take you five or ten years to understand the importance of saying your mantra from the beginning to the end of your meditation, without ceasing.

You will meet alternative doctrines but I would urge you to stay with the tradition which tells us that if we would find a central reality, then we must learn to be deeply silent. We must learn to be disciplined and we must learn to leave our thoughts and imagination entirely behind. The faithful recitation of the mantra is the way. It takes time to learn the wisdom and deep truthfulness of this radically simple teaching. As I say, it has taken me a good part of thirty years to understand the importance of it.

The Way of Unknowing

🏵 OCTOBER 19

The mystery of God is one of infinite generosity, a pouring out of infinite love, and we have to prepare our hearts to make them as generous and as loving as we can. So as we say our mantra, we let go of our thoughts, plans and problems in order to clear the way for God. This means that we must learn to say the mantra without expectations, without demands. In other words, we must become 'poor in spirit' and for most of us this is the greatest challenge. It will probably even be a quite unprecedented experience of a wholly selfless act: doing something with no concern whatever for what we are going to get out of it.

When you are beginning it is very easy to say, 'Well, I'll try it. I'll meditate for six months and if it works out, I'll continue.' But if we want really to begin, we have to learn *from the beginning* to say the mantra unconditionally. It is a great act of faith. And naturally, in spite of all good intentions, we most of us start out with less than perfect attitudes. What, therefore, is of over-riding importance is that we remain as faithful as we can, as generous as we can, as undemanding as we can; and that we return daily to the practice. If you seriously want to learn to meditate, it is necessary to meditate for a minimum of twenty minutes each morning and each evening. The optimum time is about thirty minutes.

The Heart of Creation

The way of meditation is the way of opening ourselves as fully as we can in this life to the gift of God. His gift, *par excellence*, is Jesus Christ. He is our light. He is our enlightenment. The fullness of His spirit dwells in our hearts and the task of Christians is to understand this in all its power and wonder in the depth of our spirit. Our gospel, the gospel that we preach, is a gospel of the glory of Christ. A glory that radiates throughout history, and a glory that shines within each of us. The light of that glory is what gives direction to the lives of each one of us.

When we meditate every morning and evening we set everything else aside and we are open to that light. We seek to follow that light and so we are illuminated by it. The marvel of meditation is that, if we can be faithful to it, everything in our lives that is not consonant with the light is burned away by it. We do not need to spend time and effort making resolutions to do this or not to do that. All our effort should be put to the single task of coming in to the full consciousness of Jesus. After that effort of faith, everything else is given to us. Everything else in our lives not compatible with the light and warmth of love will fall away, if we will only be faithful to the daily pilgrimage away from division and self-consciousness and into the consciousness of Jesus. Then, just as we must go beyond ourselves into the consciousness of Christ, so He Himself takes us beyond Himself, in His consciousness, into God, to the Father.

The Way of Unknowing

In the vision proclaimed by Jesus each one of us is invited to understand the sacredness of our own being and life. That is why the second priority is of such great importance: namely, that we should allow our spirit the space within which to expand. In the tradition of meditation this space for expansion of spirit is to be found in silence, and meditation is both a *way* of silence and a *commitment* to silence which grows in every part of our lives. It becomes a silence that we can only describe as the infinite silence of God, the eternal silence.

And, as I am sure you will find from your own experience, it is in this silence that we begin to find the humility, the compassion, the understanding that we need for our expansion of spirit. Thoughtful men and women everywhere in the world today are beginning to see that spiritual growth, spiritual awareness, is the highest priority for our time.

Moment of Christ

❧ OCTOBER 22

What our encounter with India and the East is teaching us is something we should never have forgotten – that the essential Christian experience is beyond the capacity of any cultural or intellectual form to express. This is the 'glorious liberty of the children of God': no restriction. It became so clear to us talking with Father Bede [Father Bede Griffiths 1906–1993] that this experience has to be restored to the heart of the Church if she is to face creatively the challenges before her: the challenge of the renewal of her contemplative religious life, the challenge of finding unity in the Spirit with all Christian communions, the challenge of embracing the non-Christian religions with the universal love of Christ present in the hearts of all people and which she has a special duty to release and identify. To meet these challenges each one of us must be personally rooted in the experience of God that Jesus personally knows and shares with us all through His Spirit.

Letters From the Heart

ꕥ OCTOBER 23

The ancient monastic word to describe the state of prayer was the Latin word *quies*, which contains the notion of being at rest, being in a state of silence, sometimes described as 'staying quiet in the Lord'. This state of being quiet suggested complete confidence and ease at being in the presence of God. In our society we are so used to striving for things, to owning things, to earning the approval of others, that it is very hard for us to think of ourselves as usefully employed if we are just 'resting in the Lord' in this state of *quies*, of being quiet. But what those of us who try to tread this pilgrimage must always remember is that just being in His presence is all-sufficient.

When we are wholly present to God, we are wholly present to ourselves and wholly present to the whole of creation. But as you know from your own human experience, being wholly present to another does require ease, confidence, relaxation. You cannot have a very up-building conversation with another person if you think the chair you are sitting on is about to collapse any moment. So being present to another requires confidence, confidence in our own capacity for relationship, confidence that the other accepts us, loves us. But that acceptance requires our own willingness to be accepted, our own fearlessness in the relationship and saying the mantra in our meditation is a way of coming to this ease, this confidence, this absolute complete fearlessness as we stay in the presence of the One who is the love that casts out all fear.

Being On The Way

The quality that every one of us needs most urgently is silence. We simply must learn how to be silent and how to remain in silence. Once you enter that silence, once you open your heart to that unpredictable and incomparable experience, you will find that each of us can only be the person we are called to be if we allow that silence to develop in our hearts. Make no mistake about it, the silence that each of us is summoned to enter is the eternal silence of God. This is the silence that each of us can find in our own hearts. Discovering it will lead you to understand that silence is itself the medium of perfect communication. It is in silence that we communicate at depth and with the truth of wholeness.

The tradition that we speak from in the monastic order tells us, and quite uncompromisingly, that the way to that silence is a way of discipline. And the discipline is a hard one for us of the twentieth century because we have to learn to leave behind, indeed to abandon, our own thoughts, words, ideas, imagination. That is the silence we need: a silence beyond all words, ideas, thoughts, and beyond all imagination. An ancient tradition tells us that the way to that imageless but wakeful silence, which is the way of meditation, is the way of learning to say, in all simplicity and concentration, our *word*. Our meditation word, our mantra.

The Way of Unknowing

OCTOBER 25

The art of meditation is the art of learning to say the mantra, learning to set it free in your heart, so that it sounds in your heart at all times as a focal point of stability within the depths of your being. The richness of the Christian vision of prayer, of meditation, of being, is that it is only in the depths of ourselves that we can encounter the mystery of God.

The whole way of meditation is a way of non-violence and so the art of saying the mantra requires sustained delicacy and strength rather than force. These have to be sustained because we have to *learn* to say it. We have to learn, through thick and through thin, through difficult times and through good times, to abandon our own thoughts, plans and ideas as well as all our own images. And so, one of the things we must learn is to approach each meditation with a freshness of spirit. Each meditation is a new beginning, a fresh setting-out on the pilgrimage beyond self, beyond limitation into the wonder of God. What we seek to do when we meditate is *simply* to say our mantra as faithfully and as generously as we can.

The Heart of Creation

✤ OCTOBER 26

St John makes it abundantly clear that each of us is invited to allow the Word of God – the truth of God – to abide actively and potently in our hearts. It is when it does so that we go beyond falsehood and sin. One of the things Christians are so guilty of is underestimating this vocation and destiny. Each of us is destined to come to fullness of life through the full power of the Spirit's love. Our task is simply to come into full contact with the Spirit of Truth by turning aside from all illusion, and the desire that breeds illusion; to be one with Him, in Him.

> While I am still in the world I speak these words, so that [those who listen to me] may have my joy within them in full measure. I have delivered thy word to them ... I pray thee, not to take them out of the world, but to keep them from the evil one ... Consecrate them by the truth; thy word is truth. As thou hast sent me into the world, I have sent them into the world, and for their sake I now consecrate myself, that they too may be consecrated by the truth.[1]

This is simply what meditation is about: being consecrated by the truth that dwells in our hearts in power.

Word Made Flesh

[1] John 17:13–19

Meditation is a very simple concept. There is nothing complicated about it, nothing esoteric. It is the simplest concept that you could imagine and the beauty of it is that it leads us to experience simplicity. In essence, meditation is simply being still at the centre of your being. The only problem connected with it is that we live in a world of almost frenetic movement, and so stillness and rootedness seem quite foreign to most of us. But in nature all growth is from the centre outwards. The centre is where we begin and again that is what meditation is about. It is making contact with the original centre of your own being. It is a return to the ground of your being, to your origin, to God. To know God, to grow and to be still are all experiences at the centre of our being.

St John of the Cross, in his reflections on the nature of meditation, wrote that 'God is the centre of my soul.' One of the great religious dilemmas of our time is that those of us who think of ourselves as religious are trying to understand God with our minds, while those of us who are not overtly religious dismiss God from our lives. What all of us have to discover is that the only way we can talk in any meaningful way about God is if we discover Him in ourselves; if we set out on a road of self-discovery which is the pilgrimage to our own essential being.

The Way of Unknowing

The faithful saying of our mantra is our response to this call of Jesus. It is work – the work of God. Above all, meditation is an all-out onslaught on egoism, on isolation and on sadness. It is an affirmation of consciousness and life through the experience of love. The Christian vision demands a community that is created and vitalised in the mind of Christ. The message this community must communicate is that it is possible for all of us to become alive with the life of Christ. It is not only possible, it is the destiny of each one of us.

The way to this vitalising Christianity – a Christianity which is a light for the nations, the salt of the world and a power for peace – is the way of prayer: the prayer that is not our prayer but is the prayer of Jesus Himself. That prayer is, even now as you read this, flowing in our hearts. Our meditation is our full acceptance of this ontological reality – the full acceptance of the gift of our own being and of the Being of God, fully embodied in Jesus. Our prayer in this vision is our life force.

The Present Christ

❦ OCTOBER 29

Meditation is the very simple process by which we prepare ourselves, in the first instance, to be at peace with ourselves so that we are capable of appreciating the peace of the Godhead within us. The view of meditation that many people are encouraged to take as a means of relaxation, of retaining inner peacefulness throughout the pressures of modern urban life, is not essentially wrong in itself. But if this is all it is seen as being, the view is very limited. The longer we meditate, the more we become aware that the source of our new-found calm in our daily lives is precisely the life of God within us.

The degree of peace we possess is directly proportional to our awareness of this fact of life, a fact of human consciousness, common to every man and every woman in the world. But to realize this fact as a present reality in our lives, we have to decide that we want to be at peace. This is the reason for the psalmist's saying: 'Be still and know that I am God.'[1]

Word Into Silence

[1] Ps. 46:10

I want to talk to you about meditation as the way of peace, the way to peace. Just listen to these words of St Paul:

> Your world was a world without hope and without God but now, in union with Christ Jesus, you who once were far off have been brought near through the shedding of Christ's blood, for He Himself is our peace.[1]

In the New Testament this peace is the greatest quality that we can possess. It is beyond understanding but for us to be able to enter into this peace we must enter into the experience of meditation itself. One of the great problems in talking about meditation is that very often people who listen to one talk have no experience of what one is talking about and as a result fail completely to understand what meditation really summons us to.

The Christian tradition and the Christian mystery summon each of us to infinite riches. Every one of us. The real thing to understand about Jesus is that He is the universal redeemer and every one of us, if only we can realise it, are redeemed, that is, made free from all our chains of fear, of guilt and we are made free in the depths of our spirit. Peace is not a static quality. Peace is full vitality. It is the sense of joyous well-being that comes to us when we find ourselves to be truly harmonious, every part of our being in harmony.

The Door to Silence

[1] Eph. 2:12

❧ OCTOBER 31

I think what all of us have to learn is that we do not have to create silence. The silence is there within us. What we have to do is to enter into it, to become silent, to become *the* silence. The purpose of meditation and the challenge of meditation is to allow ourselves to become silent enough to allow this interior silence to emerge. Silence is the language of the Spirit.

These words of St Paul writing to the Ephesians are charged with the power of silence:

> With this in mind, then, I kneel in prayer to the Father, from whom every family in heaven and on earth takes its name, that out of the treasures of His glory He may grant you strength and power through his Spirit in your inner being, that through faith Christ may dwell in your hearts in love.[1]

The words we use in trying to communicate the Christian message in the Christian experience have to be charged with strength and power, but they can only be charged with strength and power if they spring from the silence of the Spirit in our inner being. Learning to say your mantra, leaving behind all other words, ideas, imaginations and fantasies, is learning to enter into the presence of the Spirit who dwells in your inner heart, who dwells there in love. The Spirit of God dwells in our hearts in silence, and it is in humility and in faith that we must enter into that silent presence. St Paul ends that passage in Ephesians with the words, 'So may you attain to fullness of being, the fullness of God himself.' That is our destiny.

Moment of Christ

[1] Eph. 3:14–16

❈ NOVEMBER 1

We must understand that the path of meditation is a way of purification. Purification is often abrasive, painful. But we have to understand that we must be stripped of everything that would hinder our openness to the pure energy of God. Egoism must go; desire must go; possessiveness must go; and that is painful. But each of us must learn to be prepared for a certain suffering that will be involved as we leave our old ways, our old selves, and open to this new life, this new way which is the way of God.

We should be encouraged, we should take heart, because the power to overcome is not only given to each of us but the power to overcome is infinite. The power that resides in the heart of each one of us to follow this way is exactly the same power that God exercised in Christ when He raised Him from the dead. By accepting the discipline of meditation by ourselves being present to ourselves, to God, every morning and every evening, we open ourselves to that power, to that vitalizing energy that is the source of all life and all love. Whatever the challenges, whatever the difficulties, whatever the suffering, that power is always with us.

Being On The Way

🎔 NOVEMBER 2

There is nothing dramatic about meditation; the most important thing is to understand its absolute ordinariness. There is nothing theatrical about it; it is absolutely ordinary. You have to start: the most important thing to do is to start. Do not ask yourself, 'Have you the resources for the journey? Have you the necessary will-power, strength of character – or whatever?' Only begin. But once you begin, everything you need for the journey is given to you. And to begin you need to build your meditation into every day. You must understand that it is impossible to learn to meditate without meditating. So the first thing is to put in the time. Meditate every morning and every evening.

In The Beginning

To meditate is just to 'stand still in the centre.' The very word 'meditation' is made up from the Latin words *stare in medio*, to abide in the centre. But it seems inadequate to say this is just 'centering ourselves' or even 'finding our centre.' We do this too, but not if it is our conscious aim – that would be too self-conscious, too desiring. We find our centre only by placing ourselves in the silence of God beyond any image of centre or circumference. What we think of as 'our' centre is too often an illusion of the self-reflecting ego, somewhere we like to take up our stand and observe God at work in us. But this can never be the way.

The challenges that face us point to the mystery of union we are summoned to enter. But we find our way into this mystery of union with others and with God only when we reach in ourselves that place where Jesus experiences His oneness with the Father. That place from which He prayed, 'I in them and Thou in me, that they may become perfectly one.'[1]

Letters From the Heart

[1] John 17:21

We are all called to tread this inner pilgrimage. Rooting our life in the spiritual reality is part of the plan of salvation – the meaning of the universe – revealed and actually completed in Jesus. Our task is simply to get on to the wavelength of this achievement. We do not have to accomplish it ourselves – to try to would be the highest hubris.

Putting ourselves into harmony with Him is the work of the mantra. The mantra is a tuning device, a harmonic to help us to resonate with Jesus. By its means we are enabled, as St Peter puts it, to let ourselves be built as living stones into a spiritual temple. By our commitment to meditating daily we take this option. By setting aside those two half-hours we move from the realm of materialistic expectations and conditions in order to enter the supreme reality of God revealed in Jesus. Reality does not exist outside of us, or even inside of us. It is in the heart where all dualities are resolved and there is simply God, perfect wholeness.

Word Made Flesh

❧ NOVEMBER 5

Meditation is simply a way of entering into freedom. It is the freedom that each of us can find if only we will undertake the discipline of the journey. Each of us can find this freedom in our own hearts. But as soon as I use the word discipline, we feel 'Isn't this a loss of freedom?' We cannot help but approach even meditation with our modern indiscipline by saying: 'Okay, I'll try it, I'll see if there's anything in it for me; if there is, I'll stick with it, if there isn't, I'll give it up and try jogging or something else.' However, we can't approach meditation in that way. Even to begin to meditate faces us with the challenge of discipline that it presents to us as modern people because we are not used to doing something unless there is a quick visible pay-off.

Meditation is just like breathing. If your life is going to be full, a spiritual discipline is as necessary to your spirit as breathing is to your body. It gives you the necessary space to be, the silence to be and, above all, the peace to be. To be at peace is to experience the reality of a tranquillity and order that is already in your own heart. Of course, this is what everyone is looking for, to be at peace, to be one, to experience, at the centre of your being, your harmony with all beings. That is precisely what meditation is about.

The Way of Unknowing

As we all know, all that matters is that we are single-minded and open-heartedly on the way, on the pilgrimage – the pilgrimage away from self into the wonder of the mystery of God. Meditation is a total commitment to *presence*. We meditate because we believe that God is, and that He is present to us. We believe too that through the human consciousness of Jesus each one of us can be deeply present to God. 'As thou Father art in me, and I in thee, so also may they be in us, that the world may believe that thou didst send me.'[1] Those words of Jesus should remind us that prayer itself, being at prayer, being in the state of prayer, is the great act of communicating the gospel. Note those words of Jesus, 'that the world may believe that thou didst send me'. The world will believe when we ourselves dwell fully in God's presence. Our meditation then is a time of ease, of quiet, and it gives each of us the capacity to be at ease in all the things of God, and in time it gives us the ease not only to speak of the things of God but to live our lives in godliness.

Being On The Way

[1] John: 17:21

The entrance to simplicity is the door of practice. Our practice is the saying of the mantra. Say it clearly, attentively. If you can, breathe it in, and breathe out in silence. Recite it from the beginning to the end. Don't analyse it, don't analyse what you are doing. Do not think about what you are doing but be one with what you are doing. That is the first step to a oneness that you will find intoxicating, a oneness with all creation, with all beauty, a oneness with all reality, a oneness with God – which is another way of saying a oneness with Love, the basic energy of everyone and everything.

The call that each of us has unveils the potential that each of us has. It is an openness to the experience of wholly undivided consciousness, the experience of unity. All that is required is that we give this way our total attention. So for the time of the meditation, say your word, sound your word, listen to your word and abandon all else.

The mantra reflects the single-mindedness of St Paul, writing to the Galatians: 'If we are in union with Christ Jesus ... the only thing that counts is faith, active in love.'[1] We say the mantra in faith and our meditation thereby becomes an activity of love.

The Way of Unknowing

[1] Gal. 5:6

We cannot approach meditation hoping that we are going to be experts, proficient within a week or two (or within a year or two). What we require is the regular practice of meditating every morning and evening and a constant commitment to the practice. You can read all the books in the world about playing the flute, but until you pick up a flute and start to play, you will not really have begun. Once you understand that meditation is an art, you begin to understand that the practice of it is much more important than all the speculation about it.

We slowly come to understand that to learn to meditate we need discipline: the discipline of sitting down and sitting still and of saying our word, our mantra, from the beginning of our meditation until the end. This is a difficult thing to understand when you begin. We want to follow our thoughts, to come to new insights. Being religious people we may want to praise God, to say some prayer. But when you meditate you must transcend all thoughts and all words, and be silent, still and humble in the depths of your own being.

The Heart of Creation

I suppose there is only one ultimate human tragedy and that is not to live to the full the gift of life that is given to us, and in meditating we seek to respond to that gift of life at the very depth of our own being. Why do we build these protective defences around ourselves? It is, I suppose, because we are not sure whether other people will accept us as we are and probably the reason for this is that we do not accept ourselves as we are. So our fears about ourselves must be dissolved. This is the importance of meditation for us. In the first place, it is a re-direction of our energy beyond ourselves to ultimate reality, to God. In other words, meditation is a putting of ourselves in touch with the source of all the energy of creation.

What does this mean in practical terms for us? It means that we learn to abandon our self-protectiveness, our self-assertiveness, our self-obsession, and to enter into the reality of God. The marvel of the Christian revelation is that God is love and that is what our meditation is about: getting into touch with that basic energy of creation flowing in the depths of our own heart, our own being, the energy who is God, who is love. This is an astonishing truth.

In the hearts of each one of us, in the depths of our own being, is to be found the source of endless, infinite love and this is the love which casts out all our fear and in casting it out enables us to become ourselves, to be the person we are called to be. To abandon all our energies and all our defences and to become ourselves, we have simply to put ourselves in full contact with this power, with this energy, that we call love.

The Door to Silence

✿ NOVEMBER 10

To learn to meditate you have to learn to be silent and not to be afraid of silence. A great difficulty presents itself to many modern people who are beginning to meditate simply because they are so unused to silence. Even at our meditation groups, we usually play some music as people assemble rather than prepare in complete silence, because many would feel very uncomfortable walking into a room of silent strangers.

Travelling to California recently I witnessed this conversation, or something like it, between two men sitting near me: one said 'Going somewhere?' to which the other rather surprisingly replied 'No.' There was an embarrassed pause after which the first person said hopefully, 'I've just been there. Now I'm going back.'

Many of us spend a great deal of time in such inane conversation because we are so frightened and feel so socially awkward of silent spaces in our meeting together. We fear silence when we are alone as well and so we often live with a constant background of radio chat shows or muzak.

In meditation we cross the threshold from background noise into silence. This is vital for us because silence is necessary if the human spirit is to thrive and to be creative. Silence releases a creative response to life, to our environment and friends because it gives our spirit room to breathe, room to be. In silence we do not have to justify ourselves, apologise or impress anyone. Just *be*.

Word Made Flesh

❧ NOVEMBER 11

In meditation we discover a harmony and an integration that become the basis of all our subsequent use of these great human gifts we have been given. The peace, the stillness and the harmony that we experience in meditation become the basis for all our action. All our judgments are now illumined, inspired by love because we know that that love is the very ground of our being. Everyone who perseveres in meditation discovers that although during our time of meditation it might appear that nothing happens, yet gradually the whole of our life is changed. We have to be patient because we might like it to be changed more rapidly.

Our thought gradually becomes clarified, relationships become more loving, and this is because, in the process of meditation, we are made free to love *by* love. The reason for all this is really very simple. When we meditate, not only do we stand back from the individual operations of our being, but we begin to learn to find a wholly new ground to stand on. We discover a rootedness of being which is not just in ourselves, because we discover ourselves rooted in God. Rooted in God who is Love. All this happens because we learn the courage to take the attention off ourselves. We learn to stop thinking about ourselves and to allow ourselves to be. To be still, to be silent, is the lesson and in that stillness and silence we find ourselves in God, in love.

The Way of Unknowing

In meditation, the greater part of what we have to do is to unlearn. What we have to do is to surrender all the false images that we have of ourselves and of God. Meditation has always been understood, in this tradition, as an art. It is the art of all arts. And it is helpful to look at it like this, because it reminds us that we are undertaking the process of learning to be at one with our art.

If you have ever seen a great violinist playing, the violinist and the violin become *one* in the exercise of the art; and as we look at it, it seems absolutely effortless. Whenever I myself have heard Isaac Stern or Yehudi Menuhin playing, in watching them I have been quite certain that I could do it just as well, it looks so easy. But of course the facility that the great artists have at being at one with their art comes from their practice, their daily practice. An artist of the eminence of Yehudi Menuhin even now practises for four hours every day.

Meditation and learning to meditate is a gradual process, and the most important element in it is the practice. We must meditate every day.

The Heart of Creation

I think all of us fear commitment because it seems to be a reducing of our options. We say to ourselves, 'Well, if I commit myself to meditating, then I'll not be able to do other things.' But I think what all of us find is that this fear dissolves in the actual commitment to be serious, to be open, to live not out of the shallows of our being, but out of its depths. What we all find in the experience of meditation is that our horizons are expanding not contracting and we find not constraint but liberty.

How does this happen? I think it happens as a result of our commitment, not to an abstract ideal or to an ideology but to simplicity, the simplicity that is required to sit down every morning, to close our eyes and to recite the one word from beginning to end. Begin your day like this, out of the essence of your own nature. Prepare for your day by *being*. Then in the evening return and give meaning to everything you have done during the day by similarly being open to your own rootedness in God and open to the ground of your own being.

The mantra will lead you into a greater silence. The silence leads you to to greater depth. In the depth you find not ideals or ideologies but a person who is God, who is Love. The Way is the way of simplicity. What we have to learn in meditation is to accept to be more and more simple every day of our lives. Listen to the words of Jesus again:

> How blessed are those who know that they are poor; the kingdom of heaven is theirs. . . . How blessed are those whose hearts are pure; they shall see God.[1]

Meditation is the way to purity of heart, leaving behind all fear and all limitation and entering – simply – into God's presence.

Moment of Christ

[1] Matt. 5:3, 8

All of us know at the deepest level of our being that we are made for union, that our perfection can only be found in union: that is, if we go beyond ourselves, we must pass over totally into the other. Now for that union faith is required, because we have to abandon self and we have to, as it were, leap over the divide between ourselves and the other. Again, almost everything in our modern education militates against that. 'Is it prudent, is it possible? Is not this a temerarious way of understanding your own vocation or destiny?' But again, what we know is that there is only the Way.

Meditation teaches us, strengthens us for the leap, so that when the leap comes we hardly know that it has happened. Meditation simplifies us. Meditation gently melts away the obstacles that prevent us leaping, melts away our fears, and it does so in an entirely gentle and imperceptible way. It might seem to us that we are making no progress; it might seem to us that we have been saying the mantra for weeks, months, years with no result. When you think that, remember this: it is not *your* way, it is *the* way. The journey we are on is not just *our* journey, it is *the* journey. The way is Jesus, the way is truth and life.

Being On The Way

Our silence, stillness and our fidelity to the simplicity of the mantra serves to lead us away from our isolated self-centred view of life. We are only 'realised' or 'fulfilled' in meditation, because we have ceased to seek or desire realisation or fulfilment. We only learn to be joyful, because we have learned not to possess nor to want to possess. The ordinary discipline of our daily meditation increasingly shifts our centre of consciousness from ourselves into the limitless Mystery of God's love.

But first a certain effort is needed to root the discipline in our being rather than just into the routine of our day. We need to have it rooted as an interior as well as an external discipline, so that we can carry it with us through the inevitably changing circumstances of life. Even monasteries change their timetables! When the rhythm of the twice-daily meditation becomes part of the fabric of our being, entirely natural and so always renewed and renewing, then our life is being transformed from the centre outwards. Then we are learning to see even the appearances of our ordinary life, work, relationships with the vision of love. The Christian is called to see all reality with the eyes of Christ.

The Present Christ

Meditation is the process in which we take time to allow ourselves to become aware of our infinite potential in the context of the Christ-event. As St Paul puts it in chapter 8 of Romans: 'And those whom He called, He has justified, and to those whom He justified, He has also given His splendour.'[1]

In meditation we open ourselves up to this splendour. Put another way, this means that in meditation we discover both who we are and why we are. In meditation we are not running away from ourselves, we are finding ourselves; we are not rejecting ourselves, we are affirming ourselves. St Augustine put this very succinctly and very beautifully when he said: 'We must first be restored to ourselves, that, making of oneself as it were a stepping stone, we may rise up and be borne to God.'[2]

Word Into Silence

[1] Rom. 8:30   [2] *Retractions* 1 (viii) 3 (Migne PL XXXII)

❀ NOVEMBER 17

We all know from our own experience, because all of us have been meditating long, that one of the principal things we have to learn from our meditation is to meditate without expectations. We have to learn that the way we are treading is the path of dispossession and we must learn to let go of our desire for wisdom, for knowledge, for holiness or whatever. A way of expressing this is to understand that once we begin to enter into the experience of prayer in our meditation, we begin to understand the limiting factors that would be involved in praying for things, for limited things. We begin to appreciate the sheer wonder of the experience of prayer itself, the wonder of entering into the limitlessness of Christ's prayer, of entering the unchartered seas of the divine reality, and we begin to learn in the experience of our meditation that praying for things is so often indulging our own desires.

The Door to Silence

Is there such a thing as petitionary prayer? Has it any value? Obviously there is such a thing as petitionary prayer. Jesus himself tells us to seek so that we will find; ask so that we will receive.[1] The more you meditate, the more you realise that all petitions that we can think of are already contained in the prayer of Jesus. His love for us and His love for the Father make Him the perfect mediator. In the time of meditation we cast all our cares, all our concerns, totally on Him, surrender them into His hands.

Petitionary prayer, as you know, is not to inform God of what we need or what we would like. God knows already what we need. He knows what we would like. Petitionary prayer is basically for the good of those who hear our petitions. The essence of the petitionary prayers, for example in the eucharistic assembly, are really not addressing God; we are addressing the assembly, the community, informing them of our concerns, of our needs. In a community where there is a general understanding of our total commitment to the prayer of Jesus and to its efficacy, it might well seem that we could ask on that stage. It could be appropriate to make a petition from time to time, I suppose. But that, too, is contained in the prayer of Jesus. Again, in meditating we are not denying the reality, or in certain circumstances the usefulness of petitionary prayer or intercessory prayer. But what we are affirming is the greatness of the love of Jesus, our conviction of His love for us and for all humankind and our total faith in Him.

Being On The Way

[1] Matt. 7:8

It is wonderful, therefore, but not surprising, that a very important aspect of meditation is its silence. It means that we can be there to listen, to hear with open attention. And it is a very fertile silence that we encounter in our meditation, one that is vibrant with God's presence, vibrant with His love; vibrant in summoning us beyond ourselves, beyond our self-limitations and revealing to us the unimaginable potentiality revealed once we ally ourselves to this enlightening power of love.

There is also another silence of God that we could describe as His testing of us. It is a magisterial silence. It is silence that purifies us and to purify us He allows us to remain in this silence of absence and loss; to experience what it is to be cut off from a sense of his reality; to experience what is to be cut off from the sense of His presence. It is a sense-less silence and faith is forced to greater depths by senselessness in any form. Part of the discipline of meditation is that we learn to be open to both of these silences. In our meditation we enter into this dual aspect of God's silence.

The Way of Unknowing

In silence you are not playing a role or fulfilling any expectations. You are just there, realising your being, open to reality. Then, in the Christian vision, you are overwhelmed by the discovery that the reality in which we have our being is love. In silence we know that our spirit is expanding into love.

To learn to be silent is to begin a journey. All you have to do is to begin. To take the first step into the silence is to begin the journey of your life, the journey into life. You are learning two things: firstly, to sit still, not because you are afraid to move or are imposing a burden on yourself, but because in stillness you seek a unity of body, mind and spirit; secondly, to recite your mantra in response to the deepening silence that arises in stillness.

As you begin to say your mantra you become aware that you are on the threshold of silence. This is a critical moment for most people, as they leave the familiar world of sounds, ideas, thoughts, words and images. You do not know what is in store for you as you cross into the silence. This is why it is so important to learn to meditate in a tradition and in a group that receives, passes on and embodies that tradition. It is for us a tradition that says 'fear not'. Jesus is the heart of a tradition that sees the purpose of meditation as being in the presence of love, the love that casts out all fear.

Word Made Flesh

Meditation is a way of returning to our own innocence and so of learning to trust as a child; as we used to trust before the experience of betrayal, before we ourselves had become betrayers. But the great message of hope of the gospel is that because our sins are forgiven, our betrayals are forgiven and we can return to that early fullness of life, through fullness of trust, wholly innocent and wholly loving. To love in innocence is to be wholly trusting. In meditation this is what we know, that we live from this power. We know that we are forgiven, we know the wonder of the difference that has been made for each of us by the life, death and resurrection of Jesus.

Each of us is invited to know this uniquely, for ourselves, and so to respond fully to the gift of our own life. Innocence is characterised by trust and Jesus says that we must trust the Father, 'putting his trust in him who sent me'. It is the fundamental challenge and invitation to the Christian because to trust we have to let go. To trust we have to come to rest in Him and to allow ourselves to be held by Him. Meditation opens up the experience, to which each of us is called, of the interior reality of the theological virtues, the reality of faith, the reality of hope, the reality of love: a triune reality realized by the innocent act of trust.

The Way of Unknowing

I think there is a real sense in which we cannot hear too often the *way* of meditating. And it is this: to learn to say your word, your mantra, from the beginning to the end of the meditation. That is something you have to relearn constantly because the temptation that most of us face is that our thoughts begin to take over. The thoughts are usually quite insidious because it can often be like, 'I wonder would I be able to say my mantra better if I was sitting in the full lotus rather than the half lotus. Now, *how* could I learn to sit in the full lotus?' Ten minutes later you think of what you are going to have for dinner or do tomorrow, and so maybe twenty minutes later you get back to saying the mantra again. What you have to learn is that *the* important thing is to say the mantra from the beginning to the end, and when you find you have strayed from it, return to it immediately, not violently but gently, faithfully.

The Heart of Creation

The call to meditation, for the early Fathers of the Church, was a call to purity of heart and that is what innocence is – purity of heart. A vision unclouded by egoism or by desire or by images, a heart simply moved by love. Meditation leads us to pure clarity – clarity of vision, clarity of understanding and clarity of love – a clarity that comes from simplicity. And to begin to meditate requires nothing more than the simple determination to begin and then to continue. *To begin* means to discover your own roots, your own potential and destiny. It is to set out on the journey both to our source and our goal.

Now let me remind you what it involves. It is the way of attention. In meditation we must go beyond thought, beyond desire and beyond imagination and in that *beyond* we begin to know that we are here and now in God, in whom 'we live, move and have our being'.[1] The way of simplicity is the way of the one word, the recitation of the one word. It is the recitation, and the faithfulness to that recitation every morning and every evening, that leads us beyond all the din of words, beyond all the labyrinth of ideas, to *oneness*.

The Heart of Creation

[1] Acts 17:28

One of the things that all of us find as we tread our path of meditation with simplicity and with humility is that there will be certain things in our lives that have to change. For example, I should think it would be very difficult to meditate if you spend three or four hours a day watching television. A great enemy of all prayer and of all recollection is a plethora of images in our minds. You will all discover, and I am sure you are already discovering it from your own experience, that it is foolishness to add indiscriminately to this plethora of images.

Listen to the words of St Paul writing to the Corinthians: 'Remember: sparse sowing, sparse reaping; sow bountifully, and you will reap bountifully.'[1] There is a marvellous harvest for all of us in our own spirit. But the call to this openness to the spirit of Jesus does ask for real generosity from each of us.

Firstly we need generosity in putting aside the half-hour for meditation every morning and every evening. And I understand very well that this does ask for a very generous response and a very creative response, given the tasks and responsibilities of your own lives. Secondly, a great generosity is called for in the actual time of your meditation to say your word, *maranatha* from the beginning to the end. So often we want to follow our own thoughts, our own insights, our own religious feeling. But we must learn to leave everything behind and to seek the spirit in our own hearts.

Moment of Christ

[1] 2 Cor. 9:6

A question that constantly recurs is what are we actually *doing* when we are meditating? What place does it have in our Christian life in general? When you begin meditating and you are told, 'You must say your word from the beginning to the end and you mustn't speak to God or think of God but simply must say your word,' you are likely to say, 'But is this prayer? Is it Christian prayer at all? Or is it just some form of relaxation or self-hypnosis?' Now, in the New Testament you find that one of its recurring themes is that prayer is the prayer of Jesus and that it is His prayer that we must learn to be part of.

Saying the mantra, saying your word, is simply a *keeping guard* over your heart so that extraneous trivia cannot enter in, even the trivia of your own pious, holy words and thoughts. Nothing must dilute the stream of prayer that is the love of Jesus for His Father. We must be undividedly open to that and the mantra is like a watchdog guarding your heart. That is why you are asked to learn to say it from the beginning to the end of each meditation.

The Way of Unknowing

✿ NOVEMBER 26

Meeting and meditating with so many who follow the extraordinary and wonderful pilgrimage in the usual course of their ordinary daily lives makes me see more clearly than ever before the true nature of this journey we are making together. We know it as a journey of faith, of expanding capacity to love and to be loved; and so also as an expanding vision of reality. And we know it too as a way that demands more and more faith. Mountains get steeper the closer you approach the summit and the path narrows. But so also the view becomes vaster, more inspiring and more humbling, strengthening us for the deeper commitment required of us for the last stages of the climb.

We know too that our journey is a way of solitude. True, it is the end to loneliness and isolation. And the solitude becomes the real material of integrity which the love of God transforms into communion, into belonging and relatedness at every level of our lives. But still it is an ascesis, a continual purification, an ongoing refining in the fire of love.

The Present Christ

🏵 NOVEMBER 27

Meditation is a discipline of *presence*. By our stillness of body and spirit each of us must take the responsibility of sitting as quietly as we can. By that discipline we learn to become wholly present to ourselves, to our situation, to our place, and by staying in that rootedness in our own being we become present to the source of our being and we become rooted in Being itself. We become rooted in God and in that rootedness we become unshakable in all the changing circumstances of life.

Now the process is a gradual one. It requires patience; it requires faithfulness; it requires discipline; and it requires humility – the humility during the time of our meditation to put aside all self-important questions, to put aside all self-importance, to experience ourselves poor, divested, as we learn to be, to be present, to the Presence. We begin to learn, not out of our own cleverness, but we begin to learn to be from the source of the only true wisdom – Wisdom itself. Now remember, when you begin the practice is most important... None of us can tread this path – no matter how long we have been on it – none of us can tread it without the daily commitment, the daily discipline, the daily faithfulness. So learn to be faithful by meditating every morning and every evening. Do not meditate for the results. The only sufficient motive for meditating – is that God *is*.

The Door to Silence

✿ NOVEMBER 28

The threshold of silence is still a critical moment because if you go back to your thoughts and images, even perhaps to your familiar prayers, you have turned away from the door to silence which leads into the pure prayer of love. Learning to return humbly to your mantra is the first step into this wonderful experience of silence as the presence of love.

I could use all the words in our vocabulary to tell you about the eternal silence of God that dwells within our innermost being, the silence of pure creation. I could say how important that silence is because in it you hear your own name spoken clearly and unmistakably for the first time. You come to know who you are. Yet all these words would fail to convey the experience itself – an experience of unselfconscious liberty in the creating presence of God.

To learn to be silent is to say your mantra and to keep saying it. So do not fear to leave your thoughts behind. Do not go back to your ideas or imaginations. Leave them to one side and say your word. We are not alone in doing this.

> And from time to time he would withdraw to lonely places for prayer . . . During this time he went out one day into the hills to pray, and spent the night in prayer to God.[1]

When we meditate in this tradition we enter into this same silence and it makes us one with Jesus in God.

Word Made Flesh

[1] Luke 5:16, 6:12

Our meditation and our daily recommitment to it is our setting out on the path of faith, which is the preparation of our heart for this moment. Day by day we leave all egoism behind and shed all divisions. We meditate in deepening silence in the humble acknowledgement that everything we can learn or experience is in the direct gift of God.

Underpinning the journey and underpinning our deepening commitment is the simple acknowledgement that God is God, God is one, God is love. The moment of revelation is our entry into the eternal now of God. It unifies our whole life 'before' and 'after', just as the one Incarnation, the one Crucifixion, the one Resurrection embraces past and future in the eternal present. At this moment we recognize what we have been seeing. We know that we are called – by name, personally – into the ocean of oneness towards God. And we recognize the call because it comes from one of ourselves who has attained this oneness. It comes from our Brother, Jesus, our Lord, our Guide.

The Present Christ

Learning to meditate is a process, and like every process it takes time. We must learn great patience and humility. After all our education and experience it is very challenging to learn just to say our word. We have to be very patient with our slowness and with our failure to persevere. I think all of us, when we start to meditate, start and stop and start again, and all of us need courage and encouragement. The courage and humility is to keep returning to it. The courageous and the humble are those who start again. Indeed, every time we meditate, every time we sit down to meditate we are starting again. Not surprisingly, therefore, perseverance makes us think and feel better about ourselves.

In learning to say the mantra we learn to let go of all our ideas, plans, thought-processes and, at the given moment, even our self-consciousness. We let go of them because we know we must enter into total silence.

The Way of Unknowing

❧ DECEMBER 1

We all come from a state we once enjoyed of simplicity, innocence and the joy of sheer goodness. This is the basis of a truly religious response to life. You can see this in the serious eyes of a child who is beginning to discover the wonder in the mystery of life, in religion, in God. Meditation is so important to all of us because, by the simplifying power of its action, it brings us again to this serious approach to religious experience.

By serious, I mean that in meditation we are not trying to manipulate God for our own purposes. We are not condescending to involve Him in our lives. We are rather discovering the wonder of His involvement in our life. We do so by saying the mantra, coming to stillness and silence, going beyond desire and coming to purity of heart. We are then simply open – but this requires everything we are – to reality in its purest and most intimate self-revelation.

Word Made Flesh

There is only the prayer of Jesus. His is the one prayer and that prayer is the stream of His consciousness fully open to the Father. The wholly extraordinary truth about the Christian proclamation is that each one of us, wherever we start from, is invited to open our consciousness fully to the consciousness of Jesus, and, in that openness, to be taken out of ourselves, beyond ourselves, into that stream of conscious love which flows between Jesus and the Father. That is the personal destiny of each one of us and in that experience we are made completely and eternally real. The paradox is to know yourself for the first time because you are lost in God. That is what the gospel tells us, 'Whoever would find their life must lose it.'[1]

Meditation is a sure way of losing your own life, losing your own consciousness of yourself as an autonomously separate, separated entity. In losing it you find yourself at one with God and at one with all creation because you are now at last one with yourself. Your consciousness is no longer divided, no longer confused. It is simplified. It is one in God.

The Way of Unknowing

[1] Matt. 10:39

❧ DECEMBER 3

When you begin to meditate, spend a couple of moments getting really comfortable. If you want to sit in a chair, sit in an upright one. If you sit on the floor, sit in a comfortable position. Then try to be as still as you can for the entire time of the meditation. It isn't all that easy for most of us when we start, but meditation involves coming to a stillness of spirit and a stillness of body. It gives you an awareness of yourself as one, as still, as whole. So you have to learn to sit as still as you can. When you are seated and are still, close your eyes and then begin to repeat, interiorly and silently in your heart, the word *Maranatha*. In some traditions, this is called a 'mantra', in others a 'prayer phrase' or 'prayer word'.

The essence of meditation and the art of meditation is simply learning to say that word to recite it, to sound it, from the beginning to the end of the meditation. It is utterly simple – say it like this: 'Ma-ra-na-tha'. Four equally stressed syllables. Most people say the word in conjunction with their breathing, but that isn't of the essence. The essence requires that you say the word from beginning to end and continue to say it right throughout your meditation time. The speed should be something that is fairly slow, fairly rhythmical – 'Ma-ra-na-tha'. And that is all you need to know in order to meditate. You have a word, and you say your word, and you remain still.

Moment of Christ

The experience of poverty is only the beginning and in meditating, what we learn to do is to build on our poverty, to deepen it. The great thing we have to understand is this: that the summons we have from Jesus is to follow the Way. Not *my* way but *the* way. That is very difficult for us as modern men and women to understand, because almost everything in our experience prepares us to look for *my* way, what will bring me happiness, satisfaction, fulfilment. But the clear call of Jesus to each of us is to follow *the* way. *The* way, as we all know, is Jesus. He is the Way: the Way that is truth and life. The marvellous thing about our destiny is this: that the Way is union with Him. It is surprising that it takes us so long, or it takes many of us so long, to understand this – to understand that there is a power-source, there is an energy, that is available to all of us – to take us we do not know where, but to take us always into deeper truth and greater and greater life.

Being On The Way

✿ DECEMBER 5

We will discover as we persevere in meditation that we cannot put God on hold, keep Him in a waiting room and say to Him, 'When I'm through with this important business I'm so absorbed in, I'll attend to you.' We cannot postpone God and say 'I'll be back in a minute.' As we commit ourselves to meditate every morning and evening we see the central significance of God's eternal *presentness* and we recognise that we have to learn to pay attention to God now, today.

This is what causes us a minor panic, because we wonder *will we be able to do it?* But there is really no cause for panic. Indeed the only cause for panic would be the reverse, if we had no encounter with the truth of God's presence and the need of response on our part. We ought to panic if we realise that we are deciding to commit ourselves to what is passing away, to the second-rate, to second-hand illusions that always seem to vanish before we encounter them. Our call is to commit ourselves to the absolute God, to the one who Is. There is no ultimate evasion of the truth that we can only commit ourselves absolutely.

The Way of Unknowing

It often seems as if we rush through life at such high speed while in our heart there is the essential interior flame of being. Our rushing often brings it to the point of extinction. But when we sit down to meditate, in stillness and simplicity, the flame begins to burn brightly and steadily. As we abandon thinking in terms of success and self-importance, the light of the flame helps us to understand ourselves and others in terms of <u>light, warmth</u> and love.

The mantra leads us to this point of stillness where the flame of being can burn bright. It teaches us what we know, but frequently forget, that we cannot live a full life unless it is <u>grounded on some underlying purpose.</u> Life has an ultimate significance and value that is only really discovered in the still steadiness of *being* which is our essential rootedness in God.

Word Made Flesh

As Christians today we need to reflect deeply on the notion of the silence of God. Before we heard the Word, the Word was already in God. We read this in the Gospel of John. And when the Word was spoken it became the revelation of a mystery that had been shrouded in darkness and silence from the beginning of the ages. There is a real sense in which our personal call to know and to serve God is of the same order. Even before God calls us to knowledge of Him and before He calls us to serve Him, God already knows and loves us in our mother's womb. Here, already, is part of the mystery of silence in which we all unconsciously participate.

Underlying the human encounter with God is this extraordinary mystery that God knows us from the very beginning. He calls us from the very beginning, speaking the Word when the time is ripe. So the silence of God is, from the first human experience of it, pregnant with love, pregnant with power. When the Word is spoken, it is a word of revelation, bringing to birth the wonder of God's love, revealed in human bodies, minds and hearts.

The Way of Unknowing

❀ DECEMBER 8

The essential Christian insight which Mary exemplifies in Luke's Gospel is poverty of spirit. This is purity of heart because it is unsullied by the intrusion of the egotistic will seeking for experience, desiring holiness, objectifying the Spirit or creating God in its own image. Mary reveals the basic simplicity of the Christian response in a poverty of spirit that consists in turning wholly to God, wholly away from self.

Mary is one of the greatest expressions in any culture of the wholly fulfilled woman, complete in her motherhood, her womanhood, and complete, too, in her spiritual maturity. And because both were complete there is no real demarcation between them. In Mary, as in Jesus, we see the expression of the essential correspondence between body and spirit which itself finds expression in the New Testament account of the Ascension and, later, in the Assumption. The importance of these accounts is that they remind us of the integration of the whole person in the Christian mystery and the continuity of this integration in the fulfilled life of the Resurrection.

Community of Love

God is our Creator and Father. Jesus is our Redeemer and Brother. And the Holy Spirit dwells within each one of us in such a way that we are – as we heard in the beautiful Liturgy of Vespers this evening – we are all of us, quite literally 'temples of holiness'. Now meditation is simply the process whereby we come to terms with these truths: truths about God, truths about ourselves, truths, too, about our neighbour. For in our daily meditations we stand aside from all that we can bring together under the term 'ephemeral immediacy' and we open ourselves fully to the grandeur and the wonder of God – to the enduring present. And in this process we both discover our own grandeur and liberate our capacity for wonder. We might equally well say that in discovering our own value we discover God, the Creator of all that is valuable. We discover, with Gerard Manley Hopkins, that 'the world is charged with the grandeur of God'.

Christian Meditation: The Gethsemani Talks

The two dangers you must avoid are, first of all, distraction, not allowing your mind to become involved in trivia. The second is that you must not allow yourself to be just nowhere. Prayer is not just floating in space. It is a full and fully conscious entry into the prayer of Jesus. It is in fact having His mind. As St Paul says, 'We possess the mind of Christ.'[1] One of the constantly recurring themes of the Buddhist scriptures is the warning to humanity not to waste life, not to allow life to slip through our fingers until we suddenly become aware that it is all over. Your life is for living. Your life is for coming to full consciousness, full enlightenment. In the teaching of St Paul, we are allowing the light of Christ to shine with its full brilliance in our heart.

Meditation is our acceptance of the gift, the gift of life, the gift of Jesus and the self-giving of His Spirit. Because the gift is infinite, it requires our full attention and complete concentration. We are not spending half an hour in the morning and half an hour in the evening going in for a 'bit of religion' or doing spirituality as part of our health programme. In these half-hours we seek to live the eternal moment. We seek to set aside everything that is passing away and to live in the eternity of God.

The Way of Unknowing

[1] 1 Cor. 2:16

The mantra leads us to attention, a spirit of attention, a mindfulness of what is, not what has been or not what might be, but what is. The first step, therefore, is mindfulness, attention. The second step – which is more like a leap or a plunge into the very basis of all that is – the second step is the realisation that God is, that God is present, that God is now and, perhaps the most wonderful of all, that God is mindful of all.

People often wonder when they begin to meditate about the apparent gap in the practice of meditation between, on the one hand, their faith in God, and on the other hand, their recitation, their perfect recitation of their mantra. It seems to us when we begin that because we are instructed to leave all thoughts, ideas and images behind in our meditation, that we must leave God behind, because when we are meditating we cannot think of Him, we cannot imagine Him, we cannot construct any image or idea of Him. Basically, what we must learn to understand is that all our images, our memories, are fantasies.

The Door to Silence

One of the weaknesses that we have is that we are always trying to settle down. One of the challenges we have to face in our Christian life is that we have to learn to be pilgrims, to be on the way. We are always trying to accumulate things, either material things or knowledge, but we have to learn to tread the path of dispossession. Jesus described the way of salvation as a narrow road and few find it. The reason why so few do find it is that it is a comparatively untravelled road.

Two principal things are required of the pilgrim. The pilgrim must not succumb to the temptation to settle down on the way: 'I have gone far enough. I am getting tired. The going is getting too tough.' All these feelings, the pilgrim must set aside.

Perhaps the most insidious temptation is for the pilgrim to say, 'This is a good plateau I have arrived at; this is a peaceful place. I must just rest up here for a bit.' What we learn as we continue is that our commitment to the pilgrimage becomes something that is absolute. The reason is simple: because the journey, the pilgrimage, arises from our commitment to someone who is infinitely greater than we are. What we discover is that we are summoned on this journey not just so that we may arrive at some place, not just so that we may have some sort of experience. Our summons is a summons to the oneness of God, our call is a call to be unified in the unity of God.

The call, the vision that Jesus prepared, is a call to absolute communion and, as pilgrims, we must always keept this ultimate destination, this ultimate destiny that each of us has clearly written in our hearts. None of us knows what we will have to endure, none of us knows what dangers we shall have to pass through. We do know, and we learn to know with ever-increasing clarity, that the power to overcome all such trials, all such difficulties, is given to us and will be given to us, and will be given to us from the power–source that each of us is invited to discover in our own hearts, the power–source that is God, the power–source that is love.

Being On The Way

🎋 DECEMBER 13

Learning to meditate is quite a demand. It means devoting time generously to what is the most important fact in life, that God is and that the Spirit of God dwells in our hearts. In meditating we accept that fact and adopt a wholly positive attitude to it. It is not only death we often suppress and deny, it is also God and therefore life. Each day needs to begin out of the acceptance of God's power in our life. Each day needs to be brought to a conclusion by returning our scattered minds to the mystery of His presence and love.

Integrity means wholeness. Meditation is a way that brings every part of our day, all our experience and all the dimensions of our being, into harmony. It is the way beyond the personal dividedness and anxiety from which we suffer as a result of our denial of God and our separation from the Spirit. Meditation proves itself, through faithful practice, as a way to deep peace and joy. It takes us across the bridge of sadness that arises from the feeling of separation. The ego arises in separateness and when the ego is transcended we realise our unity with God.

Word Made Flesh

By the Incarnation God has touched our lives in Jesus, and the great importance of the feast of Christmas is that it is the celebration of our humanity, redeemed by being touched by God. God assumes the mortality of the human condition in Jesus so that we can burst through the bonds of death in Him. Indeed, He bursts through all the chains that keep us bound by the earth.

What we learn from His life is that the destiny of each one of us is to begin to live our lives fully now, in our present earthly, mortal condition. To live our lives now, as free men and women, not bound by fear or enchained by desire, but utterly in harmony with the liberating power of God's own energy. This energy of God cannot be bounded by any human limitation. It is the eternal life-source, not just constantly renewed in each one of us but always expanding in each one of us.

Our invitation, our destiny, is to place our lives in complete harmony with this divine energy. And so, the Christian experience cannot be contained by any set of propositions, by any library of books, by any formulas or any creeds. It can only be adequately expressed in the human experience of Jesus Himself. He alone, of all human beings, was able to say of God, 'Abba, Father.'[1]

The Way of Unknowing

---

[1] Mark 14:36

Silence at first seems an emptiness and an absence. Sometimes it seems extraordinarily negative. And you might well ask, 'Am I really to spend this hour like this every day – and is it necessary to meditate for a half-hour in the morning and a half-hour in the evening?' Other questions arise too as a result: 'Am I, in effect, turning my back on human relationships during this time? Am I being asked to abandon my own rational capacity? Am I being asked to let go of everything I've learnt? There seems so much at stake. Am I to let go of all my studies, all my professional training? Am I to abandon my own creativity?' This is what it can all seem like, at first glance. It seems that we are abandoning one by one, each and every one of our human potentialities. For what? For stillness, for silence. For nothing.

Now it is quite certain that there is no way we can come to a satisfactory answer to this sort of question, apart from the actual practice of meditation. It is only in the practice and in faith that one can find the answer but finding it does call from each of us a real leap into the dark, into the silence. It is only in the actual experience of this that we can find any satisfactory answer. This may not seem the best approach to a dialogue about meditation. But however much we can valuably say about meditation there comes a point where dialogue itself must fall silent.

The Way of Unknowing

One of the great difficulties about learning to meditate is that it is so simple. In our society most people think that only very complex things are worthwhile. To meditate you have to learn to be simple, and that provides a real challenge for all of us.

The simplicity that is involved in learning to meditate is turning away from multiplicity and from all the options that are before us and concentrating in utter simplicity of being. Think of learning to ride a bike. To learn how to ride it you have first of all to learn to balance yourself on the bike. And later you have to concentrate both on keeping your balance and steering a straight course. The extraordinary thing is that as you do devote all your energies to being balanced and steady you discover unexpected harmony and a new freedom. The same is true with meditation. Like learning to ride a bike you have to be willing to learn. You have to be willing to concentrate. You have to learn to direct all your energies to the simple task of being balanced and travelling steadily in one direction.

To be *on the way* in meditation you have to be simple enough to turn aside from everything else so that you can really be harmonious and free.

Moment of Christ

❧ DECEMBER 17

Our task is to persevere – not grudgingly or self-importantly, but with simple faith and self-renewing love. The figure of Mary is a central one in our understanding of Christmas. Above all, she is a great example of interiority with a direct meaning for each of us. Just as she carried the human Christ within her, so we must bear and worship Christ in our own hearts, remembering that He is just as truly present within us as He was bodily present in His mother.

Mary in the gospels has another meaning for us: her silence is both the medium and the response to the presence of Jesus within us. The true silence of our meditation is creative and fertile. As it deepens and grows, so does the presence and power of the risen Christ expand the kingdom of love in our heart.

Our task is to be silent, to be still, and to allow His transforming presence to emerge within us, out of the living, creative centre of our being.

Letters From the Heart

❧ DECEMBER 18

The mystery of the Incarnation and the sheer wonder of the Christian proclamation of truth is that Christ shares His experience with each one of us. And He actively invites each one of us to enter into His own experience of the Father. He invites us not just to make some sort of intellectual assent or volitional intention. He invites us to *share*, to share with His experience in all its fullness, to share and to be carried away by the infinite thrust of his energy as He knows the Father and loves the Father, and as He in His turn is known and loved infinitely. And this is what we are all called to.

In meditation we develop full attention, full commitment because what we set out for is to enter the eternal moment of God's self-communication in Jesus. We are called not just to consider this but to share it, to enter into it at the very depth of our being. And the result for us is deep, supreme, unshakable joy. Our minds and hearts are expanded beyond all isolation into oneness, into union. The Way is the way of daily fidelity.

The Way of Unknowing

The mantra is, as experience proves, an act of pure love, universal love. Everyone who meditates faithfully through all the personal storms and challenges of their personal life begins to know this. They come also to know that they are meditating through the crises and tragedies of their world. It is so because the Spirit moves among it, giving it that completion, that redemption which is the centre of God's design.

The communion we discover in the solitude of our own hearing and responding is not only communion with ourselves. That is perhaps the first sign we have of it – a deeper personal harmony and freedom. But it persists beyond, to the communion we share with all men and women, with all the dead and all the living and the yet unborn. With them we share the great and mysterious gift of life in the flesh and in the Spirit.

And as we awaken to this deeper and higher sense of wholeness we sense the ultimate all-embracing communion which contains all this and of which these are epiphanies. The communion we have with God and the communion within God – this is the great truth we encounter. All we can say in the end is what we said at the beginning – that the meaning of life is the mystery of love.

The Present Christ

Wherever we are on the path – whether we are just beginning and meditating twice every day for twenty minutes, or whether we have been on the path for some time and we meditate for thirty minutes or meditate three times a day – wherever we are, all that is required is that we give ourselves totally *now* to our commitment. It seems, when we begin, that this is asking a lot, but the feast of Christmas reminds us that God in his gift to us does not just give us a lot, he gives us everything of himself, in Jesus. Somehow we must understand that and we must understand it in the silence of our own heart. We must understand it in the eternal silence of God.

And so when we meditate each morning and evening, we each of us receive, as fully as we are now able to, the gift of God in Jesus. To receive it requires a generosity on our part that is not less than the generosity of God. That is why we must say our mantra with the greatest attention we can, with the greatest love we can. The words of Jesus constantly inspire us to deepen our generosity:

The Way of Unknowing

The German mystic, Silesius, reflecting upon the feast of the Nativity, said that it may be that Jesus was born in Bethlehem but that will be of no avail to us, unless He is born in our hearts. There is the whole purpose of Christian meditation, that we *accept* the freedom that the Incarnation has achieved for each of us. To accept it, we have to follow in the way of Jesus.

We have to be reduced to the single activity of being; being the person we are called to be and being that person fully. Being who we are means accepting the gift of our creation by God, accepting the gift of our redemption by Jesus and accepting fully the gift of the Spirit, the Holy Spirit dwelling in our hearts. For this Trinitarian acceptance we must turn from everything that is less than the fullness of the Godhead. We must concentrate and we must be concentrated. We must be reduced to nothing so that we may pass through, to become all. The feast of the Nativity is the feast of the reduction of God to man, so that many may enter into Godliness.

The Heart of Creation

❦ DECEMBER 22

In this Christmastide, in a time when we are all thinking of the new life of Christ and our own rebirth in grace as the result of his birth in the flesh, I thought it would be appropriate to put down before you some thoughts on the Spirit of St Benedict, a spirit that flows so directly from a knowledge of the Incarnate Word born in us through the love of God.

For Benedict, the first quality we all require if we would respond to Christ and be open to His life in our hearts is the capacity to listen. The first word of the Rule is 'Listen!' And as you all know, this capacity is one of the great fruits of meditation, which teaches us that the condition of true listening is *silence*. We can only listen to the word spoken to us by another if we ourselves are silent of all words.

The wonder of Benedict's spirit as it speaks to us in the Rule is that his understanding of the prayerful heart is so naturally and humanly integrated into this whole vision of life. He does not see silence in the monastery, for example, just as a regulation to be obeyed but wisely knows that there are times when charity will demand words. Instead, he sees silence as the fundamental condition of our heart, attentiveness to a reality larger than the limits of our immediate activities or concerns, a heart wrapped in silence and wholly attentive to the word of the Master.

Letters From the Heart

At Christmastime we become more sharply aware of the mysterious blend of the ordinary and the sublime in the monastic life and indeed all life that is really Christian. It is important, though, to see it as a blend, not as an opposition.

It is tempting to treat the birth of Christ as something romantically outside the full meaning of His life, something pre-Christian. In the rich and beautiful gospel accounts of his birth we can be tempted to see this part of His life as merely consoling or idyllic. But it is part of the human mystery that nothing is outside the Mystery. By the Incarnation God accepted this aspect of the human condition and so the birth and childhood of Christ are part of the mystery of His life – a life that culminated on the cross and reached its transcendent completion in the Resurrection and Ascension.

Our meditation teaches us how fully every part of us has to be involved in the radical conversion of our life. It teaches us that we have to put our whole heart into this work of the Spirit if we are genuinely to respond to the call to leave the shallows and enter into the deep, direct knowledge that marks a life lived in the mystery of God. Then everything in our life acquires this depth dimension of divine Presence. We are foolish to look for 'signs' on the way, a form of spiritual materialism that Jesus rebuked, because if we *are* on the way, in the bright cloud of God's presence, then all things are signs. Everything mediates the love of God.

The Present Christ

🎄 DECEMBER 24

As we prepare each year for the feast of Christmas we have a precious opportunity to reflect upon the marvellous context of the Christian vision. The Incarnation, the birth of Jesus, is the revelation of God. It is the showing of His power, His wisdom, His love in the man Jesus. The Incarnation is like a pouring out of God on earth and, as the life of Jesus proves, God holds nothing back. The generosity of God is incarnated in the generosity of Jesus. In His life we see His availability to the crowds, His compassion for the sick, for the mourning. His utter selflessness, we know, comes to a climax in His death on the cross.

Christ was born at Bethlehem and that is a marvellous, historical fact. But it is a fact that is completed. It was completed in the past so that now He must be *born* in our hearts. Our hearts must be made ready for Him. There must be room for Him in the inn of our heart. That is all meditation is: a readying and opening of our heart for the birth of Christ.

And it is because He is the infinite God that we must let go of everything else, so that there is space for Him in our hearts. The mystery is that when He is come to birth in our hearts, everything is come to birth with Him. Our hearts are filled with all His love, all His compassion, all His forgiveness. We know ourselves forgiven, loved and understood by the infinite God and by His Son, our brother. Filled with this experiential knowledge we cannot fail to communicate and share it with anyone to whom we turn, with whom our lives are interwoven.

The Heart of Creation

> Christmas is the feast
> of the divine
> explosion,
> the
> love
> of
> God
> revealed
> in the poverty of Christ.

With all the materialistic pressures involved in Christmas today we can easily think of it as a period of hectic preparation, a day of celebration and a brief aftermath. We can forget that it is more than a feast. It is a season. And like all seasons its essence is a cycle of preparation, achievement and then the incorporation of what has been achieved into the larger season of which it is a part, the season of our life.

The Present Christ

'Do I have a responsibility to communicate meditation to others?' I think the answer to that is that once we are on the way, we cannot help but communicate it. I do not think we need to be too self-conscious about going out of our way, as it were, to communicate meditation. I think if we really do say our mantra faithfully, humbly, in simplicity, every morning and every evening, in God's good time and in His plan we cannot help but communicate it.

One of the other questions that we might go into in greater detail is, 'Is this a very narrow way?' 'Does meditation make you narrow-minded?' I think it is a very narrow way. It is a way where we do reduce the focal point of our attention to one thing, to God, to the mystery of His love, the mystery of His presence. The beginning process of meditation is a narrowing down to one-pointedness, to single-mindedness, and when we have reached that one-pointedness, that single-mindedness, we are propelled through.

Now we see everything with a divine perspective; whereas before meditation, life often seemed to be diminishing, passing away, so often life seemed to be the expending of a diminishing amount of energy. After the experience of narrowing our consciousness to the supreme fact of God's existence and His love, our experience of life is not of a diminishing energy, but of an expanding energy: the energy of God's creative love.

Being On The Way

Perhaps the most valuable first lesson to learn is that the coming of Jesus, which we celebrated at Christmas, has transformed the ordinary. If we can see this clearly, we can see our own spiritual journey, our own religious practice, our personal life, all shot through with the transforming potentiality of Christ's redemptive love.

In order to see this clearly, we have to understand how *ordinary* meditation is. Just as breathing is necessary for bodily life, so meditation is necessary for the development and sustenance of our spiritual life. To say the mantra is a very ordinary thing. It is of the same order as eating, breathing, sleeping. It remains esoteric only to those who have not yet undertaken the journey. To those who have begun, it is as ordinary and as wonderful as daylight. Like the other functions necessary for a balanced and healthy life, it requires a regular, daily commitment. But it is unique among these functions. It is the great integrating function wherein all our other processes are held in balance and aligned on the centre. Achieving or realising, the balance is the first step. From there on, we progress steadily into the heart of the divine.

The Present Christ

🎋 DECEMBER 28

People often ask, 'I don't seem to be making any progress in my meditation. What should I do about it?' Perhaps the most important progress we have to make in our meditation is to abandon the idea of making progress. We have to understand that we are always beginning. Every time we sit down to meditate we begin again. Every meditation is a setting out, a re-setting out, and because it is a re-setting out it always remains fresh, always a further entry into the mystery which is infinite, inexhaustible. It is important to understand that although we do speak of meditation as a journey it is an unusual journey, because it is a pilgrimage to where we *are*. It is a return to our roots, to our rootedness. It is a pilgrimage to the only place where we can really be, that is where we are. Meditation, as you all know, is a focusing of our attention into the *now*. It is becoming wholly present to the *now* to the now of what is. When we try to speak of it, we describe it with all sorts of words – pure consciousness, pure awareness, purity of heart.

Being On The Way

What we do in meditation and in the lifelong process of meditation is to refine our perception down to the single focal point which is Christ. Christ is our way, our goal, our guide. But He is our goal only in the sense that once we are wholly with Him, wholly at one with Him, we pass with Him to the Father. In meditation we come to that necessary single-pointedness and find it is Christ.

It is impossible to talk about meditation as it is impossible to talk about the Christian experience in any adequate terms. As one philosopher put it, 'As soon as we begin to speak of the mysteries of Christ, we hear the gates of heaven closing.' Yet we have to try to speak, though we speak only to bring people to silence. The silence of our meditation is our way into the indescribable mystery to be found within the heart of each one of us, if only we will undertake this pilgrimage to one-pointedness, to single-mindedness.

Meditation is like breaking through the sound barrier. When you come to that point there can be a lot of turbulence. It is at this moment that the discipline you have learned by saying your mantra and by faithfully continuing to say it, will enable you to be entirely open to the love of Jesus which takes you through it. We need discipline to love and to be open to love because we need discipline to be free. As we approach that point it seems that we require great courage. It seems that we require great perseverance. What we come to know is that all the courage and all the capacity to persevere are freely ours in Jesus.

Moment of Christ

❧ DECEMBER 30

Death itself, especially the death of someone we have loved, teaches us what love teaches us. It reveals to us that the more deeply we love and enter into communion, so the more radically we must become detached and non-possessive. To continue to fall in love we must continue to fall away from the ego. It is the final and the most demanding of the lessons that life teaches. It is the meaning of the absolute finality of the Cross, the single-pointedness of the Cross that yet opens up into the infinite universe of the Resurrection.

Both in the experience of love and of death we discover the reality of losing self. The wonder of each is to discover that we *can* lose self. In fact, we discover that the very reason for our creation is that we *do* lose self. And this is exactly what our meditation teaches us so well. To lose self, we must stop thinking about ourselves. We must place our centre outside of ourselves, beyond ourselves in another, in *the* Other.

Community of Love

The vision is intoxicating. We must beware of just being intoxicated. We must set out on the path and we must stay on the path, not with demands but with fidelity, not with expectations but in profound poverty of spirit, not with mere curiosity but with faith: a willingness to enter in, to taste and to see. Listen to St John's First Letter:

> It was there from the beginning. We have heard it. We have seen it with our own eyes. We looked upon it and felt it with our own hands and it is of this we tell. Our theme is the word of life. This life was made visible. We have seen it and bear our testimony and we here declare to you the eternal Life which dwelt with the Father and was made visible to us. What we have seen and heard we declare to you so that you and we together may share in a common life: that life which we share with the Father and His Son, Jesus Christ, and we write this in order that the joy of us all may be complete.[1]

When we meditate in a few moments, by our stillness, by our discipline, by our transcendence we enter into that sharing of the life of Jesus and His Father.

Being On The Way

[1] 1 John 1:1–4

True, I am living here & now this mortal life, but my real life is the faith I have in the Son of God. Galatians 2: 19b-20

" On things of no account, an unaccountable deal bestowing" (p. 193)

Aug 9;
Aug 25; Aug 27;
Sept 5, 30;
October 9; 13, 28, 29,
November 9 & 10, 24,
December 4 & 4, 7, 12, 13,
January 7th, 27,
February 9th, 15th, 23;
March 28;

& We pray to the Word of God who came
down all our sins in the ocean of his
love

> Help us to set our hearts where they
> will find fulfilment not betrayal

May He enlighten the eyes of your minds
Ephesians C1 V 18

You do not belong to yourselves
Corinthians C6, v 19

True, I am living, here and now,
It is mortal life, but my real life
is the faith I have in the Son of God,
who loved me, & gave himself for me
Galatians Ch 2; V 19b—20